German

at your Fingertips

compiled by

LEXUS

with

Horst Kopleck,
Chris Stephenson
and Peter Terrell

Routledge & Kegan Paul
London and New York

First published in 1987 by
Routledge & Kegan Paul
11 New Fetter Lane, London EC4P 4EE

Published in the USA by
Routledge & Kegan Paul Inc.
in association with Methuen Inc.
29 West 35th Street, New York, NY 10001

Set in Linotron 202 Baskerville
by Morton Word Processing Ltd, Scarborough
and printed in Great Britain
by The Guernsey Press Co. Ltd
Guernsey, Channel Islands

© LEXUS Ltd 1987

Library of Congress Cataloging in Publication Data

German at your fingertips.—(Fingertips)

1. German language—Conversation and phrase books—English.
I. Kopleck, Horst   II. Lexus (Firm)
PF3121.G47   1987   438.3'421   86-21914

British Library CIP Data also available
ISBN 0-7102-0954-1

German

at your Fingertips

Other titles in this series

Dutch at your Fingertips
French at your Fingertips
Greek at your Fingertips
Italian at your Fingertips
Portuguese at your Fingertips
Spanish at your Fingertips

Contents

GERMAN PRONUNCIATION

Because you are likely to want to speak most of the German given in this book, rather than just to understand its meaning, an indication of the pronunciation has been given in square brackets. If you pronounce this as though it were English, the result will be clearly comprehensible to a German person.

In some cases, however, we have decided that it was not necessary to give the entire pronunciation for a word or phrase. This may be because it would more or less duplicate the ordinary German spelling, or because the pronunciation of a particular word or words has already been given within the same entry. In these cases we have simply shown how to pronounce the problematic parts of the word or phrase.

Some comments on the pronunciation system used:

VOWELS

a	as in 'hat'
ah	as in 'father'
ay	as in 'day'
ine	as in 'mine'
oo	as in 'book' or 'took'
$\overline{oo}$	as in 'soon' or 'boom'
œ	as in 'huge' or 'few'
ow	as in 'how'
uh	a short sound like the 'er' in 'mother'
y	as in 'by'

CONSONANTS

CH	like the ch in the Scottish pronunciation of 'loch'
g	as in 'get'
j	like the 's' in 'leisure'

When part of the pronunciation is given in quotes (e.g. 'eye') this means that this should be read exactly as the English word.

When the print for a letter or letters is in bold type this means that this part of the word should be stressed.

For nouns which have the indefinite article 'ein' in the translation we have added *m* or *nt* afterwards in brackets to indicate the gender of the word.

English – German

A

a, an ein(e) *[ine(-uh)]*; **10 marks a bottle** 10 Mark pro Flasche; *see page 108*

about: about 25 etwa 25 *[etvah]*; **about 6 o'clock** gegen 6 Uhr *[gaygen]*; **is the manager about?** ist der Geschäftsführer in der Nähe? *[ist dair gesheftsforer in dair nay-uh]*; **I was just about to leave** ich wollte gerade gehen *[ich vollt-uh grahd-uh gayen]*; **how about a drink?** wie wär's mit einem Drink? *[vee vairss mit ine-em]*

above oben *[ohben]*; **above the village** oberhalb des Dorfes *[ohberhalp]*

abroad im Ausland *[im owsslant]*; **when I go abroad** wenn ich ins Ausland fahre *[venn ich inss ... fahr-uh]*

abscess ein Abszeß (m) *[aps-tsess]*

absolutely: it's absolutely perfect es ist absolut perfekt *[absoloot pairfekt]*; **you're absolutely right** Sie haben vollkommen recht *[zee hahben follkommen recht]*; **absolutely!** vollkommen!

absorbent cotton die Watte *[vatt-uh]*

accelerator das Gaspedal *[gahss-pedahl]*

accept akzeptieren *[aktsepteeren]*

acceptable: this is not acceptable das ist nicht annehmbar *[dass ist nicht annaymbar]*

accident der Unfall *[oonfal]*; **there's been an accident** es hat einen Unfall gegeben *[gegayben]*; **sorry, it was an accident** tut mir leid, das war ein Versehen *[toot meer lyte, dass vahr ine fairzayen]*

accommodation(s) die Unterkunft *[oonter-koonft]*; **we need accommodation(s) for four** wir brauchen Zimmer für vier Personen *[veer browchen tsimmer foor feer pairzohnen]*

accurate genau *[genow]*

ache: I have an ache here ich habe hier Schmerzen *[ich hahb-uh heer shmairtsen]*; **it aches** es tut weh *[ess toot vay]*

across: across the street über die Straße *[oober dee shtrahss-uh]*; **it's across the**

street es ist gegenüber *[gaygenoober]*

actor der Schauspieler *[showshpeeler]*

actress die Schauspielerin *[showshpeelerin]*

adapter ein Adapter (m)

address die Adresse *[address-uh]*; **what's your address?** was ist Ihre Adresse?

address book das Adreßbuch *[addressbooch]*

admission: how much is admission? was kostet der Eintritt? *[vass kosstet dair ine-tritt]*

adore: I adore ... ich liebe ... *[ich leeb-uh]*

adult der Erwachsene *[airvaksen-uh]*

advance: I'll pay in advance ich zahle im voraus *[ich tsahl-uh im forowss]*

advertisement eine Anzeige *[an-tsyge-uh]*

advise: what would you advise? was würden Sie empfehlen? *[vass voorden zee empfaylen]*

aeroplane das Flugzeug *[flooktsoyk]*

affluent wohlhabend *[vohl-hahbent]*

afraid: I'm afraid of heights ich habe Angst vor großen Höhen *[ich hahb-uh angst for grohssen hur-en]*; **don't be afraid** haben Sie keine Angst *[hahben zee kyne-uh]*; **I'm not afraid** ich habe keine Angst; **I'm afraid I can't help you** es tut mir leid, ich kann Ihnen nicht helfen *[ess toot meer lyte ich kan eenen nicht helfen]*; **I'm afraid so** ich fürchte ja *[ich foorcht-uh yah]*; **I'm afraid not** leider nicht *[ly-der nicht]*

after: after you nach Ihnen *[nach eenen]*; **after 9 o'clock** nach 9 Uhr; **not until after 9 o'clock** nicht vor 9 Uhr *[nicht for]*

afternoon der Nachmittag *[nachmittahk]*; **in the afternoon** am Nachmittag; **good afternoon** guten Tag *[gooten tahk]*; **this afternoon** heute Nachmittag *[hoyt-uh]*

aftershave das After-shave

after sun cream die Après-Lotion
[ap**ray**-lohts-yohn]

afterwards danach [dan**a**cн]

again wieder [v**ee**der]

against gegen [g**ay**gen]

age das Alter [**a**l-ter]; **not at my age!** nicht
in meinem Alter! [nicнt in m**y**nem]; **it
takes ages** es dauert eine Ewigkeit [ess
dow**ert** **ine**-uh **a**yvicнkyte]; **I haven't
been here for ages** ich bin ewig nicht
mehr hier gewesen [icн bin **a**yvicн nicнt
mair heer gev**a**yzen]

agency die Agentur [ahgent**oo**r]

ago: a year ago vor einem Jahr [for **ine**-em
yahr]; **it wasn't long ago** es ist noch
nicht lange her [nocн nicнt l**a**ng-uh hair]

agony: it's agony es ist eine Qual [ess ist
ine-uh kvahl]

agree: do you agree? sind Sie einverstan-
den? [zint zee **ine**-fairshtanden]; **I agree**
ich stimme zu [icн shtimm-uh ts**oo**]; **sauerkraut doesn't agree with me** Sauerkraut bekommt mir nicht [meer nicнt]

aggressive aggressiv [aggress**ee**f]

AIDS Aids

air die Luft [looft]; **by air** mit dem
Flugzeug [mit daym fl**oo**ktsoyk]

air-conditioning die Klimaanlage
[kl**ee**ma-anlahg-uh]

air hostess die Stewardess

airmail: by airmail per Luftpost [pair
l**oo**ftposst]

airmail envelope der Luftpost-Briefum-
schlag [l**oo**ftposst br**ee**f-oomshlahk]

airplane das Flugzeug [fl**oo**ktsoyk]

airport der Flughafen [fl**oo**k-hahfen]

airport bus der Flughafenbus [fl**oo**k-
hahfenbooss]

airport tax die Flughafengebühr [fl**oo**k-
hahfen-geb**oo**r]

alarm der Alarm

alarm clock ein Wecker (m) [v**e**cker]

alcohol der Alkohol [alkoh**oh**l]

alcoholic: is it alcoholic? enthält es Alkohol? [ent**he**lt ess alkoh**oh**l]

alive lebendig [leb**e**ndicн]; **is he still
alive?** lebt er noch? [laypt air nocн]

all: all the hotels alle Hotels [**a**l-uh]; **all
my friends** alle meine Freunde; **all my
money** mein ganzes Geld [myne g**a**ntsess
gelt]; **all of it** alles [**a**l-ess]; **all of them**
alle; **all right** in Ordnung [in **o**rdnoong];
I'm all right (I'm fine) mir geht's gut

[meer gayts g**oo**t]; (no more food etc) danke;
that's all das ist alles; **it's all changed**
alles hat sich verändert [zicн fair**e**ndert];
thank you — not at all vielen Dank —
keine Ursache [kyne-uh **oo**rzacн-uh]

allergic: I'm allergic to ... ich bin aller-
gisch gegen ... [all**air**gish g**ay**gen]

allergy eine Allergie [allerg**ee**]

all-inclusive inklusive [inklooz**ee**v-uh]

allowed erlaubt [air**low**pt]; **is it allowed?** ist es erlaubt?; **I'm not allowed
to eat salt** ich darf kein Salz essen [icн
darf kyne zalts **e**ssen]

almost fast [fasst]

alone allein [al-**ine**]; **are you alone?** sind
Sie allein? [zint zee]; **leave me alone**
lassen Sie mich in Ruhe [lassen zee micн
in r**oo**-uh]

already schon [shohn]

Alsace-Lorraine Elsaß-Lothringen [el-
zass-l**oh**-tringen]

also auch [owcн]

alteration eine Änderung [**e**nderoong]

alternative: is there an alternative? gibt
es eine Alternative? [gipt ess **ine**-uh al-
tairnat**ee**v-uh]; **we had no alternative**
wir hatten keine andere Wahl [veer h**a**t-
ten kyne-uh **a**nder-uh vahl]

alternator die Lichtmaschine [licнt-
masheen-uh]

although obwohl [opv**oh**l]

altogether insgesamt; **what does that
come to altogether?** was macht das zusammen? [vass macнt dass ts**oo**zammen]

always immer

a.m.: at 8 a.m. um 8 Uhr morgens

amazing (surprising) erstaunlich
[airsht**own**licн]; (very good) fantastisch

ambassador der Botschafter [b**oh**t-
shaffter]

ambulance ein Krankenwagen (m)
[kr**a**nken-vahgen]; **get an ambulance!**
rufen Sie einen Krankenwagen [r**oo**fen
zee]

America Amerika [am**a**ireeka]

American (adj) amerikanisch [amerik**ah**-
nish]; (man) der Amerikaner [—k**ah**ner];
(woman) die Amerikanerin [—k**ah**nerin]

American plan Vollpension [f**o**llpangz-
yohn]

among unter [**oo**nter]

amp: a 13-amp fuse eine 13-Ampere-
Sicherung [amp**ai**r]

an(a)esthetic die Narkose *[nahrkohz-uh]*
ancestor der Vorfahr *[forfahr]*
anchor der Anker
anchovies Sardellen *[zardellen]*
ancient alt
and und *[oont]*
angina die Angina *[angeena]*
angry wütend *[vootent]*; **I'm very angry about it** ich bin darüber sehr verärgert *[ich bin dahroober zair fair-airgert]*; **please don't be angry** seien Sie bitte nicht böse *[zy-en zee bitt-uh nicht burz-uh]*
animal ein Tier *(nt)* *[teer]*
ankle der Knöchel *[knurchel]*
anniversary: it's our (wedding) anniversary today heute ist unser Hochzeitstag *[hoyt-uh ist oonzer hochtsytes-tahk]*
annoy: he's annoying me er belästigt mich *[air belesticht mich]*; **it's so annoying** es ist so ärgerlich *[ess ist zoh airgerlich]*
anorak ein Anorak *(m)*
another: can we have another room? können wir ein anderes Zimmer haben? *[kurnen veer ine anderess tsimmer hahben]*; **another bottle, please** noch eine Flasche bitte *[noch ine-uh flash-uh bitt-uh]*
answer die Antwort *[antvort]*; **there was no answer** es hat sich niemand gemeldet *[ess hat zich neemant gemeldet; **what was his answer?** was hat er geantwortet? *[vass hat air ge-antvortet]*
ant: ants Ameisen *[ah-myzen]*
antibiotics Antibiotika *[—bee-ohteeka]*
anticlimax eine Enttäuschung *[ent-toyshoong]*
antifreeze das Frostschutzmittel *[frost-shoots-mittel]*
anti-histamine das Antihistamin
antique: is it an antique? ist es antik? *[ist ess anteek]*
antique shop ein Antiquitätengeschäft *(nt)* *[antikvitayten-gesheft]*
antisocial: don't be antisocial seien Sie kein Spielverderber *[zyen zee kyne shpeel-fairdairber]*
any: have you got any rolls/milk? haben Sie Brötchen/Milch?; **I haven't got any** ich habe keine *[ich hahb-uh kyne-uh]*
anybody jeder *[yayder]*; **can anybody**

help? kann jemand helfen? *[yaymant helfen]*; **there wasn't anybody there** es war keiner da *[ess vahr kyner da]*
anything etwas *[etvass]*; **I don't want anything** ich möchte nichts *[ich murcht-uh nichts]*; **don't you have anything else?** haben Sie etwas anderes?
apart from abgesehen von *[apgezayen fon]*
apartment eine Wohnung *[vohnoong]*
aperitif ein Aperitif *(m)*
apology eine Entschuldigung *[entshool-digoong]*; **please accept my apologies** ich möchte mich entschuldigen *[ich murcht-uh mich entshooldigen]*
appalling entsetzlich *[entzetslich]*
appear: it would appear that ... es scheint, als ob ... *[ess shynt alss op]*
appendicitis eine Blinddarmentzündung *[blint-darm-entsoondoong]*
appetite der Appetit *[appeteet]*; **I've lost my appetite** ich habe keinen Appetit mehr *[kynen ... mair]*
apple ein Apfel *(m)*
apple pie ein Apfelkuchen *(m)* *[—koochen]*
application form ein Antragsformular *(nt)* *[antrahks-formoolahr]*
appointment der Termin *[tairmeen]*; **I'd like to make an appointment** ich möchte einen Termin vereinbaren *[fair-ine-bahren]*
appreciate: thank you, I appreciate it recht vielen Dank *[recht feelen dank]*
approve: she doesn't approve das gefällt ihr nicht *[dass gefelt eer nicht]*
apricot eine Aprikose *[aprikohz-uh]*
April der April *[a-prill]*
aqualung ein Tauchgerät *(nt)* *[towch-gerrayt]*
archaeology die Archäologie *[archay-ologee]*
architect der Architekt *[archeetekt]*
are *see page 113*
area: I don't know the area ich kenne mich in der Gegend nicht aus *[ich kenn-uh mich in dair gaygent nicht owss]*
area code die Vorwahl *[forvahl]*
argument der Streit *[shtryte]*
arm der Arm
around *see* about
arrangement: will you make the arrangements? können Sie das regeln?

[kurnen zee dass raygeln]

arrest verhaften *[fairhaften]*; **he's been arrested** er ist verhaftet worden

arrival die Ankunft *[ankoonft]*

arrive: when do we arrive? wann kommen wir an? *[van kommen veer an]*; **has my parcel arrived yet?** ist mein Paket schon angekommen? *[ist myne pakayt shohn angekommen]*; **let me know as soon as they arrive** sagen Sie mir, wenn sie eintreffen *[zahgen zee meer venn zee ine-treffen]*; **we only arrived yesterday** wir sind erst gestern angekommen

art die Kunst *[koonst]*

art gallery die Kunstgalerie *[koonstgalleree]*

arthritis die Arthritis *[artreetis]*

artificial künstlich *[koonstlich]*

artist der Künstler *[koonstler]*

as: as fast as you can so schnell Sie können *[zoh shnell zee kurnen]*; **as much as you can** soviel Sie können *[zohfeel]*; **as you like** wie Sie wollen *[vee zee vollen]*; **as it's getting late** weil es spät wird *[vyle ess shpayt veert]*

ashore: to go ashore an Land gehen *[an lant gayen]*

ashtray ein Aschenbecher (*m*) *[ashenbecher]*

aside from außer *[owsser]*

ask fragen *[frahgen]*; **that's not what I asked for** das hatte ich nicht bestellt *[dass hatt-uh ich nicht beshtellt]*; **could you ask him to phone me back?** können Sie ihn bitten, mich zurückzurufen? *[kurnen zee een bitten mich tsoorooktsooroofen]*

asleep: he's still asleep er schläft noch *[air shlayft noch]*

asparagus der Spargel *[shpahrgel]*

aspirin ein Kopfschmerzmittel (*nt*) *[kopfshmairtsmittel]*

assault: she's been assaulted sie ist überfallen worden *[zee ist ooberfal-en vorden]*; **indecent assault** das Notzuchtverbrechen *[noht-tsoocht-fairbrechen]*

assistant (*helper*) der Assistent *[assistent]*; (*in shop*) der Verkäufer *[fairkoyfer]*

assume: I assume that ... ich nehme an, daß ... *[ich naym-uh an dass]*

asthma das Asthma

astonishing erstaunlich *[airshtownlich]*

at: at the café im Café; **at the hotel** im

Hotel; **at 8 o'clock** um 8 Uhr *[oom acht oor]*; **see you at dinner** wir sehen uns beim Abendessen *[veer zayen oonss byme ahbentessen]*; **at his party** auf seiner Party *[owff zyner]*; **at the station** am Bahnhof

Atlantic der Atlantik

atmosphere die Atmosphäre *[atmosfair-uh]*

attractive attraktiv *[atrakteef]*; **you're very attractive** ich finde dich sehr attraktiv *[ich find-uh dich zair]*

aubergine eine Aubergine *[ohbairjeen-uh]*

auction die Versteigerung *[fair-shtygeroong]*

audience das Publikum *[pooblikoom]*

August der August *[owgoost]*

aunt: my aunt meine Tante *[myne-uh tant-uh]*

au pair (*girl*) das Au-pair-Mädchen *[—maydchen]*

Australia Australien *[owsstrahlee-en]*

Australian (*adj*) australisch *[owsstrahlish]*; (*man*) der Australier *[owsstrahleeer]*; (*woman*) die Australierin *[—lee-erin]*

Austria Österreich *[urster-ryche]*

Austrian (*adj*) österreichisch *[ursterrychish]*; (*man*) der Österreicher *[ursterrycher]*; (*woman*) die Österreicherin *[—in]*

authorities die Behörden *[behurden]*

automatic automatisch *[owtomahtish]*; (*car*) der Automatikwagen *[owtomahtikvahgen]*

automobile das Auto *[owto]*

autumn der Herbst *[hairpst]*; **in the autumn** im Herbst

available: when will it be available? wann wird es erhältlich sein? *[van veert ess airheltlich zyne]*; **when will he be available?** wann wird er zu sprechen sein? *[van veert air tsoo shprechen zyne]*

avenue die Allee *[allay]*

average: the average German der durchschnittliche Deutsche *[dair doorch-shnittlich-uh doytsh-uh]*; **an above average hotel** ein überdurchschnittliches Hotel *[ine ooberdoorch-shnittliches]*; **a below average hotel** ein unterdurchschnittliches Hotel *[ine oonter-doorch-shnittliches]*; **the food was only average** das Essen

war nur mittelmäßig *[vahr noor mittel-maysich]*; **on average** im Durchschnitt
awake: is she awake yet? ist sie schon wach? *[ist zee shohn vach]*

away: is it far away? ist es weit? *[vyte]*; **go away!** gehen Sie weg! *[gay-en zee vek]*
awful furchtbar *[foorchtbar]*
axle die Achse *[ax-uh]*

B

baby das Baby
baby-carrier eine Säuglingstragetasche *[zoyglingstrahg-uh-tash-uh]*
baby-sitter der Babysitter; **can you get us a baby-sitter?** können Sie uns einen Babysitter besorgen? *[kurnen zee oonss]*
bachelor der Junggeselle *[yoong-gezell-uh]*
back: I've got a bad back mir tut der Rücken weh *[meer toot dair rocken vay]*; **at the back** hinten; **in the back of the car** hinten im Auto; **I'll be right back** ich bin gleich zurück *[ich bin glyche tsoo-rock]*; **when do you want it back?** wann wollen Sie es zurückhaben? *[van vollen zee ess tsoorock-hahben]*; **can I have my money back?** kann ich mein Geld zurückbekommen? *[kan ich myne gelt tsoo-rockbekommen]*; **come back!** kommen Sie zurück!; **I go back home tomorrow** ich fahre morgen nach Hause zurück *[ich fahr-uh morgen nach howz-uh tsoo-rock]*; **we'll be back next year** wir kommen nächstes Jahr wieder *[veer kommen naychstess yahr veeder]*; **when is the last bus back?** wann fährt der letzte Bus zurück? *[van fairt dair letst-uh booss]*; **he backed into me** er hat mich rückwärts angefahren *[air hat mich rockvairts angefahren]*
backache die Rückenschmerzen *[rocken-shmairtsen]*
back door die Hintertür *[hintertoor]*
backgammon das Backgammon
backpack der Rucksack *[roockzack]*
back seat der Rücksitz *[rockzits]*
back street die Seitenstraße *[zyten-shtrahss-uh]*
bacon der Speck *[shpeck]*; **bacon and eggs** Eier mit Speck *['eye'-er]*
bad schlecht *[shlecht]*; **this meat's bad**

dieses Fleisch ist schlecht; **a bad headache** schlimme Kopfschmerzen *[shlimm-uh kopf-shmairtsen]*; **it's not bad** es ist nicht schlecht; **too bad!** Pech! *[pech]*
badly: he's been badly injured er ist schwer verletzt worden *[air ist shvair fair-letst vorden]*
bag die Tasche *[tash-uh]*; *(handbag)* die Handtasche *[hant-tash-uh]*; *(suitcase)* die Reisetasche *[ryze-uh-tash-uh]*
baggage das Gepäck *[gepeck]*
baggage allowance das zugelassene Gepäck *[tsoogelassen-uh gepeck]*
baggage checkroom *(for leaving bags)* die Gepäckaufbewahrung *[gepeck-owffbevahroong]*
baker der Bäcker *[becker]*
balcony der Balkon *[balkong]*; **a room with a balcony** ein Zimmer mit Balkon; **on the balcony** auf dem Balkon *[owff daym]*
bald kahl
ball ein Ball *(m)* *[bal]*
ballet das Ballett *[bal-ett]*
ball-point pen ein Kugelschreiber *(m)* *[koogel-shryber]*
Baltic die Ostsee *[ost-zay]*
banana eine Banane *[banahn-uh]*
band *(mus)* die Band *[bend]*
bandage ein Verband *(m)* *[fairbant]*; **could you change the bandage?** können Sie den Verband wechseln? *[kurnen zee dayn fairbant veckseln]*
bandaid das Hansaplast *(tm)*
bank *(money)* die Bank; **when are the banks open?** wann haben die Banken geöffnet? *[hahben … ge-urfnet]*
bank account das Bankkonto
bar die Bar; **let's meet in the bar** wollen wir uns in der Bar treffen? *[vollen veer]*

oonss in dair]; **a bar of chocolate** eine Tafel Schokolade *[ine-uh tahfel shokolahd-uh]*

barbecue der Grill

barber der Frisör *[frizz-ur]*

bargain: it's a real bargain das ist wirklich billig *[dass ist veerklich billich]*

barmaid die Bardame *[bardahm-uh]*

barman der Barkeeper

barrette eine Haarspange *[hahr-shpang-uh]*

bartender der Barkeeper

basic: the hotel is rather basic das Hotel ist ziemlich einfach *[dass hotel ist tseemlich ine-fach]*; **will you teach me some basic phrases?** können Sie mir einige grundlegende Ausdrücke beibringen? *[kurnen zee meer ine-iguh groontlaygend-uh owssdrock-uh by-bringen]*

basket ein Korb (m) *[korp]*

bath das Bad *[baht]*; **can I take a bath?** kann ich ein Bad nehmen? *[kan ich ine baht naymen]*

bathing das Baden *[bahden]*

bathing costume der Badeanzug *[bahd-uh-antsook]*

bathrobe der Bademantel *[bahd-uh-mantel]*

bathroom das Bad *[baht]*; **a room with a private bathroom** ein Zimmer mit eigenem Bad *[ine tsimmer mit 'eye'gen-em baht]*; **can I use your bathroom?** kann ich Ihre Toilette benutzen? *[kan ich eer-uh twalett-uh benootsen]*

bath salts das Badesalz *[bahd-uh-zalts]*

bath towel ein Badehandtuch (nt) *[bahd-uh-hant-tooch]*

battery eine Batterie *[batteree]*; **the battery's flat** die Batterie ist leer *[ist lair]*

bay die Bucht *[boocht]*

be sein *[zyne]*; **be reasonable** seien Sie vernünftig *[zy-en zee fairnoonftich]*; **don't be lazy** seien Sie nicht so faul *[nicht zoh fowl]*; **where have you been?** wo sind Sie gewesen? *[voh zint zee gevayzen]*; **I've never been to ...** ich war noch nie in ... *[ich vahr noch nee in]*; *see* **I, you, he** *etc and pages 113, 114*

beach der Strand *[shtrant]*; **on the beach** am Strand; **I'm going to the beach** ich gehe zum Strand

beach towel ein Badetuch (nt) *[bahd-uh-tooch]*

beach umbrella ein Sonnenschirm (m) *[zonnensheerm]*

beads die Perlen *[pairlen]*

beans die Bohnen; **runner beans** die Stangenbohnen *[shtangen—]*; **broad beans** dicke Bohnen *[dick-uh]*

beard der Bart

beautiful (person) schön *[shurn]*; (food) wunderbar *[voonderbar]*; (beach, weather) herrlich *[hairlich]*; **thank you, that's beautiful** vielen herzlichen Dank *[feelen hairtslichen dank]*

beauty salon der Schönheitssalon *[shurnhytes-zallong]*

because weil *[vile]*; **because of the weather** wegen des Wetters *[vaygen dess vetters]*

bed das Bett; **single bed/double bed** ein Einzelbett/ein Doppelbett *[ine-tsel-bet/doppel-bet]*; **you haven't made my bed** mein Bett ist nicht gemacht worden *[myne bet ist nicht gemacht vorden]*; **I'm going to bed** ich gehe zu Bett *[ich gay-uh tsoo bet]*; **he's still in bed** er ist noch im Bett *[air ist noch im bet]*

bed and breakfast Übernachtung mit Frühstück *[oobernachtoong mit frooshtock]*

bedclothes das Bettzeug *[bet-tsoyk]*

bed linen die Bettwäsche *[betvesh-uh]*

bedroom das Schlafzimmer *[shlahf-tsimmer]*

bee eine Biene *[been-uh]*

beef das Rindfleisch *[rintflyshe]*

beer ein Bier (nt) *[beer]*; **two beers, please** zwei Bier bitte

beer cellar der Bierkeller *[beerkeller]*

beer mat ein Bierdeckel (m) *[beer—]*

beer mug ein Bierkrug (m) *[beerkrook]*; (in South Germany) eine Maß *[mahss]*

before: before breakfast vor dem Frühstück *[for]*; **before I leave** bevor ich abreise *[befor ich ap-ryzuh]*; **I haven't been here before** ich bin noch nie hier gewesen *[noch nee heer gevayzen]*

begin: when does it begin? wann fängt es an? *[van fenkt ess an]*

beginner der Anfänger *[anfenger]*; **I'm just a beginner** ich bin erst Anfänger *[airst]*

beginners' slope der Anfängerhügel *[anfengerhoogel]*

beginning: at the beginning am Anfang

behavio(u)r das Benehmen [benaymen]

behind hinten; the driver behind me der Fahrer hinter mir

beige beige

Belgian (adj) belgisch; (man) der Belgier [bel-gee-er]; (woman) die Belgierin

Belgium Belgien [bel-gee-en]

believe: I don't believe you ich glaube Ihnen nicht [ich glowb-uh eenen nicht]; I believe you ich glaube Ihnen

bell (door) die Klingel; (church) die Glocke [glock-uh]

belly-flop ein Bauchklatscher (m) [bowch-klatsher]

belong: that belongs to me das gehört mir [dass gehurt meer]; who does this belong to? wem gehört das? [vaym]

belongings: all my belongings alle meine Sachen [al-uh myne-uh zachen]

below unten [oonten]; below the knee unter dem Knie [oonter daym k-nee]

belt ein Gürtel (m) [goortel]

bend (in road) die Kurve [koorv-uh]

berries die Beeren [bairen]

berth eine Kabine [kabeen-uh]

beside: beside the church neben der Kirche [nayben dair keerch-uh]; sit beside me setzen Sie sich zu mir [zetsen zee zich tsoo meer]

besides: besides that außerdem [owsserdaym]

best beste [best-uh]; the best hotel in town das beste Hotel der Stadt; that's the best meal I've ever had das ist das Beste, was ich jemals gegessen habe [yaymahls gegessen hahb-uh]

bet: I bet you 50 marks ich wette mit Ihnen um 50 Mark [ich vett-uh mit eenen oom]

better besser; that's better das ist besser; are you feeling better? geht es Ihnen besser? [gayt ess eenen]; I'm feeling a lot better ich fühle mich viel besser [ich fool-uh mich feel]; I'd better be going now ich gehe jetzt besser

between zwischen [tsvishen]

beyond jenseits [yaynzytes]; beyond the mountains hinter den Bergen [dayn bairgen]

bicycle ein Fahrrad (nt) [fahr-raht]; can we rent bicycles here? kann man hier Fahrräder leihen? [fahr-rayder ly-en]

bidet das Bidet [beeday]

big groß [grohss]; a big one ein großes; that's too big das ist zu groß; it's not big enough es ist nicht groß genug

bigger größer [grurser]

bike ein Rad (nt) [raht]; (motorbike) ein Motorrad (nt) [motohr-raht]

bikini ein Bikini (m)

bill die Rechnung [rechnoong]; could I have the bill, please? kann ich bitte bezahlen? [kan ich bitt-uh betsahlen]

billfold die Brieftasche [breef-tash-uh]

billiards das Billard [billyart]

binding (ski) die Bindung [bindoong]

bingo Bingo

bird ein Vogel (m) [fohgel]

biro (tm) ein Kugelschreiber (m) [koogel-shryber]

birthday der Geburtstag [geboorts-tahk]; it's my birthday es ist mein Geburtstag; when is your birthday? wann haben Sie Geburtstag?; happy birthday! herzlichen Glückwunsch zum Geburtstag! [hairtslichen glockvoonsh tsoom]

biscuit ein Plätzchen (nt) [plets-chen]

bit: just a little bit for me für mich nur ein bißchen [foor mich noor ine bisschen]; a big bit ein großes Stück [ine grohssess shtock]; a bit of that cake ein Stück von diesem Kuchen [deezem koochen]; it's a bit too big for me es ist etwas zu groß für mich [ess ist etvass tsoo grohss foor mich]; it's a bit cold today es ist ein bißchen kalt heute

bite (by flea, dog) der Biß [biss]; I've been bitten (by insect) ich bin gestochen worden [ich bin geshtochen vorden]; do you have something for bites? haben Sie etwas gegen Insektenstiche? [hahben zee etvass gaygen inzektenshtich-uh]

bitter (taste etc) bitter

bitter lemon ein Bitter Lemon (nt)

black schwarz [shvartz]; see coffee

black and white (photograph) schwarzweiß [shvarts-vyce]

Black Forest der Schwarzwald [shvartsvallt]

Black Forest gateau die Schwarzwälder Kirschtorte [shvarts-velder keershtortuh]

blackout: he's had a blackout er hatte einen Ohnmachtsanfall [air hatt-uh ineen ohnmachts-anfal]

bladder die Blase [blahz-uh]

blanket die Decke *[deck-uh]*; **I'd like another blanket** ich hätte gern noch eine Decke

blast! verdammt! *[fairdamt]*

blazer ein Blazer *(m)*

bleach *(for loo etc)* das Scheuermittel *[shoyermittel]*

bleed bluten *[blooten]*; **he's bleeding** er blutet *[air blootet]*

bless you! Gesundheit! *[gezoont-hyte]*

blind blind *[blint]*

blinds die Jalousie *[jalloozee]*

blind spot der tote Winkel *[dair toht-uh vinkel]*

blister die Blase *[blahz-uh]*

blocked *(road, pipe)* verstopft *[fairshtopft]*

block of flats der Wohnblock *[vohn-block]*

blond *(adj)* blond *[blont]*

blonde eine Blondine *[blondeen-uh]*

blood das Blut *[bloot]*; **his blood group is ...** seine Blutgruppe ist ... *[—groop-uh]*; **I have high blood pressure** ich habe hohen Blutdruck *[ich hahb-uh hoh-en blootdroock]*

Bloody Mary ein Cocktail aus Wodka und Tomatensaft *[ine cocktail owss vodka oont tomahtenzaft]*

blouse eine Bluse *[blooz-uh]*

blow-dry fönen *[furnen]*

blue blau *[blow]*

blusher das Rouge

board: full board die Vollpension *[follpangzyohn]*; **half-board** die Halbpension *[halp-pangzyohn]*

boarding house eine Pension *[pangzyohn]*

boarding pass eine Bordkarte *[bortkart-uh]*

boat ein Schiff *(nt)* *[shiff]*; *(small)* ein Boot *(nt)* *[boht]*

boat trip eine Schiffsreise *[shiffs-ryze-uh]*; **a boat trip down the Rhine** eine Schiffsreise auf dem Rhein *[owff daym]*

body der Körper *[kurper]*

boil *(on skin)* ein Furunkel *(m)* *[fooroonkel]*; **to boil the water** das Wasser kochen *[dass vasser kochen]*

boiled egg ein gekochtes Ei *[gekochtess 'eye']*

boiling hot kochend heiß *[kochent hyce]*

bomb eine Bombe *[bomb-uh]*

bone ein Knochen *(m)* *[k-nochen]*

bonnet die Haube *[howb-uh]*

book ein Buch *(nt)* *[booch]*; *(verb)* buchen *[boochen]*; **I'd like to book a table for two** ich möchte einen Tisch für zwei Personen bestellen *[ich murcht-uh ine-en tish foor tsvy pairzohnen beshtellen]*

bookshop, bookstore eine Buchhandlung *[booch-handloong]*

boot ein Stiefel *(m)* *[shteefel]*; *(of car)* der Kofferraum *[koffer-rowm]*

booze der Alkohol *[alkohohl]*; **I had too much booze** ich habe zuviel getrunken *[ich hahb-uh tsoofeel getroonken]*

border *(of country)* die Grenze *[grents-uh]*

border crossing der Grenzübergang *[grents-oobergang]*

border guard der Grenzsoldat *[grents-zoldaht]*

bored: I'm bored ich langweile mich *[ich langvyle-uh mich]*

boring langweilig *[langvyle-ich]*

born: I was born in ... ich bin in ... geboren *[ich bin in ... geboren]*

borrow: may I borrow ...? kann ich ... leihen? *[kan ich ... ly-en]*

boss der Chef

both beide *[byde-uh]*; **I'll take both of them** ich nehme beide *[ich naym-uh]*; **we'll both come** wir kommen beide

bother: sorry to bother you es tut mir leid, Sie belästigen zu müssen *[ess toot meer lyte zee belestigen tsoo moossen]*; **it's no bother** das ist kein Problem *[dass ist kyne problaym]*; **it's such a bother** es ist so ein Ärger *[ess ist zoh ine airger]*

bottle eine Flasche *[flash-uh]*; **a bottle of wine** eine Flasche Wein *[vyne]*

bottle-opener ein Flaschenöffner *(m)* *[flashen-urfner]*

bottom *(of person)* der Hintern; **at the bottom of the hill** am Fuß des Berges *[am fooss dess bairgess]*

bottom gear der erste Gang *[airst-uh]*

bouncer der Rausschmeißer *[rowss-shmysser]*

bow *(of ship)* der Bug *[book]*

bowels die Eingeweide *[ine-gevyde-uh]*

bowling *(ten pin)* das Bowling

bowls *(game)* Boule *[bool]*

box eine Schachtel *[shachtel]*; *(big)* eine Kiste *[kist-uh]*

box lunch ein Mittagessen *(nt)* zum Mitnehmen *[mittahk-essen tsoom*

*mi*tnaymen]
box office die Kasse [kass-uh]
boy ein Junge (m) [yoong-uh]
boyfriend: my boyfriend mein Freund [myne froynt]
bra ein BH (m) [bay-hah]
bracelet ein Armband (nt) [armbant]
brake die Bremse [bremz-uh]; **there's something wrong with the brakes** mit den Bremsen stimmt etwas nicht [mit dayn bremzen shtimmt etvass niCHt]; **can you check the brakes?** können nen Sie die Bremsen überprüfen? [kurnen zee dee bremzen ooberproofen]; **I had to brake suddenly** ich mußte plötzlich bremsen [iCH moost-uh plurtsliCH]
brake fluid die Bremsflüssigkeit [brems-flossiCHkyte]
brake lining der Bremsbelag [brems-belahk]
brandy ein Weinbrand (m) [vyne-brant]
brave mutig [mootiCH]
bread das Brot [broht]; **could we have some bread and butter?** können wir etwas Brot und Butter haben? [kurnen veer etvass broht oont bootter hahben]; **some more bread, please** noch etwas Brot bitte; **white bread** das Weißbrot [vyce-broht]; **brown bread** das Graubrot [growbroht]; **wholemeal bread** das Vollkornbrot [follkornbroht]; **rye bread** das Roggenbrot [roggenbroht]
break brechen [breCHen]; **I think I've broken my ankle** ich glaube, ich habe mir den Knöchel gebrochen [iCH glowb-uh iCH hahb-uh meer dayn k-nurCHel gebroCHen]; **it keeps breaking** es geht dauernd kaputt [ess gayt dow-airnt kappoot]
breakdown die Panne [pann-uh]; **I've had a breakdown** ich habe eine Panne; **nervous breakdown** der Nervenzusammenbruch [nairfen-tsoozammen-brooCH]
breakfast das Frühstück [frooshtook]; **English/full breakfast** ein englisches Frühstück; **continental breakfast** ein kleines Frühstück [ine klyne-ess]
break in: somebody's broken in es ist eingebrochen worden [ess ist ine-gebroCHen vorden]
breast die Brust [broost]
breast-feed stillen [shtillen]

breath der Atem [ahtem]; **out of breath** außer Atem [owsser ahtem]
breathe atmen [ahtmen]; **I can't breathe** ich bekomme keinen Atem [iCH bekomm-uh kynen ahtem]
breathtaking (view etc) atemberaubend [ahtem-berrowbent]
breeze die Brise [breez-uh]
breezy (cool) kühl [kool]
bride die Braut [browt]
bridegroom der Bräutigam [broytigam]
bridge die Brücke [brook-uh]; (card game) Bridge
brief kurz [koorts]
briefcase eine Aktentasche [akten-tash-uh]
bright (light etc) hell; **bright red** hellrot [hell-roht]
brilliant (idea) glänzend [glentsent]; (person) großartig [grohss-ahrtiCH]
bring bringen; **could you bring it to my hotel?** können Sie es in mein Hotel bringen lassen? [kurnen zee ess in myne hotel bringen lassen]; **I'll bring it back** ich bringe es zurück [iCH bring-uh ess tsoo-roock]; **can I bring a friend too?** kann ich einen Freund mitbringen? [kan iCH ine-en froynt mitbringen]
Britain Großbritannien [grohss-britanee-en]
British britisch
brochure eine Broschüre [broshoor-uh]; **do you have any brochures on ...?** haben Sie Broschüren über ...? [hahben zee broshooren oober]
broke: I'm broke ich bin pleite [iCH bin plyte-uh]
broken kaputt; **you've broken it** Sie haben es kaputtgemacht [zee hahben ess kappoot-gemaCHt]; **it's broken** es ist kaputt; **broken nose** eine gebrochene Nase [gebroCHen-uh nahz-uh]
brooch eine Brosche [brosh-uh]
brother: my brother mein Bruder [myne brooder]
brother-in-law: my brother-in-law mein Schwager [myne shvahger]
brown braun [brown]; **I don't go brown** ich werde nicht braun [vaird-uh]
brown paper das Packpapier [pack-pappeer]
browse: may I just browse around? kann ich mich nur mal umsehen? [kan

ich mich noor mahl oomzayen]

bruise ein blauer Fleck *[blower fleck]*

brunette eine Brünette *[broonett-uh]*

brush eine Bürste *[boorst-uh]*; *(artist's)* ein Pinsel *(m)*

Brussels sprouts der Rosenkohl *[rohzenkohl]*

bubble bath das Schaumbad *[showmbaht]*

bucket ein Eimer *(m) [ime-er]*

buffet das Büfett *[boofett]*

bug *(insect)* die Wanze *[vants-uh]*; **she's caught a bug** sie hat sich angesteckt *[zee hat zich angeshteckt]*

building das Gebäude *[geboyd-uh]*

bulb eine Birne *[beern-uh]*; **we need a new bulb** wir brauchen eine neue Birne

bump: I bumped my head ich habe mir den Kopf gestoßen *[ich hahb-uh meer dayn kopf geshtohssen]*

bumper die Stoßstange *[shtohss-shtang-uh]*

bumpy *(road)* holprig *[hollprich]*

bunch of flowers ein Blumenstrauß *(m) [bloomen-shtrowss]*

bungalow der Bungalow *[boongalo]*

bunion ein Ballen *(m) [bal-en]*

bunk das Bett

bunk beds ein Etagenbett *(nt) [etahjen-bet]*

buoy eine Boje *[boh-yuh]*

burglar ein Einbrecher *(m) [ine-brecher]*

burn: do you have an ointment for burns? haben Sie eine Salbe für Brandwunden? *[hahben zee ine-uh zalb-uh foor brant-voonden]*

burnt: this meat is burnt das Fleisch ist angebrannt; **my arms are so burnt** meine Arme sind ganz verbrannt *[myne-uh arm-uh zint gants fairbrannt]*

burst: a burst pipe ein geplatztes Rohr *[ine geplatstes]*

bus der Bus *[booss]*; **is this the bus for ...?** ist das der Bus nach ...?; **when's the next bus?** wann fährt der nächste Bus? *[van*

fairt dair naychst-uh booss]

bus driver der Busfahrer *[booss-fahrer]*

business das Geschäft *[gesheft]*; **I'm here on business** ich bin geschäftlich hier *[ich bin gesheftlich heer]*

bus station der Busbahnhof *[boossbahn-hohf]*

bus stop die Bushaltestelle *[booss-hallt-uh-shtell-uh]*; **will you tell me which bus stop I get off at?** können Sie mir sagen, wo ich aussteigen muß? *[kurnen zee meer zahgen voh ich owss-shtygen mooss]*

bust *(of woman)* der Busen *[boozen]*

bus tour eine Busreise *[booss-ryze-uh]*

busy *(street)* belebt *[belaypt]*; *(restaurant etc)* vielbesucht *[feel-bezoocht]*; **I'm busy this evening** ich habe heute Abend keine Zeit *[ich hahb-uh hoyt-uh ahbent kyne-uh tsyte]*; **the line was busy** es war besetzt *[ess vahr bezetst]*

but aber *[ahber]*; **not ... but ...** nicht ... sondern ... *[nicht ... zondern]*

butcher der Metzger

butter die Butter *[bootter]*

butterfly ein Schmetterling *(m) [shmetterling]*

button ein Knopf *(m) [k-nopf]*

buy: I'll buy it ich kaufe es *[ich kowf-uh ess]*; **where can I buy ...?** wo kann ich ... bekommen? *[voh kan ich]*

by: by train/car/plane mit dem Zug/Auto/Flugzeug *[mit daym]*; **who's it written by?** wer hat das geschrieben? *[vair hat dass geshreeben]*; **it's by Mahler** es ist von Mahler *[fon]*; **I came by myself** ich bin allein gekommen *[ich bin al-ine]*; **a seat by the window** ein Platz am Fenster; **by the sea** am Meer *[am mair]*; **can you do it by Wednesday?** können Sie es bis Mittwoch machen?

bye-bye auf Wiedersehen *[owff-veeder-zayn]*

bypass eine Umgehungsstraße *[oom-gayoongs-shtrahss-uh]*

C

cab ein Taxi (*nt*)
cabaret das Varieté *[varee-etay]*
cabbage der Kohl
cabin eine Kabine *[kabeen-uh]*
cable (*elec*) ein Kabel (*nt*) *[kahbel]*
cablecar die Drahtseilbahn *[drahtzyle-bahn]*
café das Café *[kaffay]*
caffeine das Koffein *[koffay-een]*
cake der Kuchen *[kōōchen]*; **a piece of cake** ein Stück Kuchen *[ine shtœck kōōchen]*
calculator ein Rechner (*m*) *[rechner]*
calendar ein Kalender (*m*) *[kalender]*
call: **what is this called?** wie heißt das *[vee hyst dass]*; **call the police!** rufen Sie die Polizei! *[rōōfen zee dee polits'eye']*; **call the manager!** ich möchte den Geschäftsführer sprechen *[ich murcht-uh dayn geshefts-fœrer shprechen]*; **I'd like to make a call to England** ich möchte gern nach England anrufen *[gairn nach eng-lant anrōōfen]*; **I'll call back later** (*come back*) ich komme später noch einmal wieder *[ich komm-uh shpayter noch ine-mahl veeder]*; (*phone back*) ich rufe später noch einmal an *[ich rōōf-uh shpayter ... an]*; **I'm expecting a call from London** ich erwarte einen Anruf aus London *[ich airvart-uh ine-en anrōōf owss]*; **would you give me a call at 7.30 tomorrow morning?** könnten Sie mich morgen früh um 7.30 Uhr wecken? *[kurnten zee mich morgen frœ ... vecken]*; **it's been called off** es ist abgesagt worden *[ess ist apgezahgt vorden]*
call box eine Telefonzelle *[telefohntsell-uh]*
calm ruhig *[rōōich]*; **calm down!** beruhigen Sie sich! *[berōōigen zee zich]*
Calor gas (*tm*) das Butangas *[bōōtahn-gahss]*
calories Kalorien *[kaloree-en]*
camera eine Kamera
camp: **is there somewhere we can**

camp? können wir hier irgendwo zelten? *[kurnen veer heer eergentvoh tselten]*; **can we camp here?** können wir hier zelten?
campbed eine Campingliege *[kemping-leeg-uh]*
camping das Camping *[kemping]*
campsite ein Campingplatz (*m*) *[kempingplats]*
can eine Dose *[dohz-uh]*; **a can of beer** eine Dose Bier
can: **can I ...?** kann ich ...? *[ich]*; **can you ...?** (*singular polite form*) können Sie ...? *[kurnen zee]*; (*singular familiar form*) kannst du ...? *[dōō]*; **can he ...?** kann er ...? *[kan air]*; **can we ...?** können wir ...? *[kurnen veer]*; **can they ...?** können sie ...?; **I can't ...** ich kann nicht ... *[nicht]*; **he can't ...** er kann nicht ...; **can I keep it?** kann ich es behalten?; **if I can** wenn ich kann *[ven]*; **that can't be right** das kann nicht stimmen *[dass kan nicht shtimmen]*
Canada Kanada
Canadian (*adj*) kanadisch *[kanahdish]*; (*man*) der Kanadier *[kanahdee-er]*; (*woman*) die Kanadierin
canal der Kanal *[kanahl]*
cancel streichen *[shtrychen]*; **can I cancel my reservation?** kann ich meine Reservierung rückgängig machen? *[kan ich myne-uh rezairveeroong rœckgengich machen]*; **can we cancel dinner for tonight?** können wir das Abendessen heute ausfallen lassen? *[kurnen veer dass ahbentessen hoyt-uh owssfal-en lassen]*; **I cancelled it** ich habe es abgesagt *[ich hahb-uh ess apgezahkt]*
cancellation die Streichung *[shtrychoong]*
candle eine Kerze *[kairts-uh]*
candy ein Bonbon (*m*); **a piece of candy** ein Bonbon
canoe ein Kanu (*nt*) *[kahnōō]*
can-opener ein Dosenöffner (*m*)

[doohzenurfner]

cap *(yachting etc)* eine Mütze *[moots-uh]*; *(of bottle)* der Deckel; *(of radiator)* der Verschluß *[fairshlooss]*; **bathing cap** eine Badekappe *[bahd-uh-kap-uh]*

capital city die Haupstadt *[howpt-shtat]*

capital letters die Blockbuchstaben *[blockboochshtahben]*

capsize: it capsized es ist gekentert

captain *(of ship, of plane)* der Kapitän *[kapitayn]*

car das Auto *[owto]*

carafe eine Karaffe *[karaff-uh]*

carat: is it 9/14 carat gold? ist es 9/14-karätiges Gold? *[ist ess noyn/feertsayn karaytiges golt]*

caravan der Wohnwagen *[vohnvahgen]*

caravan site ein Campingplatz *(m)* *[kempingplats]*

carbonated mit Kohlensäure *[kohlenzoyr-uh]*

carburettor, carburetor der Vergaser *[fairgahzer]*

card: do you have a (business) card? haben Sie eine Karte? *[hahben zee ine-uh kart-uh]*

cardboard box ein Pappkarton *(m)*

cardigan eine Strickjacke *[shtrickyack-uh]*

cards die Karten; **do you play cards?** spielen Sie Karten? *[shpeelen zee]*

care: goodbye, take care auf Wiedersehen, mach's gut *[owff veederzayn, machss goot]*; **will you take care of this bag for me?** können Sie bitte auf diese Tasche aufpassen? *[kurnen zee bitt-uh owff deez-uh ... owff-passen]*; **care of ...** bei ... *[by]*

careful: be careful seien Sie vorsichtig *[zy-en zee forzichtich]*

careless: that was careless of you das war unvorsichtig von Ihnen *[dass vahr oonforzichtich fon eenen]*; **careless driving** leichtsinniges Autofahren *[lychtzinniges owto-fahren]*

car ferry die Autofähre *[owto-fair-uh]*

car hire eine Autovermietung *[owto-fairmeetoong]*

car keys die Autoschlüssel *[owto-shloossel]*

carnation eine Nelke *[nelk-uh]*

carnival ein Volksfest *(nt)* *[follksfest]*

car park ein Parkplatz *(m)* *[parkplats]*

carpet der Teppich *[teppich]*

car rental *(shop)* eine Autovermietung *[owto-fairmeetoong]*

carrot eine Möhre *[mur-uh]*

carry tragen *[trahgen]*; **could you carry this for me?** können Sie das für mich tragen?

carry-all eine Tasche *[tash-uh]*

carry-cot eine Säuglingstragetasche *[zoyglingstrahg-uh-tash-uh]*

carry-on: what a carry-on! so ein Theater! *[zoh ine tayahter]*

car-sick: I get car-sick beim Autofahren wird mir schlecht *[byme owtofahren veert meer schlecht]*

carton *(of cigarettes)* eine Stange *[shtang-uh]*; **a carton of milk** eine Tüte Milch *[ine-uh toot-uh milch]*

carving die Schnitzerei *[shnitser'eye']*

carwash *(place)* die Autowaschanlage *[owto-vashanlahg-uh]*

case *(suitcase)* ein Koffer *(m)*; **in any case** in jedem Fall *[in yaydem fal]*; **in that case** in dem Fall *[in daym fal]*; **it's a special case** das ist ein besonderer Fall *[dass ist ine bezonderer fal]*; **in case he comes back** falls er zurückkommt *[falss air tsoorrock-komt]*; **I'll take two just in case** ich nehme zwei, für alle Fälle *[ich naym-uh tsvy foor al-uh fel-uh]*

cash das Bargeld *[bargelt]*; **I don't have any cash** ich habe kein Bargeld; **I'll pay cash** ich zahle in bar *[ich tsahl-uh]*; **will you cash a cheque/check for me?** können Sie mir einen Scheck einlösen? *[kurnen zee meer ine-en sheck ine-lurzen]*

cashdesk die Kasse *[kass-uh]*

cash dispenser ein Geldautomat *(m)* *[gelt-owtomaht]*

cash register die Kasse *[kass-uh]*

casino ein Spielkasino *(nt)* *[shpeel-kazeenoh]*

cassette eine Kassette *[kassett-uh]*

cassette player ein Kassettenrecorder *(m)*

cassette recorder ein Kassettenrecorder *(m)*

castle das Schloß *[shloss]*

casual: casual clothes legere Kleidung *[layjair-uh klydoong]*

cat eine Katze *[kats-uh]*

catastrophe die Katastrophe *[katastrohf-uh]*

catch: the catch has broken der Verschluß ist kaputt *[fairshlooss ist kapoott]*; **where do we catch the bus?** wo können wir den Bus bekommen? *[vo kurnen veer dayn booss bekommen]*; **he's caught some strange illness** er hat sich eine seltsame Krankheit geholt *[air hat ziCH ine-uh zeltzam-uh krankhyte gehohlt]*

catching: is it catching? ist es ansteckend? *[ist ess anshteckent]*

cathedral der Dom *[dohm]*

Catholic katholisch *[kattohlish]*

cauliflower der Blumenkohl *[bloomenkohl]*

cause der Grund *[groont]*

cave eine Höhle *[hurl-uh]*

caviar der Kaviar *[kaviar]*

ceiling die Decke *[deck-uh]*

celebrations die Feiern *[fy-ern]*

celery der Sellerie *[zelleree]*

cellophane das Cellophan (*tm*) *[tsellofahn]*

cemetery der Friedhof *[freet-hohf]*

center das Zentrum *[tsentroom]*; *see also* **centre**

centigrade Celsius *[zelzee-oss]*; *see page 121*

centimetre, centimeter der Zentimeter *[tsentimayter]*; *see page 119*

central zentral *[tsentrahl]*; **we'd prefer something more central** wir möchten gern etwas zentraler wohnen *[veer murCHten gairn etvass tsentrahler vohnen]*

central heating die Zentralheizung *[tsentrahlhytsoong]*

central station der Hauptbahnhof *[howpt-bahnhohf]*

centre das Zentrum *[tsentroom]*; **how do we get to the centre?** wie kommt man zum Zentrum? *[tsoom]*; **in the centre (of town)** im Stadtzentrum *[im shtat—]*

century das Jahrhundert *[yahr-hoondert]*; **in the 19th/20th century** im 19./20. Jahrhundert *[noyntsaynten/tsvantsiCHsten]*

ceramics die Keramik *[kairahmik]*

certain sicher *[ziCHer]*; **are you certain?** sind Sie sicher?; **I'm absolutely certain** ich bin absolut sicher

certainly sicher *[ziCHer]*; **certainly not** ganz bestimmt nicht! *[gants beshtimmt niCHt]*

certificate eine Bescheinigung; *[beshynigoong]*; **birth certificate** die Geburtsurkunde *[geboorts-oorkoond-uh]*

chain eine Kette *[kett-uh]*

chair ein Stuhl (*m*) *[shtool]*

chairlift der Sessellift *[zessel-lift]*

chalet ein Chalet (*nt*)

chambermaid das Zimmermädchen *[tsimmer-maydCHen]*

champagne der Champagner *[shampanyer]*

chance: quite by chance durch Zufall *[doorCH tsoofal]*; **no chance!** kommt nicht in Frage! *[komt niCHt in frahg-uh]*

change: could you change this into marks? können Sie das in Mark umtauschen? *[kurnen zee dass in mark oomtowshen]*; **I haven't any change** ich habe kein Kleingeld *[iCH hahb-uh kyne klyne-gelt]*; **can you give me change for a 50 mark note?** können Sie mir einen 50-Mark-Schein wechseln? *[kurnen zee meer ine-en foonftsiCH mark shyne veckseln]*; **can I change this for ...?** kann ich das gegen ... umtauschen? *[kan iCH dass gaygen ... oomtowshen]*; **do we have to change (trains)?** müssen wir umsteigen? *[moossen veer oomshtygen]*; **for a change** zur Abwechslung *[tsoor apvecksloong]*; **you haven't changed the sheets** die Laken sind nicht gewechselt worden *[dee lahken zint niCHt geveckselt vorden]*; **the place has changed so much** der Ort hat sich sehr verändert *[hat ziCH zair fairendert]*; **do you want to change places with me?** möchten Sie den Platz mit mir tauschen? *[murCHten zee dayn plats mit meer towshen]*

changeable (*person*) unbeständig *[oonbeshtendiCH]*; (*weather*) veränderlich *[fairenderliCH]*

channel: the English Channel der Ärmelkanal *[airmel-kanahl]*

chaos das Chaos *[kah-oss]*

chap: he's a nice chap er ist ein netter Kerl *[kairl]*; **the chap at reception** der Mann am Empfang

chapel die Kapelle *[kapell-uh]*

charge: is there an extra charge? muß man eine Zusatzgebühr bezahlen? *[mooss man ine-uh tsoozatsgeboor betsahlen]*; **what do you charge?** wieviel

berechnen Sie? *[veefeel berecHnen zee]*;
who's in charge here? ·ver ist hier
zuständig? *[vair ist heer tsōōshtendicH]*
charmer: he's a real charmer er ist wirklich charmant *[air ist veerklicH shar-
mant]*
charming (*person*) reizend *[rytsent]*
chart die Tabelle *[tabell-uh]*
charter flight ein Charterflug (*m*) *[shar-
terflōōk]*
chassis das Chassis
cheap billig *[billicH]*; **do you have something cheaper?** haben Sie etwas billige-
res? *[hahben zee etvass billigeress]*
cheat: I've been cheated ich bin betrogen
worden *[icH bin betrohgen vorden]*
check: will you check? könnten Sie das
nachprüfen? *[kurnten zee dass
nacH-prœfen]*; **will you check the steering?** könnten Sie die Lenkung überprüfen?; **we checked in** wir haben uns
angemeldet *[veer hahben oonss angemel-
det]*; **we checked out** wir haben uns
abgemeldet *[veer hahben oonss apgemel-
det]*; **I've checked it** ich habe es nachge-
prüft *[icH hahb-uh ess nacH-geprœft]*
check (*money*) der Scheck *[sheck]*; **will
you take a check?** nehmen Sie Schecks?
[naymen zee shecks]
check (*bill*) die Rechnung *[recHnoong]*;
may I have the check please? kann ich
bitte die Rechnung haben?
checkbook das Scheckheft *[sheckheft]*
checked (*shirt etc*) kariert *[karreert]*
checkers Dame *[dahm-uh]*
check-in (*at airport*) die Abfertigung *[ap-
fairtigoong]*
checkroom die Garderobe *[garderohb-
uh]*
cheek die Backe *[back-uh]*; **what a cheek!**
so eine Frechheit! *[zoh ine-uh
frecH-hyte]*
cheeky frech *[frecH]*
cheerio tschüs *[tshœss]*
cheers (*thank you*) danke *[dank-uh]*; (*toast*)
prost! *[prohst]*
cheer up! lassen Sie den Kopf nicht hän-
gen! *[zee dayn kopf nicHt hengen]*
cheese der Käse *[kayz-uh]*
cheesecake der Käsekuchen *[kayz-uh-
kōōcHen]*
chef der Chefkoch *[shefkocH]*
chemist eine Apotheke *[apotayk-uh]*

cheque der Scheck *[sheck]*; **will you take
a cheque?** nehmen Sie Schecks? *[nay-
men zee shecks]*
cheque book das Scheckheft *[sheckheft]*
cheque card die Scheckkarte *[sheck-kart-
uh]*
cherry eine Kirsche *[keersh-uh]*
chess Schach *[shacH]*
chest die Brust *[broost]*
chewing gum ein Kaugummi (*m*)
[kow-goomee]
chicken ein Hähnchen (*nt*) *[hayncHen]*
chickenpox die Windpocken
[vintpocken]
child das Kind *[kint]*; **children** die
Kinder
child minder eine Tagesmutter *[tahgess-
mootter]*
child minding service der Babysitter-
dienst *[—deenst]*
children's playground ein Kinderspielplatz (*m*) *[kindershpeelplats]*
children's pool das Kinder-
schwimmbecken *[kindershvimmbecken]*
children's portion (*of food*) ein Kinder-
teller (*m*)
children's room das Kinderzimmer
[kindertsimmer]
chilled (*wine*) gekühlt *[gekoolt]*; **it's not
properly chilled** es ist nicht kühl genug
[ess ist nicHt kœl genōōk]
chilly (*weather*) kühl *[kœl]*
chimney der Schornstein *[shornshtyne]*
chin das Kinn
china das Porzellan *[portsellahn]*; (*adj*)
Porzellan-
chips die Pommes frites *[pom frit]*; **(potato) chips** die Chips
chiropodist der Fußpfleger *[fōōss-
pflayger]*
chocolate die Schokolade *[shockolahd-
uh]*; **a chocolate bar** eine Tafel Schokolade *[ine-uh tahfel shockolahd-uh]*; **a
box of chocolates** eine Pralinenschach-
tel *[pralleenenshacHtel]*; **hot chocolate**
der Kakao *[kackow]*
choke (*car*) der Choke
choose: it's hard to choose die Auswahl
ist schwer *[dee owssvahl ist shvair]*; **you
choose for us** entscheiden Sie für uns
[entshyden zee fœr oonss]
chop: pork/lamb chop ein Schweine-
/Lammkotelett (*nt*) *[shvyne-uh-/lamm-*

kotlett]

Christian name der Vorname *[fornahm-uh]*

Christmas Weihnachten *[vynaCHten]*; **merry Christmas** frohe Weihnachten *[froh-uh]*; **Christmas Eve** der Heilig-abend *[hylicHahbent]*

church die Kirche *[keercH-uh]*; **where is the Protestant/Catholic Church?** wo ist die evangelische/katholische Kirche? *[dee ayfangaylish-uh/katohlish-uh]*

cider der Apfelwein *[apfel-vyne]*

cigar eine Zigarre *[tsigarr-uh]*

cigarette eine Zigarette *[tsigarett-uh]*; **tipped/plain cigarettes** Zigaretten mit/ohne Filter

cigarette lighter ein Feuerzeug (*nt*) *[foyer-tsoyk]*

cine-camera eine Schmalfilmkamera *[shmahl-filmkamerah]*

cinema das Kino *[keeno]*

circle der Kreis *[kryce]*; (*cinema: seats*) der Balkon *[balkong]*

citizen der Bürger *[boorger]*; **I'm a British/American citizen** ich bin britischer/amerikanischer Staatsbürger *[icH bin britisher/amerikahnisher shtahtsboorger]*

city die Stadt *[shtatt]*

city centre, city center die Innenstadt *[innenshtatt]*

claim (*insurance*) der Anspruch *[anshproocH]*

claim form (*insurance*) ein Antragsformular (*nt*) *[antrahks-formoolahr]*

clarify klären *[klairen]*

classical (*music*) klassisch *[klassish]*

clean sauber *[zowber]*; **may I have some clean sheets?** kann ich neue Bettlaken bekommen? *[kan icH noy-uh bettlahken bekommen]*; **our room hasn't been cleaned today** unser Zimmer ist heute nicht gesäubert worden *[oonzer tsimmer ist hoyt-uh nicHt gezoybert vorden]*; **it's not clean** es ist nicht sauber; **can you clean this for me?** (*clothes*) können Sie das für mich reinigen? *[kurnen zee dass for micH rynigen]*

cleaning solution (*for contact lenses*) die Reinigungslösung *[rynigoongs-lurzoong]*

cleansing cream die Reinigungscreme *[rynigoongs-kraym-uh]*

clear: it's not very clear (*meaning*) das ist nicht sehr deutlich *[dass ist nicHt zair doytlicH]*; **ok, that's clear** (*understood*) okay, alles klar *[okay al-ess klahr]*

clever klug *[klook]*

cliff die Klippe *[klipp-uh]*

climate das Klima *[kleema]*

climb: it's a long climb to the top der Aufstieg dauert sehr lang *[dair owffshteek dowert zair]*; **we're going to climb ...** wir wollen ... besteigen *[veer vollen ... beshtygen]*

climber der Bergsteiger *[bairkshtyger]*

climbing boots die Bergstiefel *[bairk-shteefel]*

climbing holiday: we're going on a climbing holiday wir gehen im Urlaub Bergsteigen *[veer gayen im oorlowp bairkshtygen]*

clinic die Klinik

clips (*ski*) die Clips

cloakroom (*for coats*) die Garderobe *[garderohb-uh]*; (*WC*) die Toilette *[twalett-uh]*

clock die Uhr *[oor]*

close: is it close? ist es in der Nähe? *[ist ess in dair nay-uh]*; **close to the hotel** in der Nähe des Hotels; **close by** in der Nähe; (*weather*) schwül *[shvool]*

close: when do you close? wann schließen Sie? *[van shleessen zee]*

closed geschlossen *[geshlossen]*; **they were closed** sie hatten geschlossen

closet der Schrank *[shrank]*

cloth (*material*) der Stoff *[shtoff]*; (*rag etc*) ein Lappen (*m*)

clothes die Kleider *[klyder]*

clothes line die Wäscheleine *[vesh-uh-lyne-uh]*

clothes peg, clothes pin eine Wä-scheklammer *[vesh-uh-klammer]*

cloud die Wolke *[volk-uh]*; **it's clouding over** es bewölkt sich *[ess bevurlkt zicH]*

cloudy wolkig *[volkicH]*

club der Klub *[kloob]*

clubhouse das Klubhaus *[kloobhowss]*

clumsy ungeschickt *[oongeshickt]*

clutch (*car*) die Kupplung *[kooploong]*; **the clutch is slipping** die Kupplung schleift *[shlyft]*

coach der Bus *[booss]*

coach party die Busreisegruppe *[booss-ryze-uh-groop-uh]*

coach trip eine Busreise [booss-ryze-uh]

coast die Küste [koost-uh]; **at the coast** an der Küste [an dair]

coastguard die Küstenwache [koosten-vacH-uh]

coat (overcoat etc) ein Mantel (m); (jacket) eine Jacke [yack-uh]

coathanger ein Kleiderbügel (m) [klyder-boogel]

cobbled street eine Straße mit Kopfsteinpflaster [shtrahss-uh mit kopfshtyne-pflaster]

cobbler der Schuster [shooster]

cockroach eine Küchenschabe [koochenshahb-uh]

cocktail ein Cocktail (m)

cocktail bar die Cocktailbar

cocoa (drink) der Kakao [kackow]

coconut eine Kokosnuß [kohkossnooss]

cod der Kabeljau [kahbel-yow]

code: what's the (dialling) code for ...? was ist die Vorwahl für ...? [vass ist dee forvahl foor]

coffee der Kaffee [kaffay]; **white coffee, coffee with milk** Kaffee mit Milch [mit milcH]; **black coffee** schwarzer Kaffee [shvartser]; **two coffees, please** zwei Kaffee bitte

coin eine Münze [moonts-uh]

Coke (tm) eine Cola

cold kalt; **I'm cold** mir ist kalt [meer]; **I have a cold** ich bin erkältet [icH bin airkeltet]

coldbox (for carrying food) eine Kühltasche [kooltash-uh]

cold cream die Feuchtigkeitscreme [foycHticHkytes-kraym-uh]

collapse: he's collapsed er ist zusammengebrochen [air ist tsoozammen-gebrocHen]

collar der Kragen [krahgen]

collar bone das Schlüsselbein [shloossel-byne]

colleague: my colleague mein Kollege [myne kollayg-uh]; **your colleague** (woman) Ihre Kollegin

collect: I've come to collect ... ich komme, um ... abzuholen [icH komm-uh oom ... ap-tsoo-hohlen]; **I collect ...** (stamps etc) ich sammle ... [icH zammluh]; **I want to call New York collect** ich möchte ein R-Gespräch nach New York führen [icH murcHt-uh ine air-geshpraycH nacH ... fooren]

collect call ein R-Gespräch (nt) [air-geshpraycH]

college das College

collision ein Zusammenstoß (m) [tsoo-zammenshtohss]

Cologne Köln [kurln]

cologne (eau de ...) das Eau de Cologne

colo(u)r die Farbe [farb-uh]; **do you have any other colours?** haben Sie noch andere Farben? [hahben zee nocH ander-uh farben]

colo(u)r film ein Farbfilm (m)

comb ein Kamm (m)

come kommen; **I come from London** ich komme aus London [icH komm-uh owss]; **where do you come from?** woher kommen Sie? [vohair kommen zee]; **when are they coming?** wann werden sie kommen? [van vairden zee]; **come here** kommen Sie her [zee hair]; **come with me** kommen Sie mit mir [meer]; **come back!** kommen Sie zurück! [tsoo-roock]; **I'll come back later** ich komme später wieder [icH komm-uh shpayter veeder]; **come in!** herein! [hairyne]; **it just came off** es ist einfach abgegangen [ess ist ine-facH apgegangen]; **he's coming on very well** (improving) er macht sich [air macHt zicH]; **it's coming on nicely** es entwickelt sich ganz gut [ess entvickelt zicH gants goot]; **come on!** kommen Sie!; **do you want to come out this evening?** möchten Sie heute abend ausgehen? [murcHten zee hoyt-uh ahbent owssgayen]; **these two pictures didn't come out** diese zwei Bilder sind nichts geworden [deez-uh tsvy bilder zint nicHts gevorden]; **the money hasn't come through yet** das Geld ist noch nicht angekommen [dass gelt ist nocH nicHt angekommen]

comfortable bequem [bekvaym]; **the hotel's not very comfortable** das Hotel ist nicht sehr komfortabel [nicHt zair komfortahbel]

Common Market der Gemeinsame Markt [dair gemyne-zahm-uh markt]

company (firm) die Firma [feerma]

comparison: there's no comparison das ist kein Vergleich [kyne fairglycHe]

compartment (train) das Abteil [aptyle]

compass ein Kompaß (m)

compensation die Entschädigung
[*entshaydigoong*]
complain sich beschweren [*ziċн beshvai-
ren*]; **I want to complain about my
room** ich möchte mich über mein Zimmer beschweren [*iċн murċнt-uh miċн
œber myne tsimmer*]
complaint die Beschwerde [*beshvaird-
uh*]
complete vollständig [*follshtendiċн*]; **the
complete set** das ganze Set [*dass gants-
uh set*]; **it's a complete disaster** es ist
eine totale Katastrophe [*ess ist ine-uh
totahl-uh katastrohf-uh*]
completely (*finished*) völlig [*fürliċн*]; (*different*) vollkommen [*follkommen*]
complicated: it's very complicated es
ist sehr kompliziert [*ess ist zair
komplitseert*]
**compliment: my compliments to the
chef** mein Kompliment dem Koch
[*myne kompliment daym koċн*]
comprehensive (*insurance*) Vollkasko
[*follkasko*]
compulsory obligatorisch [*obligatohrish*]
computer der Computer [*komp-yōōter*]
concern: we are very concerned wir
sind sehr besorgt [*veer zint zair bezorkt*]
concert das Konzert [*kontsairt*]
concrete der Beton [*betohn*]
concussion die Gehirnerschütterung [*ge-
heern-airshœtteroong*]
condenser (*car*) der Kondensator [*kon-
denzahtor*]
condition der Zustand [*tsōōshtant*]; **it's
not in very good condition** es ist nicht
in sehr gutem Zustand [*niċнt in zair
gōōtem*]
conditioner (*for hair*) der Festiger
condom ein Kondom (*nt*) [*kondohm*]
conductor (*on train*) der Zugführer
[*tsōōkfœrer*]
conference die Konferenz [*konfairents*]
confirm: can you confirm that? können
Sie das bestätigen? [*kurnen zee dass
beshtaytigen*]
confuse: it's very confusing es ist sehr
verwirrend [*ess ist zair fairvirrent*]
congratulations! herzlichen Glückwunsch! [*hairtsliċнen glœckvoonsh*]
conjunctivitis die Bindehautentzündung
[*bind-uh-howtentsœndoong*]

connecting flight der Anschlußflug
[*anshlooss-flōōk*]
connection die Verbindung [*fairbindoong*]
connoisseur der Kenner
conscious bei Bewußtsein [*bevoostzyne*]
consciousness: he's lost consciousness
er hat das Bewußtsein verloren [*air hat
dass bevoostzyne fairlohren*]
constipation die Verstopfung
[*fairshtopfoong*]
consul der Konsul [*konzool*]
consulate das Konsulat [*konzoolaht*]
contact: how can I contact …? wie kann
ich … erreichen? [*vee kan iċн … air-
ryċнen*]; **I'm trying to contact …** ich
versuche, … zu erreichen [*iċн fair-
zōōċн-uh*]
contact lenses die Kontaktlinsen
continent: over here on the continent
hier im Ausland [*heer im owsslant*]
contraceptive ein Verhütungsmittel (*nt*)
[*fairhœtoongsmittel*]
contract der Vertrag [*fairtrahk*]
convenient günstig [*gœnstiċн*]
cook: it's not properly cooked es ist
nicht gar [*ess ist niċнt gar*]; **it's beauti-
fully cooked** es ist hervorragend zube-
reitet [*ess ist hairfor-rahgent
tsōōberytet*]; **he's a good cook** er ist ein
guter Koch [*air ist ine gōōter koċн*]
cooker der Herd [*hairt*]
cookie ein Plätzchen (*nt*) [*plets-cнen*]
cool kühl [*kool*]
corduroy der Kord [*kort*]
cork der Korken
corkscrew ein Korkenzieher (*m*)
[*korkentsee-er*]
corn (*foot*) ein Hühnerauge (*nt*)
[*hœnerowg-uh*]
corner: on the corner an der Ecke [*eck-
uh*]; **in the corner** in der Ecke; **a corner
table** ein Ecktisch [*ecktish*]
cornflakes die Corn-flakes (*tm*)
coronary ein Herzinfarkt (*m*)
[*hairtsinfarkt*]
correct richtig [*riċнtiċн*]; **please correct
me if I make a mistake** bitte korrigieren
Sie mich, wenn ich einen Fehler mache
[*bitt-uh korrigeeren zee miċн ven iċн
ine-en fayler maċн-uh*]
corridor der Gang
corset das Korsett [*korzet*]

cosmetics die Kosmetika *[kosmaytika]*

cost: what does it cost? was kostet das? *[vass kostet dass]*

cot ein Kinderbett *(nt)*

cotton die Baumwolle *[bowmvoll-uh]*

cotton buds die Wattestäbchen *[vat-uh-shtaypcнen]*

cotton wool die Watte *[vat-uh]*

couch *(sofa)* die Couch

couchette ein Liegewagen *(m)* *[leeg-uh-vahgen]*

cough der Husten *[hoōsten]*

cough drops die Hustendrops *[hoōsten-drops]*

cough medicine ein Hustenmittel *(nt)* *[hoōstenmittel]*

could: could you ...? könnten Sie ...? *[kurnten zee]*; **could I have ...?** könnte ich ... haben? *[kurnt-uh icн ... hahben]*; **I couldn't ...** ich konnte nicht ... *[icн konnt-uh nicнt]*

country das Land *[lant]*; **in the country** auf dem Land *[owff daym lant]*

countryside die Landschaft *[lantshafft]*

couple *(man and woman)* das Paar *[pahr]*; **a couple of ...** ein paar ...

courier der Reiseleiter *[ryze-uh-lyter]*

course *(of meal)* der Gang; **of course** natürlich *[natoorlicн]*

court *(law)* das Gericht *[gericнt]*; *(tennis)* der Platz *[plats]*

courtesy bus *(hotel to airport etc)* ein gebührenfreier Bus *[geboorenfryer booss]*

cousin: my cousin mein Vetter *[fetter]*

cover charge das Gedeck

cow die Kuh *[koō]*

crab die Krabbe *[krab-uh]*

cracked: it's cracked es ist gebrochen *[ess ist gebrocнen]*

cracker *(biscuit)* ein Kräcker *(m)* *[krecker]*

craftshop ein Handwerksladen *(m)* *[hantvairkslahden]*

cramp *(in leg etc)* ein Krampf *(m)*

crankshaft die Kurbelwelle *[koōrbel-vell-uh]*

crash: there's been a crash es hat einen Zusammenstoß gegeben *[ess hat ine-en tsoōzammenstohss gegayben]*

crash course ein Schnellkurs *(m)* *[shnell-koorss]*

crash helmet ein Sturzhelm *(m)* *[shtoorts-helm]*

crawl *(swimming)* das Kraulen *[krowlen]*

crazy verrückt *[fair-roockt]*

cream *(on milk)* der Rahm; *(on cakes)* die Sahne *[zahn-uh]*; *(for skin)* die Creme *[kraym-uh]*; *(colour)* cremefarben *[kraym-uh-farben]*

cream cheese der Frischkäse *[frishkayz-uh]*

crèche eine Kinderkrippe *[kinderkripp-uh]*

credit card die Kreditkarte *[kredeet-kart-uh]*

crib *(for baby)* das Kinderbett

crisis die Krise *[kreez-uh]*

crisps die Chips *[ships]*

crockery das Geschirr *[gesheer]*

crook: he's a crook er ist ein Gauner *[air ist ine gowner]*

crossing *(by sea)* die Überfahrt *[oberfart]*

crossroads die Kreuzung *[kroytsoong]*

crosswalk der Fußgängerüberweg *[foōss-genger-obervayk]*

crowd die Menge *[meng-uh]*

crowded voll *[foll]*

crown *(on tooth)* eine Krone *[krohn-uh]*

crucial: it's absolutely crucial es ist äußerst wichtig *[ess ist oysserst vicнticн]*

cruise eine Kreuzfahrt *[kroytsfart]*

crutch die Krücke *[kroock-uh]*; *(of body)* der Unterleib *[oonterlype]*

cry weinen *[vynen]*; **don't cry** weinen Sie nicht *[zee nicнt]*

cuckoo clock eine Kuckucksuhr *[koockoocksoōr]*

cucumber eine Gurke *[goork-uh]*

cuisine die Küche *[koocн-uh]*

cultural kulturell *[kooltoorel]*

cup eine Tasse *[tass-uh]*; **a cup of coffee** eine Tasse Kaffee *[ine-uh tass-uh kaffay]*

cupboard der Schrank *[shrank]*

cure: have you got something to cure it? haben Sie etwas dagegen? *[hahben zee etvass dagaygen]*

curlers die Lockenwickler *[lockenvickler]*

current *(elec)* der Strom *[shtrohm]*; *(in sea)* die Strömung *[shtrurmoong]*

curry der Curry

curtains die Vorhänge *[forheng-uh]*

curve die Kurve *[koorv-uh]*

cushion ein Kissen *(nt)*

custom der Brauch *[browcн]*

Customs der Zoll *[tsoll]*

cut: I've cut myself ich habe mich geschnitten *[icн hahb-uh micн geshnit-*

ten]; **could you cut a little off here?**
könnten Sie hier etwas abschneiden?
[kurnten zee heer etvass apshnyden]; **we
were cut off** wir wurden unterbrochen
[veer voorden oonterbrochen]; **the engine keeps cutting out** der Motor setzt
ständig aus *[dair motohr zetst shtendich
owss]*
cutlery das Besteck *[beshteck]*
cutlet ein Schnitzel (*nt*) *[shnitsel]*
cycle: can we cycle there? kann man

dorthin mit dem Rad fahren? *[kan man
dort-hin mit daym raht fahren]*
cycling das Radfahren *[rahtfahren]*
cyclist der Radfahrer *[rahtfahrer]*
cylinder (*car*) der Zylinder *[tsoolinder]*;
(*for Calor gas*) eine Flasche *[flash-uh]*
cylinder-head gasket die Zylinderkopf-
dichtung *[tsoolinderkopf-dichtoong]*
cynical zynisch *[tsoonish]*
cystitis eine Blasenentzündung
[blahzenentsoondoong]

D

damage: you've damaged it Sie haben es
beschädigt *[zee hahben ess beshay-
dicht]*; **it's damaged** es ist beschädigt;
there's no damage es ist kein Schaden
entstanden *[kyne shahden entshtanden]*
damn! verdammt! *[fairdamt]*
damp feucht *[foycht]*
dance der Tanz *[tants]*; **do you want to
dance?** möchten Sie tanzen? *[murchten
zee tantsen]*
dancer: he's a good dancer er ist ein
guter Tänzer *[air ist ine gooter tentser]*
dancing: we'd like to go dancing wir
möchten gern tanzen gehen *[veer
murchten gairn tantsen gayen]*
dandruff die Schuppen *[shooppen]*
Dane (*man*) der Däne *[dayn-uh]*; (*woman*)
die Dänin *[daynin]*
dangerous gefährlich *[gefairlich]*
Danish dänisch *[daynish]*
Danube die Donau *[dohnow]*
dare: I don't dare ich traue mich nicht
[ich trow-uh mich nicht]
dark dunkel *[doonkel]*; **dark blue** dunkel-
blau; **when does it get dark?** wann wird
es dunkel? *[van veert]*; **after dark** nach
Einbruch der Dunkelheit *[nach
inebrooch dair doonkel-hyte]*
darling Liebling *[leepling]*
dashboard das Armaturenbrett *[arma-
tooren-bret]*
date: what's the date? welches Datum ist
heute? *[velches dahtoom ist hoyt-uh]*;
on what date? wann? *[van]*; **can we**

make a date? können wir einen Termin
vereinbaren? *[kurnen veer ine-en
tairmeen fairyne-bahren]*; (*romantic*)
können wir uns verabreden? *[oonss
fairap-rayden]*
dates (*to eat*) die Datteln
daughter: my daughter meine Tochter
[myne-uh tochter]
daughter-in-law die Schwiegertochter
[shveegertochter]
dawn das Morgengrauen *[morgen-
growen]*; **at dawn** bei Tagesanbruch
[by tahgesanbrooch]
day der Tag *[tahk]*; **the day after** am Tag
danach *[am tahk danach]*; **the day before** am Tag zuvor *[tsoofor]*; **every day**
jeden Tag *[yayden]*; **one day** eines Tages
[ine-ess tahgess]; **can we pay by the
day?** können wir tageweise bezahlen?
*[kurnen veer tahg-uh-vyze-uh betsah-
len]*; **have a good day!** einen schönen
Tag! *[ine-en shurnen tahk]*
daylight robbery die Halsabschneiderei
[halssapshnyder'eye']
day trip ein Tagesausflug (*m*)
[tahgessowssflook]
dead tot *[toht]*
deaf taub *[towp]*
deaf-aid ein Hörgerät (*nt*) *[hurgerayt]*
deal (*business*) das Geschäft *[gesheft]*; **it's a
deal** abgemacht *[apgemacht]*; **will you
deal with it?** können Sie sich darum
kümmern? *[kurnen zee zich]*
dealer (*agent*) der Händler *[hendler]*

dear lieb *[leep]*; *(expensive)* teuer *[toyer]*;
Dear Sir Sehr geehrter Herr X *[zair ge-airter hair]*; **Dear Madam** Sehr geehrte
Frau X *[zair ge-airt-uh frow]*; **Dear
Klaus** Lieber Klaus *[leeber klowss]*
death der Tod *[toht]*
decadent dekadent *[dekadent]*
December der Dezember *[daytsember]*
decent: that's very decent of you das ist
sehr nett von Ihnen *[dass ist zair net fon
eenen]*
decide: we haven't decided yet wir haben uns noch nicht entschieden *[veer
hahben oonss nocH nicHt entsheeden]*;
you decide for us entscheiden Sie für
uns *[entshyden zee for oonss]*; **it's all
decided** es steht alles schon fest *[ess
shtayt al-ess shohn fest]*
decision die Entscheidung *[entshy-
doong]*
deck das Deck
deckchair ein Liegestuhl *(m)* *[leeg-uh-
shtool]*
declare: I have nothing to declare ich
habe nichts zu verzollen *[icH hahb-uh
nicHts tsoo fairtsollen]*
decoration *(in room)* die Ausstattung
[owss-shtattoong]
deduct abziehen *[aptsee-en]*
deep tief *[teef]*; **is it deep?** ist es tief?
deep-freeze die Tiefkühltruhe *[teefkool-
troo-uh]*
definitely bestimmt *[beshtimmt]*;
definitely not ganz bestimmt nicht
degree *(university)* der Abschluß *[ap-
shlooss]*; *(temperature)* der Grad *[graht]*
dehydrated *(person)* ausgetrocknet *[owss-
getrocknet]*
de-icer ein Defroster *(m)*
delay: the flight was delayed der Flug
hatte Verspätung *[dair flook hatt-uh
fairshpaytoong]*
deliberately absichtlich *[apzicHtlicH]*
delicacy: a local delicacy eine
Spezialität dieser Gegend *[ine-uh
shpetsee-alitayt deezer gaygent]*
delicious köstlich *[kurstlicH]*
deliver: will you deliver it? können Sie
es zustellen? *[kurnen zee ess
tsooshtellen]*
**delivery: is there another mail deli-
very?** kommt noch eine Postzustellung?
*[kommt nocH ine-uh posst-tsooshtel-
loong]*
de luxe Luxus-
denims die Jeans
Denmark Dänemark *[dayn-uh-mark]*
dent: there's a dent in it es hat eine Beule
[ess hat ine-uh boyl-uh]
dental floss die Zahnseide *[tsahnzyde-
uh]*
dentist der Zahnarzt *[tsahnartst]*
dentures das Gebiß *[gebiss]*
deny: he denies it er bestreitet es *[air
beshtrytet ess]*
deodorant ein Deodorant *(m)*
department store ein Kaufhaus *(nt)*
[kowfhowss]
departure die Abreise *[apryze-uh]*
departure lounge die Abflughalle
[apflookhal-uh]
depend: it depends es kommt darauf an
[ess kommt darowff an]; **it depends on
...** es hängt von ... ab *[ess hengt fon ... ap]*
deposit *(downpayment)* die Anzahlung
[antsahloong]
depressed bedrückt *[bedrookt]*
depth die Tiefe *[teef-uh]*
description die Beschreibung *[beshry-
boong]*
deserted *(beach etc)* verlassen *[fairlassen]*
dessert der Nachtisch *[nacHtish]*
destination das Reiseziel *[ryze-uh-tseel]*
detergent ein Reinigungsmittel *(nt)*
[rynigoongsmittel]
detour ein Umweg *(m)* *[oomvayk]*
devalued abgewertet *[apgevairtet]*
**develop: could you develop these
films?** können Sie diese Filme
entwickeln? *[kurnen zee deez-uh
film-uh entvickeln]*
diabetic der Diabetiker *[dee-abaytiker]*
diagram das Diagramm *[dee-agram]*
dialect der Dialekt *[dee-alekt]*
dialling code die Vorwahl *[forvahl]*
diamond ein Diamant *(m)* *[dee-amant]*
diaper eine Windel *[vindel]*
diarrhoea, diarrhea der Durchfall
[doorcHfal]; **do you have something to
stop diarrhoea?** haben Sie etwas gegen
Durchfall? *[hahben zee etvass gaygen]*
diary der Terminkalender *[tairmeen-
kalender]*; *(for personal thoughts)* das Tage-
buch *[tahg-uh-boocH]*
dictionary ein Wörterbuch *(nt)* *[vurter-
boocH]*; **a German/English dictionary**

ein deutsch-englisches Wörterbuch *[doytsh-eng-lishess]*

didn't *see* **not** *and page 117*

die sterben *[shtairben]*; **I'm absolutely dying for a drink** ich brauche unbedingt etwas zu trinken *[ich browch-uh oonbedingt etvass tsoo trinken]*

diesel (*fuel*) der Diesel

diet die Diät *[dee-ayt]*; **I'm on a diet** ich mache eine Diät *[ich mach-uh ine-uh]*

difference der Unterschied *[oontersheet]*; **what's the difference between …?** was ist der Unterschied zwischen …? *[tsvishen]*; **it doesn't make any difference** das ist egal *[aygahl]*; **I can't tell the difference** ich kann keinen Unterschied erkennen *[ich kan kynen … airkennen]*

different: they are very different sie sind sehr verschieden; **it's different from this one** es ist anders als dieses *[ess ist anders als deezess]*; **may we have a different table?** können wir einen anderen Tisch haben? *[kurnen veer ine-en anderen tish hahben]*; **ah well, that's different** ah, das ist etwas anderes *[ah, dass ist etvass anderess]*

difficult schwer *[shvair]*

difficulty die Schwierigkeit *[shveerichkyte]*; **without any difficulty** ohne Schwierigkeit; **I'm having difficulties with …** ich habe Schwierigkeiten mit …

digestion die Verdauung *[fairdowoong]*

dinghy (*rubber*) ein Schlauchboot (*nt*) *[shlowchboht]*; (*sailing*) ein Dingi (*nt*) *[dingee]*

dining car der Speisewagen *[shpyze-uh-vahgen]*

dining room das Speisezimmer *[shpyze-uh-tsimmer]*

dinner (*evening meal*) das Abendessen *[ahbentessen]*

dinner jacket eine Smokingjacke *[smohkingyack-uh]*

dinner party die Abendgesellschaft *[ahbentgezelshafft]*

dipped headlights das Abblendlicht *[apblentlicht]*

dipstick der Ölmeßstab *[urlmess-shtahp]*

direct direkt *[deerekt]*; **does it go direct?** ist es eine Direktverbindung? *[ist ess ine-uh deerekt-fairbindoong]*

direction die Richtung *[richtoong]*; **in which direction is it?** in welcher Richtung ist es?; **is it in this direction?** ist es in dieser Richtung?

directory: telephone directory das Telefonbuch *[telefohnbooch]*; **directory enquiries** die Auskunft *[owsskoonft]*

dirt der Schmutz *[shmoots]*

dirty schmutzig *[shmootsich]*

disabled behindert

disagree: it disagrees with me (*food*) es bekommt mir nicht *[meer nicht]*

disappear verschwinden *[fairshvinden]*; **it's just disappeared** es ist einfach verschwunden *[ine-fach fairshvoonden]*

disappointed: I was disappointed ich war enttäuscht *[ich var ent-toysht]*

disappointing enttäuschend *[ent-toyshent]*

disaster die Katastrophe *[katastrohf-uh]*

discharge (*pus*) der Eiter *['eye'ter]*

disc jockey der Diskjockey

disco eine Diskothek *[diskotayk]*

disco dancing das Disco-Tanzen *[—tantsen]*

discount ein Rabatt (*m*) *[rabbat]*

disease die Krankheit *[krankhyte]*

disgusting widerlich *[veederlich]*

dish (*plate*) der Teller; (*meal*) das Gericht *[gericht]*

dishcloth ein Spültuch (*nt*) *[shpooltooch]*

dishonest unehrlich *[oonairlich]*

dishwashing liquid ein Spülmittel (*nt*) *[shpoolmittel]*

disinfectant ein Desinfektionsmittel (*nt*) *[dezinfekts-yohnsmittel]*

disk: disk film eine Film-Disc

dislocated shoulder ein ausgekugelter Arm *[ine owssgekoogelter arm]*

dispensing chemist eine Apotheke *[apotayk-uh]*

disposable nappies Papierwindeln *[pappeervindeln]*

distance die Entfernung *[entfairnoong]*; **what's the distance from … to …?** wie weit ist es von … nach …? *[vee vyte ist ess fon … nach]*; **in the distance** weit weg *[vyte veck]*

distilled water destilliertes Wasser *[destilleertess vasser]*

distributor (*in car*) der Verteiler *[fairtyler]*

disturb: the disco is disturbing us die Diskothek stört uns *[dee diskotayk shturt oonss]*

diversion eine Umleitung *[oomlytoong]*

diving board das Sprungbrett *[shproongbret]*

divorced geschieden *[gesheeden]*

dizzy: I feel dizzy mir ist schwindlig *[meer ist shvindlicH]*; **dizzy spells** Schwindelanfälle *[shvindel-anfell-uh]*

do tun *[tōōn]*; **what do you do?** *(job)* was machen Sie beruflich? *[vass macHen zee berōōflich]*; **what shall I do?** was soll ich tun? *[zoll icH tōōn]*; **what are you doing tonight?** was machen Sie heute abend? *[macHen zee hoyt-uh ahbent]*; **how do you do it?** wie machen Sie das? *[vee]*; **will you do it for me?** können Sie das für mich tun? *[kurnen zee]*; **who did it?** wer hat es getan? *[vair hat ess getahn]*; **the meat's not done** das Fleisch ist nicht durch *[dass flyshe ist nicHt doorcH]*; **do you have …?** haben Sie …?

docks der Hafen *[hahfen]*

doctor der Arzt *[artst]*; **he needs a doctor** er braucht einen Arzt *[air browcHt ine-en]*; **can you call a doctor?** können Sie einen Arzt rufen? *[kurnen zee … rōōfen]*

document das Dokument *[dokōōment]*

dog der Hund *[hoont]*

doll eine Puppe *[poop-uh]*

dollar der Dollar

donkey ein Esel *(m) [ayzel]*

don't! nicht! *[nicHt]; see* **not** *and page 117*

door die Tür *[tœr]*

doorman der Portier *[portyay]*

dormobile *(tm)* das Campomobil *[kempomobeel]*

dosage die Dosis *[dohzis]*

double: double room ein Doppelzimmer *(nt) [doppel-tsimmer]*; **double bed** ein Doppelbett *(nt)*; **double brandy** ein doppelter Weinbrand *[vynebrant]*; **double r** *(in spelling name)* Doppel-r *[air]*; **it's all double dutch to me** ich verstehe nur Bahnhof *[icH fairshtay-uh nōōr bahnhohf]*

doubt: I doubt it ich bezweifle das *[icH betsvyfe-luh dass]*

douche die Spülung *[shpœloong]*

doughnut ein Berliner *(m) [bairleener]*

down: get down! runter da! *[roonter da]*; **he's not down yet** *(out of bed)* er ist noch nicht aufgestanden *[air ist nocH nicHt owffgeshtanden]*; **further down the road** weiter die Straße entlang *[vyter dee shtrahss-uh entlang]*; **I paid 20% down** ich habe 20% angezahlt *[icH hahb-uh tsvantsicH protsent angetsahlt]*

downmarket *(hotel etc)* weniger anspruchsvoll *[vayniger anshproocHsfoll]*

downstairs unten *[oonten]*

dozen ein Dutzend *(nt) [dootsent]*; **half a dozen** 6 Stück *[zecks shtœck]*

drain der Abfluß *[apflooss]*

draughts *(game)* Dame *[dahm-uh]*

draughty: it's rather draughty es zieht sehr *[ess tseet zair]*

drawing pin eine Heftzwecke *[heft-tsveck-uh]*

dreadful furchtbar *[foorcHtbar]*

dream der Traum *[trowm]*; **it's like a bad dream** es ist wie ein böser Traum *[ess ist vee ine burzer trowm]*; **sweet dreams** träume süß *[troym-uh sœss]*

dress *(woman's)* ein Kleid *(nt) [klyte]*; **I'll just get dressed** ich ziehe mich nur schnell an *[icH tsee-uh micH nōōr shnell an]*

dressing *(for wound)* ein Verband *(m) [fairbant]*; *(for salad)* die Soße *[zohss-uh]*

dressing gown ein Bademantel *(m) [bahd-uh-mantel]*

drink trinken; *(alcoholic)* ein Drink *(m)*; **what are you drinking?** *(can I get you one)* was möchten Sie zu trinken? *[vass murcHten zee tsōō trinken]*; **I don't drink** ich trinke keinen Alkohol *[icH trink-uh kynen alkohohl]*; **a long cool drink** ein kühler Longdrink *[ine kœler]*; **may I have a drink of water?** kann ich ein Glas Wasser haben? *[ine glahss vasser hahben]*; **drink up!** trinken Sie aus! *[zee owss]*; **I had too much to drink** ich habe zuviel getrunken *[icH hahb-uh tsōōveel getroonken]*

drinkable trinkbar

drive: we drove here wir sind mit dem Auto gekommen *[veer zint mit daym owto gekommen]*; **I'll drive you home** ich fahre Sie nach Hause *[icH fahr-uh zee nacH howz-uh]*; **do you want to come for a drive?** kommen Sie mit auf eine Spazierfahrt? *[kommen zee mit owff ine-uh shpatseerfahrt]*; **is it a very long drive?** muß man lange fahren? *[mooss*

man *lang-uh* **fa**hren]
driver der Fahrer
driver's license der Führerschein
[f**ω**rershyne]
drive shaft die Kardanwelle [k**a**rdanvell-
uh]
driving licence der Führerschein
[f**ω**rershyne]
drizzle: it's drizzling es nieselt [ess
n**ee**zelt]
drop: just a drop nur ein Tropfen [n**oo**r
ine tropfen]; **I dropped it** ich habe es
fallenlassen [i**cн** ha**h**b-uh ess f**a**l-en las-
sen]; **drop in some time** kommen Sie
doch einmal vorbei [**k**ommen zee do**cн**
ine-mahl for-by]
drown: he's drowning er ist am Ertrin-
ken [air ist am airtr**i**nken]
drug ein Medikament (nt) [medikam**e**nt];
(hashish etc) eine Droge [dr**oh**g-uh]
drugstore eine Drogerie [dr**oh**ger-ee]
drunk betrunken [betr**oo**nken]
drunken driving Trunkenheit am Steuer
[tr**oo**nkenhyte am sht**o**yer]

dry trocken
dry-clean chemisch reinigen [k**a**ymish
rynigen]
dry-cleaner eine chemische Reinigung
[k**a**ymish-uh rynigoong]
duck eine Ente [ent-uh]
due: when is the bus due? wann kommt
der Bus? [van kommt dair booss]
dumb stumm [sht**oo**m]; (stupid) blöd
[blurt]
dummy (for baby) ein Schnuller (m)
[shn**oo**ler]
durex (tm) ein Kondom (nt) [kond**oh**m]
during während [v**ai**rent]
dust der Staub [sht**ow**p]
dustbin die Mülltonne [m**oo**ltonn-uh]
Dutch holländisch [h**o**llendish]
Dutchman der Holländer [h**o**llender]
Dutchwoman die Holländerin
[h**o**llenderin]
duty-free zollfrei [ts**o**llfry]; **duty-free
goods** zollfreie Waren [—uh v**a**hren]
duvet das Federbett [f**a**yderbet]
dynamo der Dynamo [d**oo**namo]

E

each: each of them jeder von ihnen [y**a**y-
der fon **ee**nen]; **one for each of us** eins
für jeden von uns [ine-ss f**ω**r y**a**yden fon
oonss]; **how much are they each?** was
kosten sie pro Stück [vass k**o**sten zee pro
sht**ω**ck]; **each time** jedesmal [y**a**ydess-
mahl]; **we know each other** wir kennen
uns [veer k**e**nnen oonss]
ear das Ohr
earache die Ohrenschmerzen [**o**hren-
shmairtsen]
early früh [fr**ω**]; **early in the morning**
früh am Morgen; **it's too early** es ist zu
früh [ts**ω**]; **a day earlier** ein Tag früher
[ine tahk fr**ω**-er]; **I need an early night**
ich muß früh ins Bett [i**cн** mooss]
early riser: I'm an early riser ich bin
Frühaufsteher [i**cн** bin fr**ω**-owfshtayer]
earring ein Ohrring (m)
earth (soil) die Erde [**a**ird-uh]
earthenware die Tonware [t**oh**nvahr-uh]

earwig der Ohrwurm [**oh**rvoorm]
east der Osten; **to the east** nach Osten
Easter Ostern [**oh**stern]
East Germany die DDR [day-day-**a**ir]
easy leicht [ly**cн**te]; **easy with the cream!**
seien Sie sparsam mit der Sahne! [z**y**-en
zee shp**a**hrzahm mit dair z**a**hn-uh]
eat essen; **something to eat** etwas zu essen; **we've already eaten** wir haben
schon gegessen [veer h**a**hben shohn ge-
g**e**ssen]
eau-de-Cologne das Eau de Cologne
eccentric exzentrisch [exts**e**ntrish]
edible eßbar [**e**ssbahr]
efficient (staff) tüchtig [t**ω**cнti**cн**]; (hotel
etc) leistungsfähig [l**y**stoongs-fayi**cн**]
egg ein Ei (nt) ['eye']
eggplant eine Aubergine [ohbairj**ee**n-uh]
Eire Irland [**ee**rlant]
either: either … or … entweder … oder …
[entv**a**yder … **oh**der]; **I don't like either**

of them ich mag keinen von ihnen *[icH mahk kynen fon eenen]*

elastic elastisch *[elastish]*

elastic band ein Gummiband *(nt)* *[goomeeband]*

Elastoplast *(tm)* das Hansaplast *(tm)*

elbow der Ellbogen *[ellbohgen]*

electric elektrisch *[elektrish]*

electric blanket eine Heizdecke *[hytesdeck-uh]*

electric cooker der Elektroherd *[elektrohairt]*

electric fire ein elektrisches Heizgerät *[elektrishes hytes-gerayt]*

electrician der Elektriker

electricity der Strom *[shtrohm]*

electric outlet die Steckdose *[shteckdohz-uh]*

elegant elegant *[elegant]*

elevator der Aufzug *[owftsook]*

else: something else etwas anderes *[etvass anderess]*; **somewhere else** woanders *[vo-anders]*; **let's go somewhere else** gehen wir woanders hin *[gayen veer]*; **what else?** was sonst? *[vass zonst]*; **nothing else, thanks** danke, das ist alles *[dank-uh dass ist al-ess]*

embarrassed verlegen *[fairlaygen]*

embarrassing peinlich *[pyne-licH]*

embassy die Botschaft *[bohtshafft]*

emergency ein Notfall *(m)* *[noht-fal]*; **dies ist ein Notfall** *[deess ist ine]*

emery board die Sandblattfeile *[zantblat-fyle-uh]*

emotional emotional *[emotsyohnahl]*

empty leer *[lair]*

end das Ende *[end-uh]*; **at the end of the road** am Ende der Straße *[dair shtrahss-uh]*; **when does it end?** wann ist es zu Ende? *[van ist ess tsoo]*

energetic energiegeladen *[energee-gelahden]*

energy die Energie *[energee]*

engaged *(toilet, telephone)* besetzt *[bezetst]*; *(person)* verlobt *[fairlohpt]*

engagement ring der Verlobungsring *[fairlohboongs-ring]*

engine der Motor *[motohr]*

engine trouble der Motorschaden *[motohrshahden]*

England England *[eng-lant]*

English englisch *[eng-lish]*; **the English** die Engländer *[eng-lender]*; **I'm English**

ich bin Engländer; *(woman)* ich bin Engländerin; **do you speak English?** sprechen Sie englisch? *[shprecHen zee]*

enjoy: I enjoyed it very much es hat mir sehr gefallen *[meer zair gefal-en]*; **enjoy yourself!** viel Spaß! *[feel shpahss]*

enjoyable unterhaltsam *[oonterhal-tzam]*; **that was a very enjoyable meal** das hat sehr gut geschmeckt *[zair goot geshmeckt]*

enlargement *(of photo)* die Vergrößerung *[fairgrurseroong]*

enormous enorm *[aynorm]*

enough genug *[genook]*; **there's not enough …** es ist nicht genug … da *[ess ist nicHt]*; **it's not big enough** es ist nicht groß genug; **thank you, that's enough** danke, das genügt *[dass genookt]*

entertainment die Unterhaltung *[oonterhal-toong]*

enthusiastic begeistert *[begystert]*

entrance der Eingang *[ine-gang]*

envelope ein Umschlag *(m)* *[oomshlahk]*

epileptic der Epileptiker

equipment *(in flat)* die Einrichtung *[ine-ricHtoong]*; *(climbing etc)* die Ausrüstung *[owss-rœstoong]*

eraser ein Radiergummi *(nt)* *[radeergoomee]*

erotic erotisch *[erohtish]*

error ein Fehler *(m)* *[fayler]*

escalator die Rolltreppe *[rol-trepp-uh]*

especially besonders *[bezonders]*

espresso (coffee) ein Espresso *(m)*

essential wesentlich *[vayzentlicH]*; **it is essential that …** es ist unbedingt notwendig, daß … *[ess ist oonbedinkt noht-vendicH dass]*

estate agent der Grundstücksmakler *[groontshtœksmahkler]*

ethnic *(restaurant)* typisch deutsch *[tœpish doytsh]*

Eurocheque der Euroscheck *[oyro-sheck]*

Eurocheque card die Euroscheckkarte *[oyro-sheck-kart-uh]*

Europe Europa *[oyro-pa]*

European europäisch *[oyropayish]*

European plan Halbpension *[halp-pangz-yohn]*

even: even the Germans sogar die Deutschen *[zogahr dee doytshen]*; **even if …** selbst wenn … *[zelpst ven]*

evening der Abend *[ahbent]*; **good evening** guten Abend *[gōōten]*; **this evening** heute Abend *[hoyt-uh]*; **in the evening** am Abend; **evening meal** das Abendessen *[ahbentessen]*

evening dress der Abendanzug *[ahbentantsōōk]*; *(woman's)* das Abendkleid *[ahbentklyte]*

eventually schließlich *[shleesslicн]*

ever: have you ever been to ...? waren Sie schon einmal in ...? *[vahren zee shohn ine-mahl]*; **if you ever come to London** sollten Sie einmal nach London kommen *[zolten zee ine-mahl nacн]*

every jeder *[yayder]*; **every day** jeden Tag *[yayden tahk]*

everyone jeder *[yayder]*

everything alles *[al-ess]*

everywhere überall *[ōōber-al]*

exact genau *[genow]*

exactly! genau! *[genow]*

exam die Prüfung *[prōōfoong]*

example ein Beispiel *(nt)* *[byshpeel]*; **for example** zum Beispiel *[tsoom]*

excellent hervorragend *[hairforrahgent]*

except außer *[owsser]*; **except Sunday** außer Sonntag

exception die Ausnahme *[owssnahm-uh]*; **as an exception** ausnahmsweise *[owssnahms-vyze-uh]*

excess baggage das Übergewicht *[ōōbergevicнt]*

excessive *(bill etc)* zu teuer *[tsōō toyer]*; **that's a bit excessive** das ist ein bißchen viel *[dass ist ine biss-cнen feel]*

exchange *(money)* umtauschen *[oomtowshen]*; *(telephone)* das Fernamt *[fairnamt]*; **in exchange** im Tausch *[towsh]*

exchange rate: what's the exchange rate? was ist der Wechselkurs *[vass ist dair veckselkoorss]*

exciting aufregend *[owff-raygent]*; *(film etc)* spannend *[shpannent]*

exclusive *(club etc)* exklusiv *[exklōōzeef]*

excursion der Ausflug *[owssflōōk]*; **is there an excursion to ...?** gibt es Ausflugsmöglichkeiten nach ...? *[gipt ess owssflōōks-murglicнkyten nacн]*

excuse me *(to get past etc)* entschuldigen Sie! *[entshooldigen zee]*; *(to get attention)* Entschuldigung! *[entshooldigoong]*;

(apology) Verzeihung *[fair-tsy-oong]*

exhaust *(car)* der Auspuff *[owsspooff]*

exhausted erschöpft *[airshurpft]*

exhibition die Ausstellung *[owssshtelloong]*

exist: does it still exist? *(café etc)* gibt es das noch? *[gipt ess dass nocн]*

exit der Ausgang *[owssgang]*

expect: what do you expect! was erwarten Sie! *[vass airvarten zee]*; **I expect so** ich glaube ja *[icн glowb-uh yah]*; **she's expecting** sie erwartet ein Kind *[zee airvartet ine kint]*

expensive teuer *[toyer]*

experience: an absolutely unforgettable experience ein absolut unvergeßliches Erlebnis *[ine absolōōt oonfairgesslicнess airlaypnis]*

experienced erfahren *[airfahren]*

expert der Experte *[expairt-uh]*

expire ablaufen *[aplowffen]*; **it's expired** es ist abgelaufen *[ess ist apgelowffen]*

explain erklären *[airklairen]*; **would you explain that to me?** könnten Sie mir das erklären? *[kurnten zee meer]*

explore erforschen *[airforshen]*; **I just want to go and explore** ich möchte mich nur mal da umsehen *[icн murcнt-uh micн nōōr mahl da oomzayen]*

export der Export *[exp**o**rt]*

exposure meter der Belichtungsmesser *[belicнtoongsmesser]*

express *(mail)* per Expreß *[pair]*

extra: can we have an extra chair? können wir noch einen Stuhl haben? *[kurnen veer nocн ine-en shtōōl hahben]*; **is that extra?** wird das extra berechnet? *[veert dass extra berecнnet]*

extraordinary außergewöhnlich *[owsser-gevurnlicн]*

extremely äußerst *[oysserst]*

extrovert extrovertiert *[extrovairteert]*

eye das Auge *[owg-uh]*; **will you keep an eye on it for me?** könnten Sie für mich darauf aufpassen? *[kurnten zee fōōr micн darowff owffpassen]*

eyebrow die Augenbraue *[owgen-brow-uh]*

eyebrow pencil ein Augenbrauenstift *(m)* *[owgenbrowen-shtift]*

eye drops die Augentropfen *[owgen-tropfen]*

eyeliner der Eyeliner

eye shadow der Lidschatten *[leed-shatten]*

eye witness der Augenzeuge *[owgentsoyg-uh]*

F

fabulous toll *[tol]*

face das Gesicht *[gezιcнt]*

face pack die Gesichtspackung *[gezιcнts-packoong]*

facilities: the hotel's facilities are excellent das Hotel ist hervorragend eingerichtet *[hairfor-rahgent ine-gerichtet]*

facing: facing the river mit Blick auf den Fluß *[mit blick owff dayn flooss]*

fact die Tatsache *[tahtzacн-uh]*

factory die Fabrik *[fabreek]*

Fahrenheit *see page 121*

faint: she's fainted sie ist ohnmächtig geworden *[zee ist ohnmecнtιcн gevorden]*; **I think I'm going to faint** ich glaube, ich falle in Ohnmacht *[icн glowb-uh icн fal-uh in ohnmacнt]*

fair *(fun-)* der Jahrmarkt *[yahrmarkt]*; *(commercial)* die Messe *[mess-uh]*; **it's not fair** das ist nicht fair *[dass ist nicнt fair]*; **ok, fair enough** na gut *[na goōt]*

fake eine Fälschung *[felshoong]*

fall: he's had a fall er ist hingefallen *[air ist hin-gefal-en]*; **he fell off his bike** er ist vom Rad gefallen *[fom raht]*; **in the fall** *(autumn)* im Herbst *[hairpst]*

false falsch *[falsh]*

false teeth das Gebiß *[gebiss]*

family die Familie *[fameelee-uh]*

family hotel eine Familienpension *[fa-meelee-en-pangz-yohn]*

family name der Familienname *[fa-meelee-en-nahm-uh]*

famished: I'm famished ich sterbe vor Hunger *[icн shtairb-uh for hoong-er]*

famous berühmt *[beroomt]*

fan *(mechanical)* der Ventilator *[ventilahtor]*; *(hand held)* der Fächer *[fecнer]*; *(football etc)* der Fan *[fen]*

fan belt der Keilriemen *[kyle-reemen]*

fancy: he fancies you du gefällst ihm *[doo gefelst eem]*

fancy dress das Kostüm *[kostoom]*

fantastic fantastisch *[fantastish]*

far weit *[vyte]*; **is it far?** ist es weit?; **how far is it to …?** wie weit ist es nach …? *[vee … nacн]*; **as far as I'm concerned** was mich betrifft *[vass micн]*

fare der Fahrpreis *[fahrpryce]*; **what's the fare to …?** was kostet eine Fahrt nach …? *[vass kostet ine-uh fahrt nacн]*

farewell party die Abschiedsparty *[apsheetsparty]*

farm der Bauernhof *[bowernhohf]*

farther weiter *[vyter]*; **farther than …** weiter als …

fashion die Mode *[mohd-uh]*

fashionable modisch *[mohdish]*

fast schnell *[shnell]*; **not so fast** nicht so schnell *[nicнt zo shnell]*

fastener *(on clothes etc)* der Verschluß *[fairshlooss]*

fat *(adjective)* dick; *(on meat)* das Fett

father: my father mein Vater *[myne fahter]*

father-in-law der Schwiegervater *[shveeger-fahter]*

fathom der Faden *[fahden]*

fattening: it's fattening das macht dick

faucet der Hahn

fault der Fehler *[fayler]*; **it was my fault** es war mein Fehler; **it's not my fault** es ist nicht meine Schuld *[ess ist nicнt myne-uh shoolt]*

faulty defekt *[dayfekt]*

favo(u)rite Lieblings- *[leeplings-]*; **this beer's my favourite** dieses Bier habe ich am liebsten *[hahb-uh icн am leepsten]*

fawn *(colour)* beige

February der Februar *[faybrōo-ar]*

fed up: I'm fed up ich habe die Nase voll *[icн hahb-uh dee nahz-uh foll]*; **I'm fed up with …** ich habe … satt *[zatt]*

feeding bottle die Flasche *[flash-uh]*

feel: I feel hot/cold mir ist heiß/kalt *[meer ist hyce/kalt]*; **I feel like a sausage**

ich habe Lust auf eine Wurst *[ich hahb-uh loost owff]*; **I don't feel like it** mir ist nicht danach *[meer ist nicht danach]*; **how are you feeling today?** wie fühlen Sie sich heute? *[vee foolen zee zich hoyt-uh]*; **I'm feeling a lot better** es geht mir viel besser *[ess gayt meer feel]*

felt-tip (*pen*) ein Filzstift (*m*) *[filts-shtift]*

fence der Zaun *[tsown]*

fender (*of car*) der Kotflügel *[kohtfloogel]*

ferry die Fähre *[fair-uh]*; **what time's the last ferry?** wann geht die letzte Fähre? *[van gayt dee letst-uh]*

festival das Festival *[festivahl]*

fetch: I'll go and fetch it ich gehe es holen *[ich gay-uh ess hohlen]*; **will you come and fetch me?** können Sie mich abholen? *[kurnen zee mich aphohlen]*

fever das Fieber *[feeber]*

feverish: I'm feeling feverish ich glaube, ich habe Fieber *[ich glowb-uh ich hahb-uh feeber]*

few: only a few nur ein paar *[noor ine pahr]*; **a few minutes** ein paar Minuten; **he's had a good few** (*to drink*) er hat einiges intus *[air hat ine-iges intooss]*

fiancé: my fiancé mein Verlobter *[myne fairlohpter]*

fiancée: my fiancée meine Verlobte *[myne-uh fairlohpt-uh]*

fiasco: what a fiasco! was für ein Fiasko!

fiddle: it's a fiddle das ist Schiebung *[dass ist sheeboong]*

field das Feld *[felt]*

fifty-fifty halbe-halbe *[halb-uh halb-uh]*

fight der Kampf

figs die Feigen *[fygen]*

figure die Figur *[figoor]*; (*number*) die Zahl *[tsahl]*; **I have to watch my figure** ich muß auf meine Figur achten *[ich mooss owff myne-uh figoor achten]*

fill füllen *[foollen]*; **fill her up please** volltanken bitte *[folltanken bitt-uh]*; **will you help me fill out this form?** können Sie mir helfen, dieses Formular auszufüllen *[kurnen zee meer helfen deezess for-moolahr owss-tsoofoollen]*

fillet das Filet *[fillay]*

filling (*tooth*) die Füllung *[foolloong]*

filling station die Tankstelle *[tankshtell-uh]*

film (*phot, movie*) der Film; **do you have this type of film?** haben Sie diesen Film?; **16mm film** ein 16-mm-Film *[sech-tsayn millimayter]*; **35mm film** ein 35-mm-Film *[foonf-oont-drysich]*

film processing die Filmentwicklung *[film-entvickloong]*

filter der Filter

filter-tipped Filter-

filthy dreckig *[dreckich]*

find finden *[finnden]*; **I can't find it** ich kann es nicht finden; **if you find it** wenn Sie es finden; **I've found a ...** ich habe ... gefunden *[ich hahb-uh ... gefoonden]*

fine: it's fine weather das Wetter ist schön *[dass vetter ist shurn]*; **a 200 mark fine** eine Geldstrafe in Höhe von 200 Mark *[ine-uh geltsrahf-uh in hur-uh fon]*; **thank you, that's fine** (*to waiter etc*) vielen Dank, das ist genug *[feelen dank dass ist genook]*; **that's fine by me** das ist mir recht *[meer recht]*; **how are you? — fine thanks** wie geht's? — danke, gut *[goot]*

finger der Finger *[fing-er]*

fingernail der Fingernagel *[fing-er-nahgel]*

finish: I haven't finished ich bin noch nicht fertig *[ich bin noch nicht fairtich]*; **when I've finished** wenn ich fertig bin *[ven]*; **when does it finish?** wann ist es zu Ende? *[van ist ess tsoo end-uh]*; **finish off your drink** trinken Sie aus *[zee owss]*

Finland Finnland *[finland]*

fire: fire! Feuer! *[foy-er]*; **may we light a fire here?** können wir hier ein Feuer machen? *[kurnen veer heer ine foy-er machen]*; **it's on fire** es brennt; **it's not firing properly** mit der Zündung stimmt etwas nicht *[mit dair tsoondoong shtimmt etvass nicht]*

fire alarm der Feueralarm *[foy-er-alarm]*

fire brigade, fire department die Feuerwehr *[foy-er-vair]*

fire escape die Feuerleiter *[foy-er-lyter]*

fire extinguisher der Feuerlöscher *[foy-er-lursher]*

firm (*company*) die Firma *[feerma]*

first erster *[airster]*; **I was first** ich war der/die erste; **at first** zuerst *[tsoo-airst]*; **this is the first time** dies ist das erste Mal *[deess ist dass airst-uh mahl]*

first aid Erste Hilfe *[airst-uh hilf-uh]*

first aid kit die Erste-Hilfe-Ausrüstung *[airst-uh hilf-uh owssroostoong]*

first class (*travel*) erste Klasse *[airst-uh

klass-uh]

first name der Vorname [fornahm-uh]

fish der Fisch [fish]

fish and chips Fisch mit Pommes frites [fish mit pom frit]

fisherman der Angler [ang-ler]; (at sea) der Fischer [fisher]

fishing das Angeln [ang-eln]

fishing boat das Fischerboot [fisherboht]

fishing net das Fischnetz [fishnets]

fishing rod die Angelrute [ang-el-rōōt-uh]

fishing tackle das Angelzeug [ang-el-tsoyk]

fishing village das Fischerdorf [fisherdorf]

fit (healthy) gesund [gezoont]; **I'm not very fit** ich bin nicht sehr gut in Form [icн bin nicнt zair gōōt]; **a keep fit fanatic** ein Fitness-Fanatiker (m); **it doesn't fit** es paßt nicht [ess passt nicнt]

fix: can you fix it? (arrange) können Sie das regeln? [kurnen zee dass raygeln]; (repair) können Sie das reparieren? [repareeren]; **let's fix a time** können wir eine Zeit ausmachen? [veer ine-uh tsyte owssmacнen]; **it's all fixed up** es ist alles arrangiert [ess ist al-ess arrongjeert]; **I'm in a bit of a fix** ich sitze ein bißchen in der Klemme [icн zits-uh ine bisscнen in dair klemm-uh]

fizzy sprudelnd [shprōōdelnt]

fizzy drink ein kohlensäurehaltiges Getränk (m) [kohlenzoy-ruh-haltiges getrenk]

flab (on body) der Speck [shpeck]

flag die Fahne [fahn-uh]

flannel (for washing) der Waschlappen [vashlappen]

flash (phot) der Blitz

flashcube ein Blitzwürfel (m) [blitz-voorfel]

flashlight eine Taschenlampe [tashen-lamp-uh]

flashy (clothes) auffallend [owffal-ent]

flat (adjective) flach [flacн]; **this beer is flat** das Bier ist schal [dass beer ist shahl]; **I've got a flat (tyre)** ich habe einen Platten; (apartment) die Wohnung [voh-noong]

flatterer der Schmeichler [shmycнler]

flatware (cutlery) das Besteck [beshteck]; (plates) das Geschirr [gesheer]

flavo(u)r der Geschmack [geshmack]

flea ein Floh (m)

flexible flexibel [flexeebel]

flies (on trousers) der Schlitz; (zip) der Reißverschluß [ryce-fairshlooss]

flight der Flug [flōōk]

flippers die Schwimmflossen [shvim-flossen]

flirt flirten [flurten]

float schwimmen [shvimmen]

flood die Flut [flōōt]

floor der Fußboden [fōōssbohden]; (storey) der Stock [shtock]; **on the floor** auf dem Boden [owff daym]; **on the second floor** (UK) im zweiten Stock; (USA) im ersten Stock

floorshow die Show

flop (failure) ein Reinfall (m) [ryne-fal]

florist ein Blumenhändler (m) [blōōmen-hendler]

flour das Mehl [mayl]

flower die Blume [blōōm-uh]

flu die Grippe [grip-uh]

fluent: he speaks fluent German er spricht fließend Deutsch [air shpricнt fleessent doytsh]

fly fliegen [fleegen]; **can we fly there?** können wir dorthin fliegen? [kurnen]

fly (insect) die Fliege [fleeg-uh]

fly spray das Fliegenspray [fleegen-shpray]

foggy: it's foggy es ist neblig [nayblicн]

fog light die Nebellampe [naybellamp-uh]

folk dancing der Volkstanz [follks-tants]

folk music die Volksmusik [follksmōō-zeek]

follow folgen; **follow me** folgen Sie mir [zee meer]

fond: I'm quite fond of ... ich mag ... sehr gern [icн mahk ... zair gairn]

food das Essen; **the food's excellent** das Essen ist hervorragend

food poisoning eine Lebensmittel-vergiftung [laybensmittel-fairgiftoong]

food store ein Lebensmittelgeschäft [laybensmittel-gesheft]

fool der Idiot [idioht]

foolish dumm [doom]

foot der Fuß [fōōss]; **on foot** zu Fuß; see page 119

football der Fußball [fōōssbal]

for: is that for me? ist das für mich? [ist

*dass f*œ*r mic*H*]*; **what's this for?** wozu dient das? *[vohts*oo *deent dass]*; **I've been here for a week** ich bin seit einer Woche hier *[zyte ine-er vo*cH*-uh heer]*; **a bus for ...** ein Bus nach ... *[na*cH*]*

forbidden verboten *[fairb*o*hten]*

forehead die Stirn *[shteern]*

foreign ausländisch *[*o*wsslendish]*

foreigner der Ausländer *[*o*wsslender]*; *(woman)* die Ausländerin

foreign exchange die Devisen *[de-veezen]*

forest der Wald *[vallt]*

forget vergessen *[fairg*e*ssen]*; **I forget, I've forgotten** ich habe es vergessen *[i*cH *hahb-uh ess]*; **don't forget** vergessen Sie (es) nicht

fork eine Gabel *[g*a*hbel]*; *(in road)* die Abzweigung *[*a*ptsvygoong]*

form *(document)* das Formular *[form*oo*-lahr]*

formal *(person)* förmlich *[f*u*rmli*cH*]*; *(dress)* formell *[form*e*l]*

fortnight zwei Wochen *[tsvy v*o*chen]*

fortunately glücklicherweise *[gl*œ*ck-li*cH*er-vyze-uh]*

fortune-teller die Wahrsagerin *[v*a*hr-zahgerin]*

forward: could you forward my mail? könnten Sie mir meine Post nachsenden? *[k*u*rnten zee meer myne-uh posst na*cH*-zenden]*

forwarding address die Nachsende-adresse *[n*a*chend-uh-address-uh]*

foundation cream die Grundierungs-creme *[groond*ee*roongs-kraym-uh]*

fountain der Brunnen *[br*oo*nnen]*

foyer *(of cinema etc)* das Foyer

fracture der Bruch *[broo*cH*]*

fractured skull der Schädelbruch *[sh*a*ydel-broo*cH*]*

fragile zerbrechlich *[tsairbre*cH*li*cH*]*

frame *(picture)* der Rahmen

France Frankreich *[fr*a*nkry*cH*e*]*

fraud ein Betrug *[betr*oo*k]*

free frei *[fry]*; *(no charge)* gratis *[gr*a*htiss]*; **admission free** Eintritt frei *[*i*ne-tritt fry]*

freeway die Schnellstraße *[shnel-shtrahss-uh]*

freezer die Gefriertruhe *[gefreertr*oo*-uh]*

freezing cold eiskalt *[*i*ce-kalt]*

French französisch *[frants*u*rzish]*

French fries die Pommes frites *[pom frit]*

Frenchman ein Franzose (*m*) *[frants*o*hz-uh]*

Frenchwoman eine Französin *[frants*u*rzin]*

frequent häufig *[hoyfi*cH*]*

fresh frisch *[frish]*; **don't get fresh with me** werden Sie bloß nicht frech! *[v*a*irden zee blohss ni*cH*t fre*cH*]*

fresh orange juice ein natürlicher Orangensaft (*m*) *[nat*œ*rli*cH*er or*o*njenzaft]*

friction tape das Isolierband *[eezohleer-bant]*

Friday Freitag *[frytahk]*

fridge der Kühlschrank *[k*œ*lshrank]*

fried egg ein Spiegelei (*nt*) *[shpeegel-'eye']*

friend der Freund/die Freundin *[froynt/froyndin]*

friendly freundlich *[fr*o*yntli*cH*]*

frog der Frosch *[frosh]*

from: I'm from New York ich bin aus New York *[i*cH *bin owss]*; **from here to the station** von hier zum Bahnhof *[fon heer tsoom]*; **the next train from ...** der nächste Zug aus ...; **as from Tuesday** ab Dienstag *[ap]*

front die Vorderseite *[f*o*rderzyte-uh]*; **in front** vorn *[forn]*; **in front of us** vor uns *[for oonss]*; **at the front** vorn

frost der Frost

frostbite die Frostbeulen *[fr*o*stboylen]*

frozen gefroren *[gefr*o*ren]*

frozen food die Tiefkühlkost *[teefk*œ*l-kost]*

fruit das Obst *[ohpst]*

fruit juice ein Fruchtsaft (*m*) *[fr*oo*cHtzaft]*

fruit machine der Spielautomat *[shpeelowtohmaht]*

fruit salad der Obstsalat *[*o*hpst-zalaht]*

frustrating: it's very frustrating es ist sehr frustrierend *[zair froostr*ee*rent]*

fry braten *[br*a*hten]*; **nothing fried** nichts Gebratenes *[ni*cH*ts gebr*a*htenes]*

frying pan die Bratpfanne *[br*a*ht-pfan-uh]*

full voll *[foll]*; **it's full of ...** es ist voller ... *[ess ist f*o*ller]*; **I'm full** ich bin satt *[i*cH *bin zatt]*

full-board Vollpension *[f*o*llpangz-yohn]*

full-bodied *(wine)* vollmundig *[f*o*ll-moondi*cH*]*

fun: it's fun es macht Spaß *[ess macht shpahss]*; **it was great fun** es hat viel Spaß gemacht *[feel]*; **just for fun** nur aus Spaß *[nōōr owss]*; **have fun!** viel Spaß!
funeral die Beerdigung *[be-airdigoong]*
funny (*strange*) seltsam *[zeltzam]*; (*comical*) komisch *[kohmish]*
furniture die Möbel *[murbel]*
further weiter *[vyter]*; **2 kilometres fur-**

ther 2 Kilometer weiter; **further down the road** weiter die Straße entlang
fuse die Sicherung *[zicheroong]*; **the lights have fused** die Sicherung ist durchgebrannt *[doorchgebrant]*
fuse wire der Schmelzdraht *[shmeltsdraht]*
future die Zukunft *[tsōōkoonft]*; **in future** in Zukunft

G

gale der Sturm *[shtoorm]*
gallon *see page 121*
gallstone der Gallenstein *[gal-enshtyne]*
gamble spielen *[shpeelen]*; **I don't gamble** ich bin kein Spieler *[ich bin kyne shpeeler]*
game (*sport*) das Spiel *[shpeel]*; (*meat*) das Wild *[vilt]*
games room das Spielezimmer *[shpeeluh-tsimmer]*
gammon der Schinken *[shinken]*
garage (*repair*) Werkstatt *[vairkshtatt]*; (*petrol*) eine Tankstelle *[tankshtell-uh]*; (*parking*) eine Garage *[garahj-uh]*
garbage der Abfall *[apfal]*
garden der Garten
garlic der Knoblauch *[k-nohblowch]*
gas das Gas *[gahss]*; (*gasoline*) das Benzin *[bentseen]*
gas cylinder die Gasflasche *[gahssflash-uh]*
gasket die Dichtung *[dichtoong]*
gas pedal das Gaspedal *[gahss-pedahl]*
gas permeable lenses luftdurchlässige Kontaktlinsen *[looftdoorchlessig-uh kontakt-linzen]*
gas station eine Tankstelle *[tankshtell-uh]*
gas tank der Tank
gastroenteritis die Magen-Darm-Entzündung *[mahgen-darm-entsoondoong]*
gate das Tor *[tohr]*; (*at airport*) der Flugsteig *[flōōkshtyke]*
gauge (*oil*) der Ölstandanzeiger *[urlshtant-antsyger]*; (*fuel*) die

Benzinuhr *[bentseenōōr]*
gay (*homosexual*) schwul *[shvōōl]*
gear (*car*) der Gang; (*equipment*) die Ausrüstung *[owssrœstoong]*; **the gears stick** die Gangschaltung klemmt
gearbox: I have gearbox trouble ich habe einen Getriebeschaden *[ich hahb-uh ine-en getreeb-uh-shahden]*
gear lever, gear shift der Schaltknüppel *[shaltknœppel]*
general delivery postlagernd *[posstlahgernt]*
generous: that's very generous of you das ist sehr großzügig von Ihnen *[dass ist zair grohsstsœgich fon eenen]*
gentleman: that gentleman over there der Herr dort *[dair hair]*; **he's such a gentleman** er ist wirklich ein Gentleman *[air ist veerklich ine]*
gents die Herrentoilette *[hairentwalett-uh]*
genuine (*antique etc*) echt *[echt]*
German (*adj*) deutsch *[doytsh]*; (*man*) der Deutsche *[doytsh-uh]*; (*woman*) die Deutsche; **the Germans** die Deutschen; **in German** auf Deutsch *[owfl]*
German measles die Röteln *[rurteln]*
Germany Deutschland *[doytsh-lant]*
get: have you got ...? haben Sie ...? *[hahben zee]*; **how do I get to ...?** wie komme ich nach ...? *[vee komm-uh ich nach]*; **where do I get them from?** wo kann ich sie bekommen? *[vo kan ich zee]*; **can I get you a drink?** kann ich Ihnen etwas zu trinken besorgen? *[kan ich eenen etvass tsōō trinken bezorgen]*; **will you**

get it for me? können Sie es mir besorgen? *[kurnen zee ess meer]*; **when do we get there?** wann kommen wir dort an? *[van kommen veer]*; **I've got to go** ich muß gehen *[icH mooss gayen]*; **where do I get off?** wo muß ich aussteigen? *[owss-shtygen]*; **it's difficult to get to** es ist schwer erreichbar *[shvair air-rycHbar]*; **when I get up** (*in morning*) wenn ich aufstehe *[ven icH owff-shtay-uh]*

ghastly entsetzlich *[entsetslicH]*

ghost das Gespenst *[geshpenst]*

giddy: it makes me giddy mir wird davon schwindlig *[meer veert dafon shvindlicH]*

gift ein Geschenk (*nt*) *[geshenk]*

gigantic riesig *[reezicH]*

gin der Gin; **a gin and tonic** ein Gin Tonic

girl ein Mädchen (*nt*) *[maydcHen]*

girlfriend die Freundin *[froyndin]*

give geben *[gayben]*; **will you give me …?** können Sie mir … geben? *[kurnen zee meer]*; **I gave it to him** ich habe es ihm gegeben *[icH hahb-uh ess eem gegayben]*; **I'll give you 30 marks** ich gebe Ihnen 30 Mark dafür *[dafoor]*; **will you give it back?** kann ich es zurückhaben? *[tsoorwockhahben]*

glad froh; **I'm so glad** das freut mich *[dass froyt micH]*

glamorous sehr attraktiv *[zair attrakteef]*

gland die Drüse *[drwz-uh]*

glandular fever das Drüsenfieber *[drwzenfeeber]*

glass das Glas *[glahss]*; **a glass of water** ein Glas Wasser

glasses eine Brille *[brill-uh]*

gloves die Handschuhe *[hantshoo-uh]*

glue der Leim *[lyme]*

gnat die Mücke *[mwck-uh]*

go gehen *[gayen]*; (*by train, car etc*) fahren; **we want to go to …** wir möchten nach … gehen/fahren *[veer murcHten nacH]*; **I'm going there tomorrow** ich gehe/fahre morgen dorthin *[icH gay-uh/fahr-uh]*; **I'm going back to Chicago tomorrow** (*by plane*) ich fliege morgen nach Chicago zurück *[fleeg-uh]*; **when does the train go?** wann fährt der Zug ab? *[van fairt dair tsook ap]*; **when does the plane go?** wann fliegt die Maschine ab? *[fleekt dee masheen-uh ap]*; **where are you going?** wohin gehen Sie? *[vohin gayen zee]*; **let's**

go gehen wir; **he's gone** (*left*) er ist gegangen; **it's all gone** es ist alles weg *[ess ist al-ess veck]*; **I went there yesterday** ich war gestern da *[icH vahr]*; **a hotdog to go** ein Hot dog zum Mitnehmen *[tsoom mitnaymen]*; **go away!** gehen Sie weg!; **it's gone off** (*food*) es ist schlecht geworden *[schlecHt gevorden]*; **we're going out tonight** wir gehen heute abend aus *[hoyt-uh ahbent owss]*; **do you want to go out tonight?** möchten Sie heute abend ausgehen? *[murcHten zee … owss-gayen]*; **has the price gone up?** ist der Preis gestiegen? *[ist dair pryce geshteegen]*

goal (*sport*) das Tor

goat die Ziege *[tseeg-uh]*

God Gott

goggles (*ski*) die Schneebrille *[shnaybrill-uh]*

gold das Gold *[gollt]*

golf Golf

golf clubs die Golfschläger *[golfshlayger]*

golf course der Golfplatz *[golf-plats]*

good gut *[goot]*; **good!** gut!; **that's no good** das ist nichts *[nicHts]*; **good heavens!** du lieber Himmel! *[doo leeber]*

goodbye auf Wiedersehen *[owff-veeder-zayn]*

good-looking gutaussehend *[gootowss-zayent]*

gooey (*food etc*) matschig *[matshicH]*

goose die Gans *[ganss]*

gooseberries die Stachelbeeren *[shtacHel-bairen]*

gorgeous großartig *[grohssarticH]*

gourmet der Feinschmecker *[fyneshmecker]*

gourmet food Essen für Feinschmecker *[essen foor fyne-shmecker]*

government die Regierung *[regeeroong]*

grammar die Grammatik *[grammatik]*

gram(me) das Gramm

granddaughter die Enkelin *[enkelin]*

grandfather der Großvater *[grohss-fahter]*

grandmother die Großmutter *[grohss-mootter]*

grandson der Enkel

grapefruit eine Grapefruit

grapefruit juice ein Grapefruitsaft (*m*) *[—zaft]*

grapes die Trauben *[trowben]*

grass das Gras *[grahss]*

grateful dankbar; **I'm very grateful to you** ich bin Ihnen sehr dankbar *[ich bin eenen zair dankbar]*

gravy die Soße *[zohss-uh]*

gray grau *[grow]*

grease *(on food)* das Fett; *(for car)* das Schmierfett *[shmeerfet]*

greasy *(cooking)* fett

great groß *[grohss]*; *(very good)* großartig *[grohssartich]*; **that's great!** das ist toll!

Great Britain Großbritannien *[grohss-britannee-en]*

Greece Griechenland *[greechenlant]*

greedy *(for food)* gefräßig *[gefrayssich]*

green grün *[groen]*

green card *(insurance)* die grüne Karte *[dee groen-uh kart-uh]*

greengrocer der Gemüsehändler *[ge-mooz-uh-hendler]*

grey grau *[grow]*

grilled gegrillt

gristle *(on meat)* der Knorpel *[k-norpel]*

grocer der Lebensmittelhändler *[laybens-mittel-hendler]*

ground der Boden *[bohden]*; **on the ground** auf dem Boden; **on the ground floor** im Erdgeschoß *[im airtgeshoss]*

ground beef das Gehackte

group die Gruppe *[groop-uh]*

group insurance die Gruppen-versicherung *[groopenfairzicheroong]*

group leader der Gruppenführer *[groopen-foorer]*

guarantee die Garantie *[garantee]*; **is it guaranteed?** ist darauf Garantie? *[ist darowff]*

guardian *(of child)* der Erziehungs-berechtigte *[airtsee-oongs-berechticht-uh]*

guest der Gast

guesthouse die Pension *[pangz-yohn]*

guest room das Gästezimmer *[gest-uh-tsimmer]*

guide *(tourist)* der Reiseleiter *[ryze-uh-lyter]*

guidebook der Reiseführer *[ryze-uh-foorer]*

guilty schuldig *[shooldich]*

guitar die Gitarre *[gitarr-uh]*

gum *(in mouth)* das Zahnfleisch *[tsahn-flyshe]*

gun das Gewehr *[gevair]*

gymnasium die Turnhalle *[toornhal-uh]*

gyn(a)ecologist der Frauenarzt *[frowenartst]*

H

hair das Haar *[hahr]*

hairbrush die Haarbürste *[hahrboorst-uh]*

haircut der Haarschnitt *[hahrshnit]*; **I need a haircut** ich muß mir die Haare schneiden lassen *[ich mooss meer dee hahr-uh shnyden]*; **just an ordinary haircut please** nur etwas beischneiden bitte *[noor etvass byshnyden bitt-uh]*

hairdresser der Frisör *[frizur]*

hairdryer der Fön *(tm)* *[furn]*

hair foam der Schaumfestiger *[showm-festiger]*

hair gel das Haargel *[hahr-gayl]*

hair grip die Haarklemme *[hahrklem-uh]*

hair lacquer das Haarspray *[hahr-shpray]*

half halb *[halp]*; **half an hour** eine halbe Stunde *[ine-uh halb-uh shtoond-uh]*; **a half portion** eine halbe Portion *[ports-yohn]*; **half a litre** ein halber Liter; **half as much** halb so viel *[zo feel]*; **half as much again** nochmal halb so viel *[nochmahl]*; *see page 118*

halfway: **halfway to Cologne** auf halbem Weg nach Köln *[owff halbem vayk nach kurln]*

ham der Schinken *[shinken]*

hamburger ein Hamburger *(m)* *[hem-burger]*

hammer der Hammer

hand die Hand *[hant]*; **will you give me a hand?** könnten Sie mir helfen? *[kurnten zee meer]*

handbag die Handtasche *[hant-tash-uh]*
hand baggage das Handgepäck *[hant-gepeck]*
handbrake die Handbremse *[hantbremz-uh]*
handkerchief ein Taschentuch *(nt)* *[tashentōōcн]*
handle *(door)* die Klinke *[klink-uh]*; *(cup)* der Henkel; **will you handle it?** können Sie das regeln? *[kurnen zee dass raygeln]*
hand luggage das Handgepäck *[hant-gepeck]*
handmade handgearbeitet *[hant-ge-arbytet]*
handsome gutaussehend *[gōōtowss-zayent]*
hanger *(for clothes)* der Bügel *[bœgel]*
hangover der Kater *[kahter]*; **I've got a terrible hangover** ich habe einen fürchterlichen Kater *[icн hahb-uh ine-en fœrcнterlicнen kahter]*
happen geschehen *[geshayen]*; **how did it happen?** wie ist es passiert? *[vee ist ess passeert]*; **what's happening** was ist los? *[lohss]*; **it won't happen again** es wird nicht wieder vorkommen *[ess veert nicнt veeder forkommen]*
happy glücklich *[glœcklicн]*; **we're not happy with the room** wir sind mit dem Zimmer nicht zufrieden *[veer zint mit daym tsimmer nicнt tsōōfreeden]*
harbo(u)r der Hafen *[hahfen]*
hard hart; *(difficult)* schwer *[shvair]*
hard-boiled egg ein hartgekochtes Ei *[hartgekocнtess 'eye']*
hard lenses harte Kontaktlinsen *[hart-uh kontakt-linzen]*
hardly kaum *[kowm]*; **hardly ever** fast nie *[fast nee]*
hardware store die Eisenwarenhandlung *['eye'zenvahren-handloong]*
harm der Schaden *[shahden]*
hassle: it's too much hassle es ist zu mühsam *[ess ist tsōō mœzam]*; **a hassle-free holiday** ein problemfreier Urlaub *[ine problaymfryer ōōrlowp]*
hat ein Hut *(m)* *[hōōt]*
hatchback ein Auto *(nt)* mit Hecktür *[owto mit hecktœr]*
hate: I hate ... ich kann ... nicht leiden *[icн kan ... nicнt lyden]*
have haben *[hahben]*; **do you have ...?** haben Sie ...? *[zee]*; **can I have some**

water? kann ich etwas Wasser haben?; **I have ...** ich habe ... *[icн hahb-uh]*; **I don't have ...** ich habe kein(e) ... *[kyne (-uh)]*; **can we have breakfast in our room?** können wir auf unserem Zimmer frühstücken? *[kurnen veer owff oonzerem tsimmer frœshtœcken]*; **have another** *(drink etc)* noch eins? *[nocн ine-ss]*; **I have to leave early** ich muß früh gehen *[icн mooss frœ gayen]*; **do I have to ...?** muß ich ...?; *see pages 113, 114*
hay fever der Heuschnupfen *[hoy-shnoopfen]*
he er *[air]*; **is he here?** ist er hier? *[ist air heer]*; *see page 111*
head der Kopf; **we're heading for Munich** wir wollen nach München *[veer vollen nacн]*
headache die Kopfschmerzen *[kopfshmairtsen]*
headlight der Scheinwerfer *[shyne-vairfer]*
headphones die Kopfhörer *[kopfhurer]*
head waiter der Oberkellner *[ohber-kellner]*
health die Gesundheit *[gezoont-hyte]*; **your health!** zum Wohl! *[tsoom vohl]*
healthy gesund *[gezoont]*
hear: can you hear me? können Sie mich hören? *[kurnen zee micн huren]*; **I can't hear you** ich kann Sie nicht verstehen *[icн kan zee nicнt fairshtayen]*; **I've heard about it** ich habe davon gehört *[icн hahb-uh dafon gehurt]*
hearing aid das Hörgerät *[hurgerayt]*
heart das Herz *[hairts]*
heart attack ein Herzinfarkt *(m)* *[hairts-infarkt]*
heat die Hitze *[hits-uh]*
heater die Heizung *[hyte-soong]*
heating die Heizung *[hyte-soong]*
heat rash der Hitzeausschlag *[hits-uh-owss-shlahk]*
heatwave die Hitzewelle *[hits-uh-vell-uh]*
heavy schwer *[shvair]*
hectic hektisch *[hecktish]*
heel *(of foot)* die Ferse *[fairz-uh]*; *(of shoe)* der Absatz *[apzats]*; **could you put new heels on these?** können Sie mir hier die Absätze erneuern? *[kurnen zee meer heer dee apsets-uh airnoyern]*
heel bar die Absatzbar *[apzatsbar]*
height *(of mountain)* die Höhe *[hur-uh]*;

(*of person*) die Größe [gr*u*rss-uh]

helicopter der Hubschrauber [h**oo**p-shr*ow*ber]

hell: oh hell! verdammt noch mal! [f*air*damt no*cH* mahl]; **go to hell!** gehen Sie zum Teufel! [g*ay*en zee tsoom t*oy*fel]

hello guten Tag [g*oo*ten tahk]; (*to get attention*) hallo; (*in surprise*) nanu! [nan*oo*]

helmet der Helm

help helfen; **can you help me?** können Sie mir helfen? [k*u*rnen zee meer]; **thanks for your help** vielen Dank für Ihre Hilfe [f*ee*len dank f*oo*r *ee*r-uh hilf-uh]; **help!** Hilfe!

helpful: he was very helpful er war sehr hilfsbereit [air vahr zair h*i*lfsberyte]; **that's helpful** das ist hilfreich [dass ist h*i*lfry*cH*e]

helping (*of food*) eine Portion [ports-y*oh*n]

hepatitis die Hepatitis [hepat*ee*tis]

her: I don't know her ich kenne sie nicht [i*cH* kenn-uh zee ni*cH*t]; **will you send it to her?** können Sie es ihr schicken? [k*u*rnen zee ess eer shicken]; **it's her** sie ist es [zee ist ess]; **with her** mit ihr; **for her** für sie; **that's her suitcase** das ist ihr Koffer; *see pages 110, 111*

herbs die Kräuter [kr*oy*ter]

here hier [heer]; **here you are** (*giving something*) bitte [bitt-uh]; **here he comes** da kommt er

hers: that's hers das gehört ihr [dass geh*u*rt eer]; *see page 112*

hey! he! [hay]

hi hallo

hiccups der Schluckauf [shl*oo*ckowff]

hide verstecken [fairsht*e*cken]

hideous scheußlich [sh*oy*ssli*cH*]

high hoch [hoh*cH*]

high beam das Fernlicht [f*ai*rnli*cH*t]

highchair (*for baby*) ein Hochstuhl (*m*) [hoh*cH*st*oo*l]

highlighter (*cosmetics*) der Töner [t*u*rner]

highway die Landstraße [l*a*ntshtrahss-uh]; (*with lanes*) die Autobahn [*ow*to-bahn]

hiking das Wandern [v*a*ndern]

hill der Berg [bairk]; **it's further up the hill** es ist weiter oben [vyter *oh*ben]

hillside der Hang

hill walking: to go hill walking eine Bergwanderung machen [bairk-vanderoong ma*cH*en]

hilly hügelig [h*oo*geli*cH*]

him: I don't know him ich kenne ihn nicht [i*cH* kenn-uh een ni*cH*t]; **will you send it to him?** können Sie es ihm schicken? [k*u*rnen zee ess eem shicken]; **it's him** er ist es [air ist ess]; **with him** mit ihm; **for him** für ihn; *see page 111*

hip die Hüfte [h*oo*ft-uh]

hire: can I hire a car? kann ich ein Auto mieten? [kan i*cH* ine *ow*to m*ee*ten]; **do you hire them out?** verleihen Sie sie? [fairl*y*en zee zee]

his: it's his drink das ist sein Drink [zyne]; **it's his** es gehört ihm [ess geh*u*rt eem]; *see pages 110, 112*

history: the history of Berlin die Geschichte Berlins [dee geshi*cH*t-uh bair-leenss]

hit: he hit me er hat mich geschlagen [air hat mi*cH* geshl*ah*gen]; **I hit my head** ich habe mir den Kopf gestoßen [i*cH* h*ah*b-uh meer dayn kopf gest*oh*ssen]

hitch: is there a hitch? gibt es da einen Haken? [gipt ess da *ine*-en h*ah*ken]

hitch-hike trampen [tr*e*mpen]

hitch-hiker der Tramper [tr*e*mper]; (*girl*) die Tramperin

hit record der Hit

hock der Rheinwein [r*y*ne-vyne]

hole das Loch [lo*cH*]

holiday der Urlaub [*oo*rl*ow*p]; (*single day*) der Feiertag [f*y*-er-tahk]; **I'm on holiday** ich bin im Urlaub

Holland Holland [h*o*llant]

home (*house*) das Zuhause [ts*oo*h*ow*z-uh]; **at home** zu Hause; (*in my own country*) bei uns [by oonss]; **I go home tomorrow** ich fahre morgen nach Hause [i*cH* f*ah*r-uh m*o*rgen na*cH* h*ow*z-uh]; **home sweet home!** daheim ist daheim [dah*y*me]

home address die Heimatadresse [h*y*mataddress-uh]

homemade selbstgemacht [z*e*lpst-gema*cH*t]

homesick: I'm homesick ich habe Heimweh [i*cH* h*ah*b-uh h*y*me-vay]

honest ehrlich [*air*li*cH*]

honestly? ehrlich? [*air*li*cH*]

honey der Honig [h*oh*ni*cH*]

honeymoon die Flitterwochen [fl*i*tter-vo*cH*en]; **it's our honeymoon** es ist unsere Hochzeitsreise [*oo*nzer-uh

hoCHtsytes-ryze-uh]; **a second honey-moon** zweite Flitterwochen *[tsvyte-uh]*
hood (*of car*) die Haube *[howb-uh]*
hoover (*tm*) der Staubsauger *[shtowp-zowger]*
hope hoffen; **I hope so** hoffentlich *[hoffentlicH]*; **I hope not** hoffentlich nicht *[nicHt]*
horn (*car*) die Hupe *[hoŏp-uh]*
horrible schrecklich *[shrecklicH]*
hors d'oeuvre die Vorspeise *[forshpyze-uh]*
horse das Pferd *[pfairt]*
horse riding Reiten *[ryten]*
hose (*for car*) der Schlauch *[shlowcH]*
hospital das Krankenhaus *[kranken-howss]*
hospitality die Gastfreundschaft *[gast-froyntshafft]*; **thank you for your hospitality** vielen Dank für Ihre Gastfreundschaft *[feelen dank foer eer-uh]*
hostel die Herberge *[hairbairg-uh]*
hot heiß *[hyce]*; (*curry etc*) scharf *[sharf]*; **I'm hot** mir ist heiß; **something hot to eat** etwas Warmes zu essen *[etvass varmess tsoŏ essen]*; **it's so hot today** es ist so heiß heute
hotdog ein Hot dog (*m*)
hotel das Hotel; **at my hotel** in meinem Hotel
hotel clerk der Mann am Empfang
hotplate die Kochplatte *[kocHplat-uh]*
hot-water bottle eine Wärmflasche *[vairm-flash-uh]*
hour die Stunde *[shtoond-uh]*; **on the hour** zur vollen Stunde *[tsoŏr follen]*
house das Haus *[howss]*

housewife die Hausfrau *[howssfrow]*
hovercraft das Luftkissenboot *[looftkissenboht]*
how wie *[vee]*; **how many?** wie viele? *[feel-uh]*; **how much?** wieviel? *[veefeel]*; **how often?** wie oft?; **how come?** wieso? *[veezo]*; **how are you?** wie geht es Ihnen? *[vee gayt ess eenen]*; **how do you do?** guten Tag! *[goŏten tahk]*; **how about a beer?** wie wär's mit einem Bier? *[vee vairss]*; **how nice!** wie schön! *[vee shurn]*; **would you show me how to ...?** könnten Sie mir zeigen, wie man ...? *[kurnten zee meer tsygen]*
humid feucht *[foycHt]*
humidity die Luftfeuchtigkeit *[looft-foycHticHkyte]*
humo(u)r: where's your sense of humo(u)r? haben Sie keinen Sinn für Humor? *[hahben zee kynen zin foer hoŏmohr]*
hundredweight *see page 120*
hungry: I'm hungry ich habe Hunger *[icH hahb-uh hoŏnger]*; **I'm not hungry** ich bin nicht hungrig *[nicHt hoongricH]*
hurry: I'm in a hurry ich habe es eilig *[icH hahb-uh ess 'eye'licH]*; **hurry up!** beeilen Sie sich! *[be-'eye'len zee zicH]*; **there's no hurry** es eilt nicht *[ess 'eye'lt nicHt]*
hurt: it hurts es tut weh *[ess toŏt vay]*; **my back hurts** mir tut der Rücken weh *[meer toŏt dair roecken vay]*
husband: my husband mein Mann *[myne man]*
hydrofoil das Tragflächenboot *[trahk-flecHenboht]*

I

I ich *[icH]*; **I am** ich bin; *see page 111*
ice das Eis *[ice]*; **with ice** mit Eis; **with ice and lemon** mit Eis und Zitrone *[oont tsitrohn-uh]*
ice-ax(e) ein Eispickel (*m*) *[ice-pickel]*
ice-cream ein Eis (*nt*) *[ice]*
ice-cream cone eine Tüte Eiskrem *[toet-uh ice-kraym]*

iced coffee ein Eiskaffee (*m*) *[ice-kaffay]*
ice-lolly ein Eis (*nt*) am Stiel *[ice am shteel]*
idea die Idee *[eeday]*; **good idea!** eine gute Idee! *[ine-uh goŏt-uh eeday]*
ideal ideal *[iday-ahl]*
identity papers die Ausweispapiere *[owssvyce-papeer-uh]*

idiot der Idiot [ideeoht]
idyllic idyllisch [idoollish]
if wenn [ven]; if you could wenn Sie können [zee kurnen]; if not wenn nicht
ignition die Zündung [tsoondoong]
ill krank; I feel ill ich fühle mich krank [ich fool-uh mich]
illegal illegal [illaygahl]
illegible unleserlich [oonlayzerlich]
illness die Krankheit [krankhyte]
imitation (leather etc) nachgemacht [nachgemacht]
immediately sofort [zofort]
immigration die Einwanderung [ine-vanderoong]
import importieren [importeeren]
important wichtig [vichtich]; it's very important es ist sehr wichtig [zair]; it's not important es ist nicht wichtig
import duty der Einfuhrzoll [ine-foor-tsoll]
impossible unmöglich [oonmurglich]
impressive beeindruckend [be-ine-droockent]
improve: it's improving es wird besser [veert]; I want to improve my German ich möchte mein Deutsch verbessern [ich murcht-uh myne doytsh fairbessern]
improvement die Verbesserung [fairbesseroong]
in: in my room in meinem Zimmer [in mynem tsimmer]; in the town centre im Stadtzentrum [im shtat-tsentroom]; in London in London; in one hour's time in einer Stunde; in August im August; in English/German auf englisch/deutsch [owff]; is he in? ist er da?
inch der Zoll [tsoll]; see page 119
include enthalten [ent-hal-ten]; does that include meals? ist das einschließlich Mahlzeiten? [ine-shleeslich mahltsyten]; is that included in the price? ist das im Preis enthalten? [pryce]
inclusive inklusive [inkloozeev-uh]
incompetent unfähig [oonfayich]
inconvenient ungünstig [oongoonstich]
increase die Zunahme [tsoonahm-uh]
incredible unglaublich [oonglowplich]
indecent unanständig [oonanshtendich]
independent unabhängig [oonap-hengich]
India Indien [indee-en]
Indian (adj) indisch [indish]; (man) der

Inder; (woman) die Inderin
indicator der Blinker
indigestion die Magenverstimmung [mahgenfairshtimmoong]
indoor pool das Hallenbad [hal-enbaht]
indoors drinnen; let's go indoors gehen wir nach drinnen
industry die Industrie [indoostree]
inefficient nicht leistungsfähig [nicht lystoongsfayich]
infection die Infektion [infekts-yohn]
infectious ansteckend [anshteckent]
inflammation die Entzündung [entsoon-doong]
inflation die Inflation [inflats-yohn]
informal (dress, function) zwanglos [tsvanglos]
information die Informationen [infor-mats-yohn-en]
information desk der Informations-schalter [informats-yohns-shallter]
information office das Auskunftsbüro [owsskoonftsbooro]
injection eine Spritze [shprits-uh]
injured verletzt [fairletst]; she's been injured sie wurde verletzt [zee voord-uh]
injury die Verletzung [fairletsoong]
innocent unschuldig [oonshooldich]
inquisitive neugierig [noygeerich]
insect ein Insekt (nt) [inzekt]
insect bite ein Insektenstich (m) [inzekenshtich]
insecticide das Insektengift [inzekten-gift]
insect repellent das Insektenbekämpfungsmittel [inzekten-bekempfoongs-mittel]
inside: inside the tent im Zelt; let's sit inside setzen wir uns nach drinnen [zetsen veer oonss nach drinnen]
insincere unaufrichtig [oonowfrichtich]
insist: I insist ich bestehe darauf [ich beshtay-uh darowff]
insomnia die Schlaflosigkeit [shlahf-lohzichkyte]
instant coffee der Pulverkaffee [poolver-kaffay]
instead: I'll have that one instead ich nehme statt dessen das da [ich naym-uh shtat dessen dass da]; instead of ... anstelle von ... [anshtell-uh fon]
insulating tape das Isolierband [eezoleerbant]

insulin das Insulin *[inzōoleen]*

insult die Beleidigung *[belydigoong]*

insurance die Versicherung *[fairzicheroong]*; **write the name of your insurance company here** schreiben Sie den Namen Ihrer Versicherung hierhin *[shryben zee dayn nahmen eerer ... heerhin]*

insurance policy die Versicherungspolice *[fairzicheroongs-poleess-uh]*

intellectual der/die Intellektuelle *[intellektōo-el-uh]*

intelligent intelligent *[intelligent]*

intentional: it wasn't intentional es war keine Absicht *[ess var kyne-uh apzicht]*

interest: places of interest Sehenswürdigkeiten *[zayens-voordichkyten]*

interested: I'm very interested in ... ich interessiere mich sehr für ... *[ich interesseer-uh mich zair foor]*

interesting interessant; **that's very interesting** das ist sehr interessant

international international *[internatsyonahl]*

interpret dolmetschen *[dolmetshen]*; **would you interpret?** könnten Sie für mich dolmetschen? *[kurnten zee foor mich]*

interpreter der Dolmetscher *[dolmetsher]*

intersection die Kreuzung *[kroytsoong]*

interval (*in play etc*) die Pause *[powz-uh]*

into in; **I'm not into that** (*don't like*) darauf stehe ich nicht so *[darowff shtay-uh ich nicht zo]*

introduce: may I introduce ...? kann ich Ihnen ... vorstellen? *[kan ich eenen ... forshtellen]*

introverted introvertiert *[—vairteert]*

invalid ein Behinderter

invalid chair der Rollstuhl *[rolshtōol]*

invitation die Einladung *[ine-lahdoong]*; **thank you for the invitation** vielen Dank für die Einladung *[feelen dank foor dee]*

invite einladen *[ine-lahden]*; **can I invite you out?** darf ich Sie einladen? *[zee]*

involved: I don't want to get involved in it ich möchte nicht darin verwickelt werden *[ich murcht-uh nicht darin fairvickelt vairden]*

iodine das Jod *[yoht]*

Ireland Irland *[eerlant]*

Irish irisch *[eerish]*

Irishman der Ire *[eer-uh]*

Irishwoman die Irin *[eerin]*

iron (*for clothes*) ein Bügeleisen (*nt*) *[boogel-'eye'-zen]*; **can you iron these for me?** könnten Sie diese Sachen für mich bügeln? *[kurnten zee deez-uh zachen foor mich boogeln]*

ironmonger der Eisenwarenhändler *['eye'-zenvahrenhendler]*

is ist; *see page 113*

island die Insel *[inzel]*; **on the island** auf der Insel *[owff dair]*

isolated isoliert *[eezoleert]*

it es *[ess]*; **is it ...?** ist es ...?; **where is it?** wo ist es?; **it's her** sie ist es; **it's only me** ich bin es nur *[nōor]*; **that's just it!** (*just the problem*) das ist es ja gerade *[dass ist ess ya gerahd-uh]*; **that's it** (*that's right*) genau! *[genow]*; *see page 111*

Italian (*adj*) italienisch *[italee-aynish]*; (*man*) der Italiener *[italee-ayner]*; (*woman*) die Italienerin

Italy Italien *[itahlee-en]*

itch: it itches es juckt *[ess yoockt]*

itinerary die Reiseroute *[ryze-uh-rōot-uh]*

J

jack (*for car*) ein Wagenheber (*m*) *[vahgenhayber]*

jacket eine Jacke *[yack-uh]*

jacuzzi der Whirlpool

jam die Marmelade *[marmelahd-uh]*;

traffic jam ein Stau (*m*) *[shtow]*; **I jammed on the brakes** ich machte eine Vollbremsung *[ich macht-uh ine-uh follbremzoong]*

January der Januar *[yanōoar]*

jaundice die Gelbsucht [gelpzoocʜт]
jaw der Kiefer [keefer]
jazz der Jazz
jazz club ein Jazzklub (m) [—kloob]
jealous (in love) eifersüchtig ['eye'-ferzœcʜticʜ]
jeans eine Jeans
jellyfish eine Qualle [kval-uh]
jet-setter ein Mitglied des Jet-set [ine mitgleet dess jet set]
jetty der Steg [shtayk]
Jew der Jude [yōōd-uh]; (woman) die Jüdin [yœdin]
jewel(le)ry der Schmuck [shmoock]
Jewish jüdisch [yœdish]
jiffy: just a jiffy! kleinen Moment! [klynen mohment]
job die Arbeit [arbyte]; **just the job!** genau das richtige! [genow dass ricʜtiguh]; **it's a good job you told me!** nur gut, daß Sie mir das gesagt haben! [nōōr gōōt dass zee meer dass gezahkt hahben]
jog: I'm going for a jog ich gehe joggen [icʜ gay-uh joggen]
jogging das Joggen
join (a club) beitreten [by-trayten]; **I'd like to join** ich möchte gern Mitglied werden [icʜ murcʜt-uh gairn mitgleet vairden]; **can I join you?** (go with) kann ich mitkommen?; (sit with) kann ich mich zu Ihnen setzen? [tsōō eenen zetsen]
joint (in bone) das Gelenk; (to smoke) der Joint
joke der Witz [vits]; **you've got to be**
joking! Sie machen wohl Witze! [zee macʜen vohl vits-uh]; **it's no joke** es ist kein Witz [ess ist kyne]
jolly: it was jolly good es war prima [ess vahr preema]; **jolly good!** toll!
journey die Reise [ryze-uh]; **have a good journey!** gute Reise! [gōōt-uh ryze-uh]
jug die Kanne [kann-uh]; **a jug of water** ein Krug mit Wasser [ine krōōk]
July der Juli [yōōlee]
jump: you made me jump Sie haben mich erschreckt [zee hahben micʜ airshreckt]; **jump in!** (to car) steigen Sie ein! [shtygen zee ine]
jumper ein Pullover (m) [pooll-ohver]
jump leads, jumper cables ein Starthilfekabel (nt) [shtart-hilf-uh-kahbel]
junction die Kreuzung [kroytsoong]
June der Juni [yōōnee]
junior: Mr Jones junior Herr Jones junior [yōōnyohr]
junk das Gerümpel [gerœmpel]
just: just one nur eins [nōōr ine-ss]; **just me** nur ich; **just for me** nur für mich [foor micʜ]; **just a little** nur ein bißchen [ine bisscʜen]; **just here** genau hier [genow heer]; **not just now** nicht jetzt [nicʜt yetst]; **he was here just now** er war gerade noch hier [air vahr gerahd-uh nocʜ heer]; **that's just right** das ist genau richtig [dass ist genow ricʜticʜ]; **it's just as good** das ist genauso gut [genowzo gōōt]; **that's just as well** das ist auch besser so [owcʜ besser zo]

K

kagul ein Windhemd (nt) [vinthemt]
keen: I'm not keen ich habe keine Lust [icʜ hahb-uh kyne-uh loost]
keep: can I keep it? kann ich es behalten? [kan icʜ ess]; **please keep it** bitte behalten Sie es; **keep the change** der Rest ist für Sie [dair rest ist foor zee]; **will it keep?** (food) hält es sich? [helt ess zicʜ]; **it's keeping me awake** es hält mich wach [ess helt micʜ vacʜ]; **it keeps on breaking** es geht dauernd kaputt [ess
gayt dowernt kappoot]; **I can't keep anything down** (food) ich kann nichts bei mir behalten [icʜ kan nicʜts by meer]
kerb der Straßenrand [shtrahssenrant]
ketchup der Ketchup
kettle ein Wasserkessel (m) [vasser—]
key der Schlüssel [shlœssel]
kid: the kids (children) die Kinder [kinder]; **I'm not kidding** ich meine das im Ernst [icʜ myne-uh dass im airnst]
kidneys die Nieren [neeren]

kill töten [*tur*ten]

kilo ein Kilo (*nt*); *see page 120*

kilometre, kilometer ein Kilometer (*m*) [*kee*lomayter]; *see page 119*

kind: that's very kind of you das ist sehr freundlich von Ihnen [zair *froy*ntlicн fon *ee*nen]; **this kind of ...** diese Art von ... [*deez*-uh art fon]

kiss ein Kuß (*m*) [*kooss*]

kitchen die Küche [*kœ*cн-uh]

kitchenette die Kochnische [*ko*cнnish-uh]

Kleenex (*tm*) ein Tempotaschentuch [*tempo*-tashent$\overline{oo}$cн]

knackered kaputt [*kappoot*]

knee das Knie [k-*nee*]

knickers ein Schlüpfer (*m*) [*shlœpfer*]

knife ein Messer (*nt*)

knitting das Stricken [*shtricken*]

knitting needles die Stricknadeln [shtricknahdeln]

knobbly knees Knubbelknie [k-*noo*belk-nee-uh]

knock: there's a knocking noise from the engine der Motor klopft [dair mo*tohr*]; **he's had a knock on the head** er hat einen Schlag auf den Kopf bekommen [air hat *ine*-en shlahk owff dayn kopf be*kommen*]; **he's been knocked over** er ist angefahren worden [air ist *angefahren* vorden]

knot (*in rope*) der Knoten [k-*noh*ten]

know (*somebody, a city etc*) kennen; (*something*) wissen [*vissen*]; **I don't know** ich weiß nicht [icн vyce *ni*cнt]; **do you know a good restaurant?** kennen Sie ein gutes Restaurant? [*kennen* zee ine]; **who knows?** wer weiß? [vair vyce]; **I didn't know that** das habe ich nicht gewußt [*hahb*-uh ... ge*voost*]

L

label das Etikett [*ettikett*]

laces (*shoes*) die Schnürsenkel [shn*œr*zenkel]

lacquer (*hair*) das Haarspray [*hahr*shpray]

ladies' (room) die Damentoilette [*dah*mentwalett-uh]

lady die Dame [*dahm*-uh]; **ladies and gentlemen!** meine Damen und Herren! [*myne*-uh *dah*men oont *herren*]

lager ein helles Bier [*beer*]; **lager and lime** (*nearest equivalent*) ein Bier (*nt*) mit Limonade [ine beer mit limon*ahd*-uh]

lake der See [*zay*]

lamb das Lamm

lamp die Lampe [*lamp*-uh]

lamppost der Laternenpfahl [*lattair*nenpfahl]

lampshade der Lampenschirm [*lampen*sheerm]

land (*not sea*) das Land [*lant*]; **when does the plane land?** wann landet das Flugzeug? [van landet dass fl$\overline{oo}$ktsoyk]

landscape die Landschaft [*lantshafft*]

lane (*car*) die Spur [shp$\overline{oo}$r]; (*narrow road*) die kleine Straße [*klyne*-uh shtr*ahss*-uh]

language die Sprache [spr*ahcн*-uh]

language course ein Sprachkurs (*m*) [shpr*acн*koorss]

large groß [*grohss*]

laryngitis die Kehlkopfentzündung [*kayl*kopfents$\overline{oo}$ndoong]

last letzter [*letster*]; **last year** letztes Jahr [*letstess* yahr]; **last Wednesday** letzten Mittwoch; **last night** gestern abend [*gestern ahbent*]; **when is the last bus?** wann fährt der letzte Bus? [van fairt dair *letst*-uh booss]; **one last drink** noch einen allerletzten Drink [nocн *ine*-en al*erletsten*]; **when were you last in London?** wann waren Sie zuletzt in London? [van *vahren* zee ts$\overline{oo}$letst]; **at last!** endlich! [*entlicн*]; **how long does it last?** wie lange dauert es? [vee lang-uh d*owert*]

last name der Nachname [n*acн*nahm-uh]

late spät [shpayt]; **sorry I'm late** tut mir leid, daß ich zu spät komme [t$\overline{oo}$t meer lyte dass icн ts$\overline{oo}$]; **don't be late** seien Sie pünktlich [zy-en zee p*œnk*tlicн]; **the**

train was late der Zug hatte Verspätung *[dair tsōōk hatt-uh fairshpaytoong]*; **we'll be back late** wir kommen erst spät zurück *[tsōōroock]*; **it's getting late** es wird spät *[veert]*; **is it that late!** ist es schon so spät?; **I'm a late riser** ich bin ein Langschläfer *[langshlayfer]*

lately in letzter Zeit *[in letster tsyte]*

later später *[shpayter]*; **later on** nachher *[nacH-hair]*; **I'll come back later** ich komme später wieder *[veeder]*; **see you later** bis später *[biss]*; **no later than Tuesday** nicht später als Dienstag

latest: the latest news die neuesten Nachrichten *[dee noy-esten nacHrichHten]*; **at the latest** spätestens *[shpaytestens]*

laugh lachen *[lacHen]*; **don't laugh** lachen Sie nicht *[zee]*; **it's no laughing matter** das ist nicht zum Lachen *[tsoom]*

launderette, laundromat der Waschsalon *[vashzallong]*

laundry (*clothes*) die Wäsche *[vesh-uh]*; (*place*) die Wäscherei *[vesher'eye']*; **could you get the laundry done?** könnten Sie die Wäsche waschen lassen? *[kurnten zee dee vesh-uh vashen]*

lavatory die Toilette *[twalett-uh]*

law das Gesetz *[gezets]*

lawn der Rasen *[rahzen]*

lawyer der Rechtsanwalt *[recHtsanvallt]*

laxative ein Abführmittel (*nt*) *[apfoor-mittel]*

lay-by der Rastplatz

laze around: I just want to laze around ich möchte nur faulenzen *[icH murcHt-uh nōōr fowlentsen]*

lazy faul *[fowl]*; **don't be lazy** seien Sie nicht so träge *[zy-en zee nicHt zo trayg-uh]*; **a nice lazy holiday** ein schöner Urlaub zum Faulenzen *[ine shurner ōōrlowp tsoom fowlentsen]*

lead (*elec*) das Kabel *[kahbel]*; **where does this road lead?** wohin führt diese Straße? *[vohin foort deez-uh shtrahss-uh]*

leaf das Blatt

leaflet der Handzettel *[hant-tsettel]*; **do you have any leaflets on ...?** haben Sie Prospekte über ...? *[hahben zee prospekt-uh oober]*

leak eine undichte Stelle *[oondicHt-uh shtell-uh]*; **the roof leaks** das Dach

ist undicht *[oondicHt]*; **the petrol tank is leaking** der Benzintank ist nicht dicht

learn: I want to learn ... ich möchte ... lernen *[icH murcHt-uh ... lairnen]*

learner: I'm just a learner ich lerne erst *[icH lairn-uh airst]*

lease mieten *[meeten]*

least: not in the least nicht im mindesten; **at least 50** mindestens 50

leather das Leder *[layder]*

leave: when does the train leave? wann fährt der Zug ab? *[van fairt dair tsōōk ap]*; **I leave tomorrow** ich reise morgen ab *[icH ryze-uh morgen ap]*; **he left this morning** er ist heute morgen abgereist *[air ist hoyt-uh morgen apgeryste]*; **may I leave this here?** kann ich das hierlassen? *[heerlassen]*; **I left my bag in the bar** ich habe meine Tasche in der Bar liegenlassen *[leegenlassen]*; **she left her bag here** sie hat ihre Tasche hiergelassen *[heergelassen]*; **leave the window open please** lassen sie das Fenster bitte geöffnet *[ge-urfnet]*; **there's not much left** es ist nicht viel übrig *[nicHt feel oobricH]*; **I've hardly any money left** ich habe kaum noch Geld *[kowm nocH gelt]*; **I'll leave it up to you** ich überlasse das Ihnen *[icH ooberlass-uh dass eenen]*

lecherous geil *[gyle]*

left links; **on the left** links

lefthand drive die Linkssteuerung *[links-shtoyeroong]*

left-handed linkshändig *[links-hendicH]*

left luggage (office) die Gepäckaufbewahrung *[gepeckowffbevahroong]*

leg das Bein *[byne]*

legal legal *[laygahl]*

legal aid die Rechtshilfe *[recHts-hilf-uh]*

lemon eine Zitrone *[tsitrohn-uh]*

lemonade die Limonade *[limonahd-uh]*

lemon tea der Zitronentee *[tsitrohnen-tay]*

lend: would you lend me your ...? könnten Sie mir Ihr ... leihen? *[kurnten zee meer eer ... ly-en]*

lens die Linse *[linz-uh]*

lens cap die Verschlußkappe *[fairshlōōsskap-uh]*

Lent die Fastenzeit *[fastentsyte]*

lesbian die Lesbierin *[lesbee-erin]*

less: less than an hour weniger als eine Stunde *[vayniger alss]*; **less than that**

nicht so viel [*nicht zo feel*]; **less hot** nicht so heiß

lesson die Stunde [*shtoond-uh*]; **do you give lessons?** geben Sie Unterricht? [*gayben zee oonterricht*]

let: would you let me use it? könnte ich es benutzen? [*kurnt-uh ich ess benootsen*]; **will you let me know?** können Sie mir Bescheid sagen? [*kurnen zee meer beshyte zahgen*]; **I'll let you know** ich werde Ihnen Bescheid sagen [*ich vairduh eenen*]; **let me try** lassen Sie es mich versuchen [*lassen zee ess mich fairzoochen*]; **let me go!** lassen Sie mich gehen! [*gayen*]; **let's leave now** wir sollten jetzt gehen [*veer zollten yetst gayen*]; **let's not go yet** bleiben wir noch ein bißchen [*blyben veer noch ine bisschen*]; **will you let me off at …?** können Sie mich an … aussteigen lassen? [*kurnen zee mich an … owss-shtygen*]; **room to let** Zimmer zu vermieten [*tsoo fairmeeten*]

letter ein Brief (m) [*breef*]; **are there any letters for me?** ist Post für mich angekommen? [*posst for mich angekommen*]

letterbox der Briefkasten [*breef—*]

lettuce der Kopfsalat [*kopfzalaht*]

level crossing der Bahnübergang [*bahnoobergang*]

lever der Hebel [*haybel*]

liable (*responsible*) haftbar

liberated: a liberated woman eine emanzipierte Frau [*ine-uh emantsipeert-uh frow*]

library die Bücherei [*boocher'eye'*]

licence, license eine Genehmigung [*genaymigoong*]; (*driving*) der Führerschein [*foorershyne*]

license plate das Nummernschild [*noomernshilt*]

lid der Deckel

lido das Freibad [*frybaht*]

lie (*untruth*) die Lüge [*loog-uh*]; **can she lie down for a while?** kann sie sich ein bißchen hinlegen? [*kan zee zich ine bisschen hinlaygen*]; **I want to go and lie down** ich möchte mich gern hinlegen [*ich murcht-uh mich gairn*]

lie-in: I'm going to have a lie-in tomorrow ich werde mich morgen ausschlafen [*ich vaird-uh mich morgen owss-shlahfen*]

life das Leben [*layben*]; **not on your life!** nie im Leben! [*nee*]; **that's life** so ist das Leben! [*zo*]

lifebelt der Rettungsgürtel [*rettoongs-goortel*]

lifeboat das Rettungsboot [*rettoongs-boht*]

lifeguard (*on beach*) der Rettungsschwimmer [*rettoongs-shvimmer*]

life insurance die Lebensversicherung [*laybensfairzicheroong*]

life jacket die Schwimmweste [*shvimvest-uh*]

lift (*in hotel*) der Aufzug [*owftsook*]; **could you give me a lift?** könnten Sie mich mitnehmen? [*kurnten zee mich mitnaymen*]; **do you want a lift?** kann ich Sie mitnehmen?; **thanks for the lift** danke fürs Mitnehmen; **I got a lift** ich bin mitgenommen worden [*vorden*]

lift pass ein Liftpaß (m) [*liftpas*]

light das Licht [*licht*]; (*not heavy*) leicht [*lycht*]; **the light was on** das Licht brannte; **do you have a light?** haben Sie Feuer? [*hahben zee foy-er*]; **a light meal** eine leichte Mahlzeit [*ine-uh lychte-uh mahltsyte*]; **light blue** hellblau [*hellblow*]

light bulb eine Glühbirne [*gloobeern-uh*]

lighter (*cigarette*) ein Feuerzeug (nt) [*foyer-tsoyk*]

lighthouse der Leuchtturm [*loycht-toorm*]

light meter der Belichtungsmesser [*belichtoongsmesser*]

lightning der Blitz

like: I'd like a beer ich möchte gern ein Bier [*ich murcht-uh gairn*]; **I'd like to …** ich möchte gern …; **would you like a …?** möchten Sie ein …? [*zee*]; **would you like to come too?** möchten Sie auch kommen?; **I like it** es gefällt mir [*ess gefelt meer*]; **I like you** ich mag dich [*ich mahk dich*]; **I don't like it** es gefällt mir nicht; **he doesn't like it** es gefällt ihm nicht; **do you like …?** mögen Sie …? [*murgen zee*]; **I like swimming** ich schwimme gern [*ich shvimm-uh gairn*]; **OK, if you like** gut, wenn Sie möchten [*ven*]; **what's it like?** wie ist es? [*vee*]; **do it like this** machen Sie es so [*zo*]; **one like that** so einen [*ine-en*]

lilo (*tm*) eine Luftmatratze [*looftmatrats-uh*]

lime cordial, lime juice ein Limonensaft (m) *[limohnenzaft]*

line (*on paper, road*) die Linie *[leenee-uh]*; (*of people*) die Reihe *[ry-uh]*; (*telephone*) die Leitung *[lytoong]*; **would you give me a line?** (*tel*) könnten Sie mir ein Amt geben? *[kurnten zee meer ... gayben]*

linen (*for beds*) die Bettwäsche *[betvesh-uh]*

linguist der Sprachforscher *[shprach-forsher]*; **I'm no linguist** ich bin nicht sprachbegabt *[nicht shprachbegahpt]*

lining das Futter *[footer]*

lip die Lippe *[lip-uh]*

lip brush der Lippenpinsel *[lippen-pinzel]*

lip gloss der Lip-Gloss

lip pencil der Konturenstift *[kontooren-shtift]*

lip salve der Lippen-Fettstift *[lippen-fet-shtift]*

lipstick der Lippenstift *[lippenshtift]*

liqueur der Likör *[likur]*

liquor der Alkohol *[alkohohl]*

liquor store eine Spirituosenhandlung *[shpiritooohzen-handloong]*

list die Liste *[list-uh]*

listen: I'd like to listen to ... ich möchte gern ... hören *[ich murcht-uh gairn ... huren]*; **listen!** hören Sie! *[huren zee]*

liter, litre der Liter; *see page 120*

litter der Abfall *[apfal]*

little klein *[klyne]*; **just a little, thanks** danke, nur ein bißchen *[noor ine bisschen]*; **just a very little** nur ein ganz kleines bißchen *[gants klyness]*; **a little cream** ein bißchen Sahne *[ine]*; **a little more** ein bißchen mehr; **a little better** etwas besser *[etvass]*; **that's too little** (*not enough*) das ist zu wenig *[tsoo vay-nich]*

live leben *[layben]*; **I live in Manchester/Texas** ich wohne in Manchester/Texas *[ich vohn-uh in]*; **where do you live?** wo wohnen Sie *[vo vohnen zee]*; **where does he live?** wo wohnt er? *[vo vohnt air]*; **we live together** wir wohnen zusammen *[veer vohnen tsoozammen]*

lively lebhaft *[layp-haft]*

liver die Leber *[layber]*

loaf ein Brot (nt) *[broht]*

lobby das Foyer *[foyay]*

lobster der Hummer *[hoommer]*

local: a local wine ein hiesiger Wein *[ine heeziger vyne]*; **a local newspaper** eine Lokalzeitung *[ine-uh lokahltsytoong]*; **a local restaurant** ein Restaurant an der Ort

lock das Schloß *[shloss]*; **it's locked** es ist abgeschlossen *[ess ist apgeshlossen]*; **I've locked myself out of my room** ich habe mich aus meinem Zimmer ausgesperrt *[ich hahb-uh mich owss mynem tsimmer owssgeshpairt]*

locker (*for luggage etc*) das Schließfach *[shleessfach]*

log: I slept like a log ich habe geschlafen wie ein Klotz *[ich hahb-uh geshlahfen vee ine klots]*

lollipop ein Lutscher (m) *[lootsher]*

London London *[lon-don]*

lonely einsam *[ine-zam]*; **are you lonely?** fühlen Sie sich einsam? *[foolen zee zich]*

long lang; **how long does it take?** wie lange dauert es? *[vee lang-uh dowert ess]*; **is it a long way?** ist es weit? *[vyte]*; **a long time** eine lange Zeit *[ine-uh lang-uh tsyte]*; **I won't be long** ich bin gleich zurück *[glyche tsoorøck]*; **don't be long** bleiben Sie nicht so lange *[blyben zee nicht zo]*; **that was long ago** das ist lange her *[hair]*; **I'd like to stay longer** ich möchte gern länger bleiben *[ich murcht-uh gairn lenger blyben]*; **long time no see!** lange nicht gesehen! *[nicht gezayen]*; **so long!** tschüs! *[tshøss]*

long distance call ein Ferngespräch (nt) *[fairn-gespraych]*

long drink ein Longdrink (m)

loo: where's the loo? wo ist die Toilette *[twalett-uh]*; **I want to go to the loo** ich möchte aufs Klo *[ich zay-uh owfss]*; **she's in the loo** sie ist auf dem Klo

look: that looks good das sieht gut aus *[dass zeet goot owss]*; **you look tired** Sie sehen müde aus *[zee zayen mood-uh owss]*; **I'm just looking, thanks** danke, ich sehe mich nur um *[ich zay-uh mich noor oom]*; **you don't look it** (*your age*) das sieht man Ihnen nicht an *[dass zeet man eenen nicht an]*; **look at me** sehen Sie mich an *[zayen zee mich an]*; **I'm looking for ...** ich suche ... *[zooch-uh]*; **look out!** passen Sie auf! *[owff]*; **can I have a look?** kann ich mal sehen?; **can I have a look around?** kann ich mich mal

umsehen? *[oomzayen]*
loose (*button, handle etc*) lose *[lohz-uh]*
loose change das Kleingeld *[klyne-gelt]*
lorry der Lastwagen *[lasstvahgen]*
lorry driver der Lastwagenfahrer *[lasstvahgenfahrer]*
lose verlieren *[fairleeren]*; **I've lost ...** ich habe ... verloren; **I've lost my way** ich habe mich verlaufen *[fairlowfen]*; (*driving*) ich habe mich verfahren *[fairfahren]*
lost property office, lost and found das Fundbüro *[foontbœro]*
lot: a lot, lots viel *[feel]*; **not a lot** nicht sehr viel *[nicht zair]*; **a lot of money** eine Menge Geld; **a lot of women** viele Frauen; **a lot cooler** viel kühler; **I like it a lot** ich mag es sehr *[ich mahk ess zair]*; **is it a lot further?** ist es noch sehr weit? *[noch zair vyte]*; **I'll take the (whole) lot** ich nehme alles *[naym-uh al-ess]*
lotion die Lotion *[lohts-yohn]*
loud laut *[lowt]*; **the music is rather loud** die Musik ist ziemlich laut
lounge (*in hotel*) der Gesellschaftsraum *[gezelshafftsrowm]*; (*airport*) der Warteraum *[vahrt-uh-rowm]*
lousy saumäßig *[zowmayssich]*
love: I love you ich liebe dich *[ich leeb-*

uh dich]; **he's fallen in love** er hat sich verliebt *[air hat zich fairleept]*; **I love Germany** ich mag Deutschland sehr gern *[ich mahk doytshlant zair gairn]*; **let's make love** willst du mit mir schlafen? *[villst doo mit meer shlahfen]*
lovely herrlich *[hairlich]*
low niedrig *[needrich]*
low beam das Abblendlicht *[apblentlicht]*
LP eine LP *[el-pay]*
luck das Glück *[glœck]*; **hard luck!** Pech! *[pech]*; **good luck!** viel Glück *[feel]*; **just my luck!** ich habe immer Pech! *[ich hahb-uh]*; **it was pure luck** es war reines Glück *[ess vahr ryness]*
lucky: that's lucky! Glück gehabt! *[glœck gehahpt]*
lucky charm ein Talisman (*m*)
luggage das Gepäck *[gepeck]*
lumbago der Hexenschuß *[hecksenshooss]*
lump die Beule *[boyl-uh]*
lunch das Mittagessen *[mittahkessen]*
lungs die Lungen *[loong-en]*
Luxembourg Luxemburg *[looksemboork]*
luxurious luxuriös *[looksooreeurss]*
luxury der Luxus *[looksooss]*

M

macho chauvinistisch *[shohveenistish]*
mad verrückt *[fairœckt]*
madam: excuse me madam entschuldigen Sie bitte *[entshooldigen zee]*
magazine eine Zeitschrift *[tsyte-shrift]*
magnificent großartig *[grohssartich]*
maid (*in hotel*) das Zimmermädchen *[tsimmermaydchen]*
maiden name der Mädchenname *[maydchen-nahm-uh]*
mail: is there any mail for me? ist Post für mich da? *[posst foor mich]*
mailbox der Briefkasten *[breefkassten]*
main: where's the main post office? wo ist die Hauptpost? *[dee howptposst]*; **that's the main thing** das ist die Haupt-

sache *[dee howptzach-uh]*; **main road** die Hauptstraße *[howptshtrahss-uh]*
make machen *[machen]*; **do you make them yourself?** machen Sie sie selbst? *[zee zee zelpst]*; **it's very well made** es ist sehr gut gemacht *[zair goot gemacht]*; **what does that make altogether?** was macht das zusammen *[vass macht dass tsoozammen]*; **I make it only 30 marks** nach meiner Rechnung sind das nur 30 Mark *[nach myner rechnoong zint dass noor]*
make-up das Make-up
make-up remover der Make-up-Entferner *[entfairner]*
male chauvinist pig der Chauvi

[shohvee]

man der Mann

manager der Geschäftsführer *[geshefts-fœrer]*; **may I see the manager?** kann ich den Geschäftsführer sprechen? *[dayn ... shpreCHen]*

manicure die Maniküre *[manikœr-uh]*

many viele *[feel-uh]*

map: a map of ... eine Karte von ... *[ine-uh kart-uh fon]*; **it's not on this map** es ist nicht auf dieser Karte *[niCHt owff deezer kart-uh]*

March der März *[mairts]*

marijuana das Marihuana

mark: there's a mark on it es ist ein Fleck darauf *[ine fleck darowff]*; **could you mark it on the map for me?** können Sie es mir auf der Karte anstreichen? *[kurnen zee ess meer owff dair kart-uh anshtryCHen]*

market der Markt

marmalade die Orangenmarmelade *[oronjen-marmelahd-uh]*

married: are you married? Sind Sie verheiratet? *[zint zee fairhyrahtet]*; **I'm married** ich bin verheiratet

mascara die Wimperntusche *[vimpern-toosh-uh]*

mass: I'd like to go to mass ich möchte gern zur Messe gehen *[iCH murCHt-uh gairn tsōōr mess-uh gayen]*

mast der Mast

masterpiece das Meisterwerk *[myster-vairk]*

matches die Streichhölzer *[shtryCHe-hurltser]*

material (*cloth*) der Stoff *[shtoff]*

matter: it doesn't matter das macht nichts *[dass maCHt niCHts]*; **what's the matter?** was ist los? *[vass ist lohss]*

mattress die Matratze *[matrats-uh]*

maximum das Maximum

May der Mai *[my]*

may: may I have another bottle? kann ich noch eine Flasche haben? *[noCH ine-uh flash-uh hahben]*; **may I?** darf ich?

maybe vielleicht *[feelyCHte]*; **maybe not** vielleicht nicht

mayonnaise die Mayonnaise *[my-onayz-uh]*

me: come with me kommen Sie mit mir *[kommen zee mit meer]*; **it's for me** es ist für mich *[fœr miCH]*; **it's me** ich bin's

[iCH binns]; **me too** ich auch *[owCH]*; *see page 111*

meal die Mahlzeit *[mahltsyte]*; **that was an excellent meal** das war ein herrliches Essen *[dass vahr ine hairliCHess essen]*

mean: what does this word mean? was bedeutet dieses Wort? *[vass bedoytet deezes vort]*; **what does he mean?** was meint er? *[vass mynt air]*

measles die Masern *[mahzern]*

measurements die Maße *[mahss-uh]*

meat das Fleisch *[flyshe]*

mechanic: do you have a mechanic here? gibt es hier einen Mechaniker? *[gipt ess heer ine-en meCHahniker]*

medicine die Medizin *[meditseen]*

medieval mittelalterlich *[—liCH]*

Mediterranean das Mittelmeer *[mittel-mair]*

medium mittlerer; (*meat*) medium *[maydee-oom]*

medium dry halbtrocken *[halp—]*

medium-sized mittelgroß *[mittelgrohss]*

meet: pleased to meet you angenehm *[angenaym]*; **where shall we meet?** wo sollen wir uns treffen? *[vo zollen veer oonss treffen]*; **let's meet up again** wir sollten uns irgendwann wiedersehen *[eergentvan veederzayen]*

meeting (*business etc*) die Besprechung *[beshpreCHoong]*

meeting place der Treffpunkt *[—poonkt]*

melon eine Melone *[melohn-uh]*

member das Mitglied *[mitgleet]*; **I'd like to become a member** ich möchte gern Mitglied werden *[iCH murCHte gairn mitgleet vairden]*

mend: can you mend this? können Sie das reparieren? *[kurnen zee dass repah-reeren]*

men's room die Herrentoilette *[herren-twalett-uh]*

mention: don't mention it gern geschehen *[gairn geshayen]*

menu die Speisekarte *[shpyze-uh-kart-uh]*

mess das Durcheinander *[doorCHyne-ander]*

message: are there any messages for me? ist eine Nachricht für mich hinterlassen worden? *[ine-uh naCHriCHt fœr miCH hinterlassen vorden]*; **I'd like to leave a**

message for ... ich möchte eine Nachricht für ... hinterlassen

metal das Metall *[metal]*

metre, meter der Meter *[mayter]; see page 119*

midday: at midday mittags *[mittahks]*

middle: in the middle in der Mitte *[in dair mitt-uh]*; **in the middle of the road** in der Mitte der Straße; **in the middle ages** im Mittelalter *[im mittel-al-ter]*

midnight: at midnight um Mitternacht *[oom mitternacht]*

might: I might want to stay another 3 days vielleicht bleibe ich noch 3 Tage länger *[feelychte blybe-uh ich noch ... lenger]*; **you might have warned me!** sie hätten mich warnen können! *[zee hetten mich vahrnen kurnen]*

migraine die Migräne *[migrayn-uh]*

mild mild *[millt]*

mile die Meile *[myle-uh]*; **that's miles away!** das ist meilenweit entfernt! *[mylen-vyte entfairnt]; see page 119*

mileometer der Kilometerzähler *[keelo-maytertsayler]*

military militärisch *[militairish]*

milk die Milch *[milch]*

milkshake ein Milchshake (*m*)

millimetre, millimeter der Millimeter *[millimayter]*

minced meat das Hackfleisch *[hackflyshe]*

mind: I don't mind es macht mir nichts aus *[ess macht meer nichts owss]*; (*either will do etc*) ist mir egal *[meer aygahl]*; **would you mind if I ...?** hätten Sie etwas dagegen, wenn ich ... *[hetten zee etvass dagaygen ven ich]*; **never mind** macht nichts *[macht nichts]*; **I've changed my mind** ich habe es mir anders überlegt *[ich hahb-uh ess meer anderss ooberlaykt]*

mine: it's mine es gehört mir *[ess gehurt meer]; see page 112*

mineral water das Mineralwasser *[minerahlvasser]*

minimum das Minimum

mint (*sweet*) ein Pfefferminz (*nt*)

minus minus *[meenooss]*; **minus 3 degrees** minus 3 Grad *[dry graht]*

minute die Minute *[minoot-uh]*; **in a minute** gleich *[glyche]*; **just a minute** Moment mal *[mohment mahl]*

mirror der Spiegel *[shpeegel]*

Miss Fräulein *[froylyne]*

miss: I miss you du fehlst mir *[doo faylst meer]*; **there is a ... missing** ein(e) ... fehlt *[ine(-uh) ... faylt]*; **we missed the train** wir haben den Zug verpaßt *[veer hahben dayn tsook fairpasst]*

mist der Nebel *[naybel]*

mistake der Fehler *[fayler]*; **I think there's a mistake here** ich glaube, da ist ein Fehler *[ich glowb-uh]*

misunderstanding das Mißverständnis *[missfairshtentniss]*

mixture die Mischung *[mishoong]*

mix-up: there's been a mix-up with ... mit ... ist irgendwas schiefgelaufen *[eergentvass sheefgelowfen]*

modern modern *[modairn]*; **a modern art gallery** eine Galerie für moderne Kunst

moisturizer die Feuchtigkeitscreme *[foychtichkytes-kraym-uh]*

moment ein Moment (*m*) *[mohment]*; **I won't be a moment** es dauert nur einen Moment *[ess dowert noor ine-en]*

monastery das Kloster *[klohster]*

Monday der Montag *[mohntahk]*

money das Geld *[gelt]*; **I don't have any money** ich habe kein Geld *[ich hahb-uh kyne]*; **do you take English/American money?** nehmen Sie englisches/amerikanisches Geld? *[naymen zee eng-lishess/amerikahnishess]*

month der Monat *[mohnaht]*

monument das Monument *[monooment]*; (*statue*) das Denkmal *[denkmahl]*

moon der Mond *[mohnt]*

moorings der Ankerplatz

moped das Moped *[mohpet]*

more mehr *[mair]*; **may I have some more?** kann ich etwas mehr haben? *[kan ich etvass mair hahben]*; **more water, please** noch etwas Wasser, bitte *[noch etvass]*; **no more** nichts mehr; **more expensive** teurer *[toyrer]*; **more than 50** über 50 *[oober]*; **more than that** mehr als das; **a lot more** viel mehr *[feel]*; **I don't stay there any more** ich wohne nicht mehr da *[vohn-uh nicht]*

morning der Morgen; **good morning** guten Morgen *[gooten]*; **this morning** heute morgen *[hoyt-uh]*; **in the morning** am Morgen

mosquito die Stechmücke *[shtecнmbck-uh]*
most: I like this one most dies gefällt mir am besten *[deess gefelt meer am besten]*; **most of the time** die meiste Zeit *[dee myste-uh tsyte]*; **most of the hotels** die meisten Hotels
mother: my mother meine Mutter *[myne-uh mootter]*
motor der Motor *[motohr]*
motorbike das Motorrad *[motohrraht]*
motorboat das Motorboot *[motohrboht]*
motorist der Autofahrer *[owto-fahrer]*
motorway die Autobahn *[owto-bahn]*
motor yacht die Motorjacht *[motohr-yacнt]*
mountain der Berg *[bairk]*; **up in the mountains** in den Bergen *[dayn bairgen]*; **a mountain village** ein Bergdorf *[ine bairkdorff]*
mountaineer der Bergsteiger *[bairk-shtyger]*
mountaineering das Bergsteigen *[bairk-shtygen]*
mouse eine Maus *[mowss]*
moustache der Schnurrbart *[shnoorbart]*
mouth der Mund *[moont]*
move: he's moved to another hotel er ist in ein anderes Hotel gezogen *[air ist in ine anderess hotel getsohgen]*; **could you move your car?** könnten Sie Ihr Auto wegfahren? *[kurnten zee eer owto veckfahren]*
movie der Film; **let's go to the movies** sollen wir ins Kino gehen? *[zollen veer inss keeno gayen]*

movie camera die Filmkamera
movie theater das Kino *[keeno]*
moving: a very moving tune eine sehr ergreifende Melodie *[zair airgryfend-uh melodee]*
Mr Herr *[hair]*
Mrs Frau *[frow]*
Ms Frau *[frow]*
much viel *[feel]*; **much better** viel besser; **not much** nicht viel *[nicнt]*; **not so much** nicht so viel
muffler (*on car*) der Auspufftopf *[owsspoof-topf]*
mug: I've been mugged ich bin überfallen worden *[ωberfal-en vorden]*
muggy drückend *[drωckent]*
Munich München *[mωncнen]*
mumps die Mumps *[moomps]*
muscle der Muskel *[mooskel]*
museum das Museum *[moozayoom]*
mushrooms die Pilze *[pilts-uh]*
music die Musik *[mōōzeek]*; **do you have the sheet music for ...?** haben Sie die Noten für ...? *[hahben zee dee nohten fωr]*
musician der Musiker *[mōōziker]*
mussels die Muscheln *[moosheln]*
must: I must ... ich muß ... *[icн mooss]*; **I mustn't ...** ich darf nicht ...; **you mustn't forget** Sie dürfen nicht vergessen *[zee dωrfen nicнt fairgessen]*
mustache der Schnurrbart *[shnoorbart]*
mustard der Senf *[zenff]*
my mein *[myne]*; *see page 110*
myself: I'll do it myself ich mache es selbst *[icн macн-uh ess zelpst]*

N

nail (*finger, for wood*) der Nagel *[nahgel]*
nail clippers ein Nagelzwicker (*m*) *[nahgeltsvicker]*
nailfile eine Nagelfeile *[nahgelfyle-uh]*
nail polish der Nagellack *[nahgellack]*
nail polish remover der Nagellack-entferner *[nahgellack-entfairner]*
nail scissors eine Nagelschere *[nahgel-shair-uh]*

naked nackt
name der Name *[nahm-uh]*; **what's your name?** wie heißen Sie *[vee hyssen zee]*; **what's its name?** wie heißt es? *[hyste]*; **my name is ...** ich heiße *[hyce-uh]*
nap: he's having a nap er macht ein Nickerchen *[air macнt ine nickercнen]*
napkin eine Serviette *[zairvee-ett-uh]*
nappy eine Windel *[vindel]*

nappy-liners die Windeleinlagen [vindel-ine-lahgen]
narrow eng
nasty (person) gemein [gemyne]; (weather, taste) furchtbar [foorchtbar]; (cut) schlimm [shlim]
national national [nats-yohnahl]
nationality die Staatsangehörigkeit [shahtsangehurichkyte]
natural natürlich [natoorlich]
naturally natürlich [natoorlich]
nature die Natur [natoor]
naturist der FKK-Anhänger [eff-kah-kah anhenger]
nausea die Übelkeit [oobelkyte]
near: is it near here? ist es in der Nähe? [dair nay-uh]; **near the window** nahe am Fenster [nah-uh]; **do you go near ...?** fahren Sie in die Nähe von ... [fahren zee in dee]; **where is the nearest subway?** wo ist die nächste U-Bahn? [vo ... naychst-uh]
nearby in der Nähe [in dair nay-uh]
nearly fast [fasst]
nearside: the nearside front wheel das rechte Vorderrad [recht-uh forder-raht]
neat (drink) pur [poor]
necessary notwendig [nohtvendich]; **is it necessary to ...?** ist es nötig, zu ...? [nurtich tsoo]; **it's not necessary** das ist nicht nötig [nicht nurtich]
neck der Hals [halss]
necklace eine Halskette [halskett-uh]
necktie eine Krawatte [kravatt-uh]
need: I need a ... ich brauche ein(e) ... [ich browch-uh ine(-uh)]; **it needs more salt** es muß mehr gesalzen werden [ess mooss mair gezaltsen vairden]; **do I need to ...?** muß ich ...? [mooss ich]; **there's no need** das ist nicht nötig [nicht nurtich]; **there's no need to shout!** Sie brauchen nicht zu schreien! [zee browchen nicht tsoo shryen]
needle die Nadel [nahdel]
negative (film) das Negativ [naygateef]
negotiation die Verhandlung [fairhand-loong]
neighbo(u)r der Nachbar/die Nachbarin [nachbar(in)]
neighbo(u)rhood die Nachbarschaft [nachbarshafft]
neither: neither of us keiner von uns [kyner fon oonss]; **neither one (of them)** keiner (von ihnen) [eenen]; **neither ... nor ...** weder ... noch ... [vayder ... noch]; **neither do I** ich auch nicht [ich owch nicht]
nephew: my nephew mein Neffe [myne neff-uh]
nervous nervös [nairvurss]
net das Netz; **£100 net** £100 netto
nettle die Nessel
neurotic neurotisch [noyrohtish]
neutral (gear) der Leerlauf [lairlowff]
never nie [nee]
new neu [noy]
news (TV etc) die Nachrichten [nachrichten]; **is there any news?** gibt es etwas Neues? [gipt ess etvass noyess]
newspaper eine Zeitung [tsytoong]; **do you have any English newspapers?** haben Sie englische Zeitungen [hahben zee eng-lish-uh tsytoongen]
newsstand der Zeitungsstand [tsytoongs-shtant]
New Year Neujahr [noy-yahr]; **Happy New Year** frohes neues Jahr [froh-ess noyess yahr]
New Year's Eve Silvester
New Zealand Neuseeland [noyzaylant]
New Zealander (man) der Neuseeländer [noyzaylender]; (woman) die Neeseelän-derin
next nächster [naychster]; **next to the post office** neben der Post [nayben]; **the one next to that** der daneben [dair danayben]; **it's at the next corner** es ist an der nächsten Ecke [dair naychsten eck-uh]; **next week/next Monday** nächste Woche/nächsten Montag
nextdoor nebenan [naybenan]
next of kin die nächsten Angehörigen [dee naychsten angehurigen]
nice (person, town) nett; (meal) gut [goot]; **that's very nice of you** das ist sehr nett von Ihnen [fon eenen]; **a nice cold drink** ein schöner kalter Drink [shurner]
nickname der Spitzname [shpitsnahm-uh]
niece: my niece meine Nichte [myne-uh nicht-uh]
night die Nacht [nacht]; **for one night** für eine Nacht [foor ine-uh]; **for three nights** für drei Nächte [necht-uh]; **good night** gute Nacht [goot-uh]; **at night** nachts

nightcap (*drink*) ein Schlummertrunk (*m*) [*shloomertroonk*]
nightclub ein Nachtklub (*m*) [*nachtkloob*]
nightdress das Nachthemd [*nacht-hemt*]
night flight der Nachtflug [*nachtflook*]
nightie das Nachthemd [*nacht-hemt*]
night-life das Nachtleben [*nachtlayben*]
nightmare der Alptraum [*alptrowm*]
night porter der Nachtportier [*nachtportyay*]
nit (*bug*) die Nisse [*niss-uh*]
no nein [*nyne*]; **I've no money** ich habe kein Geld [*ich hahb-uh kyne gelt*]; **there's no more** es ist nichts mehr da [*nichts mair*]; **no more than ...** nicht mehr als ...; **oh no!** (*upset*) nein!
nobody keiner [*kyner*]
noise der Lärm [*lairm*]
noisy laut [*lowt*]; **it's too noisy** es ist zu laut
non-alcoholic alkoholfrei [*alkohohlfry*]
none keiner [*kyner*]; **none of them** keiner von ihnen [*fon eenen*]
nonsense der Unsinn [*oonzin*]
non-smoking Nichtraucher [*nichtrowcher*]
non-stop (*drive etc*) nonstop
no-one keiner [*kyner*]
nor: nor do I ich auch nicht [*ich owch nicht*]
normal normal [*normahl*]
north der Norden; **to the north** nach Norden
northeast der Nordosten [*nort-ossten*]; **to the northeast** nach Nordosten
Northern Ireland Nordirland [*norteerlant*]
North Germany Norddeutschland [*nort-doytshlant*]

Norway Norwegen [*norvaygen*]
northwest der Nordwesten [*nortvesten*]; **to the northwest** nach Nordwesten
nose die Nase [*nahz-uh*]
nosebleed Nasenbluten [*nahzenblooten*]
not nicht [*nicht*]; **I don't smoke** ich rauche nicht [*ich rowch-uh nicht*]; **he didn't say that** das hat er nicht gesagt [*gezahkt*]; **it's not important** es ist nicht wichtig; **not that one** nicht diesen [*deezen*]; **not for me** nicht für mich; *see page 117*
note (*bank note*) der Schein [*shyne*]
notebook ein Notizbuch (*nt*) [*nohteetsbooch*]
nothing nichts [*nichts*]
November der November
now jetzt [*yetst*]; **not just now** jetzt nicht
nowhere nirgendwo [*neergentvo*]
nudist der FKK-Anhänger [*eff-kah-kah anhenger*]
nudist beach der FKK-Strand [*eff-kah-kah shtrant*]
nuisance: he's being a nuisance er belästigt mich [*air belesticht mich*]
numb taub [*towp*]
number die Nummer [*noommer*]; **what number?** welche Nummer? [*velch-uh*]
number plate das Nummernschild [*noommern-shilt*]
nurse die Krankenschwester [*krankenshvester*]
nursery (*at airport etc*) der Kinderhort
nursery slope der Anfängerhügel [*anfengerhoogel*]
nut eine Nuß [*nooss*]; (*for bolt*) eine Schraubenmutter [*shrowbenmootter*]
nutter: he's a nutter er ist verrückt [*air ist fairroockt*]

O

oar das Ruder [*rooder*]
obligatory obligatorisch [*obligatohrish*]
oblige: much obliged herzlichen Dank [*hairtslichen dank*]
obnoxious (*person*) widerwärtig [*veedervairtich*]

obvious: that's obvious das ist offensichtlich [*offenzichtlich*]
occasionally gelegentlich [*gelaygentlich*]

o'clock *see page 118*
October der Oktober
odd (*number*) ungerade [*oo*ngrahd-uh]; (*strange*) seltsam [*zeltzam*]
odometer der Kilometerzähler [keelo-**may**tertsayler]
of von [*fon*]; the name of the hotel der Name des Hotels [dair na**hm**-uh dess hotels]; have one of mine nehmen Sie eins von meinen [ine-ss fon m**y**nen]; *see page 107*
off: it just broke off es ist einfach abgebrochen [ine-faсн **a**pgebroснen]; 20% off 20% Ermäßigung [airm**a**yssigoong]; the lights were off das Licht war aus [dass lie**h**t var owss]; just off the main road ganz in der Nähe der Hauptstraße [gants in dair n**a**y-uh dair h**o**wpt-shtrahss-uh]
offend: don't be offended nehmen Sie das nicht übel [n**a**ymen zee dass nieht **oo**bel]
office das Büro [b**oo**ro]
officer (*said to policeman*) Herr Wachtmeister [v**a**снtmyster]
official der Beamte [be-**a**mt-uh]; is that official? ist das amtlich? [**a**mtlieh]
off-season die Nebensaison [n**a**yben-zayzong]
off-side: the front off-side wheel das linke Vorderrad [link-uh f**o**rder-raht]
often oft; not often nicht oft
oil das Öl [url]; it's losing oil es verliert Öl [fairl**ee**rt]; will you change the oil? könnten Sie einen Ölwechsel machen? [k**u**rnten zee ine-en urlvecksel m**a**снen]; the oil light's flashing das Öllämpchen blinkt [**u**rllempснen]
oil painting ein Ölgemälde (*nt*) [**u**rlge-mayld-uh]
oil pressure der Öldruck [**u**rldroock]
ointment die Salbe [z**a**lb-uh]
OK okay; are you OK? sind Sie okay?; that's OK thanks danke, das ist in Ordnung [in **o**rdnoong]; that's OK by me das ist mir recht [meer reснt]
old alt; how old are you? wie alt sind Sie? [vee alt zint zee]
old-age pensioner der Rentner
old-fashioned altmodisch [**a**ltmohdish]
old town die Altstadt [**a**ltshtatt]
olive die Olive [ol**ee**v-uh]
olive oil das Olivenöl [ol**ee**venurl]

omelet(te) ein Omelett (*nt*)
on auf [*owff*]; on the beach am Strand [am shtrant]; on Friday am Freitag; on television im Fernsehen; I don't have it on me ich habe es nicht bei mir [iсн h**a**hb-uh ess nieht by meer]; this drink's on me dieser Drink ist auf meine Rechnung [d**ee**zer drink ist owff m**y**ne-uh reснnoong]; a book on Hamburg ein Buch über Hamburg [**oo**ber]; the light was on das Licht war an [lieht vahr an]; what's on in town? was läuft in der Stadt? [vass loyft in dair shtatt]; it's just not on! (*not acceptable*) das ist nicht drin! [nieht drin]
once einmal [ine-mahl]; at once sofort [z**o**fort]
one eins [ine-ss]; that one das da; the green one der/die/das grüne [dair/dee/dass gr**oo**n-uh]; the one with the black dress on die mit dem schwarzen Kleid; the one in the blue shirt der mit dem blauen Hemd
onion eine Zwiebel [tsv**ee**bel]
only: only one nur einer [n**oo**r ine-er]; only once nur einmal; it's only 9 o'clock es ist erst neun Uhr [airst]; I've only just arrived ich bin gerade erst angekommen [iсн bin ger**a**hd-uh airst]
open (*adj*) offen; when do you open? wann machen Sie auf? [van m**a**снen zee owff]; in the open (*open air*) im Freien [im fry-en]; it won't open es geht nicht auf [ess gayt nieht owff]
opening times die Öffnungszeiten [**u**rfnoongstsyten]
opera die Oper [**oh**per]
operation (*med*) eine Operation [operats-y**oh**n]
operator (*tel*) die Vermittlung [fairm**i**tt-loong]
opportunity die Gelegenheit [gel**a**ygen-hyte]
opposite: opposite the church gegenüber der Kirche [gaygen**oo**ber dair keerсн-uh]; it's directly opposite es ist genau gegenüber [gen**o**w]
oppressive (*heat*) drückend [dr**oo**ckent]
optician der Augenarzt [**o**wgenartst]
optimistic optimistisch [optim**i**stish]
or oder [**oh**der]
orange (*fruit*) eine Orange [or**o**nj-uh]; (*colour*) orange

orange juice ein Orangensaft (*m*) *[oron-jenzaft]*

orchestra das Orchester *[orkester]*

order: could we order now? können wir jetzt bestellen? *[kurnen veer yetst beshtellen]*; **I've already ordered** ich habe schon bestellt *[icн hahb-uh shohn]*; **I didn't order that** das habe ich nicht bestellt; **it's out of order** (*elevator etc*) es ist außer Betrieb *[owsser betreep]*

ordinary normal *[normahl]*

organization die Organisation *[organee-zats-yohn]*

organize organisieren *[organeezeeren]*; **could you organize it?** könnten Sie das organisieren? *[kurnten zee dass]*

original: is it an original? ist es ein Original? *[ine originahl]*

ornament (*for room etc*) ein Ziergegenstand (*m*) *[tseergaygenshtant]*

ostentatious protzig *[protsicн]*

other: the other waiter der andere Kellner *[dair ander-uh]*; **the other one** der/die/das andere; **do you have any others?** haben Sie noch andere? *[hahben zee nocн]*; **some other time, thanks** danke, vielleicht ein anderes Mal *[feelycнt ine anderess mahl]*

otherwise sonst *[zonst]*

ouch! autsch! *[owtsh]*

ought: he ought to be here soon er müßte bald hier sein *[air moosst-uh balt heer zyne]*

ounce *see page 120*

our unser *[oonzer]*; *see page 110*

ours unserer *[oonzerer]*; *see page 112*

out: he's out (*of building etc*) er ist nicht im Hause *[air ist nicнt im howz-uh]*; **get out!** raus! *[rowss]*; **I'm out of money** mir ist das Geld ausgegangen *[meer ist dass gelt owssgegangen]*; **a few kilometres out of town** einige Kilometer außerhalb der Stadt *[ine-ig-uh keelomayter owsserhalp dair shtatt]*

outboard (motor) der Außenbordmotor *[owssenbort-motohr]*

outdoors draußen *[drowssen]*

outlet (*elec*) die Steckdose *[shteckdohz-uh]*

outside: can we sit outside? können wir draußen sitzen? *[drowssen]*

outskirts: on the outskirts of ... am Stadtrand von ... *[am shtattrant fon]*

oven der Ofen *[ohfen]*

over: over here hier *[heer]*; **over there** dort; **over 100** über 100 *[oober]*; **I'm burnt all over** ich bin ganz verbrannt *[icн bin gants fairbrannt]*; **the holiday's over** der Urlaub ist vorbei *[for-by]*

overcharge: you've overcharged me Sie haben mir zuviel berechnet *[zee hahben meer tsoofeel berecнnet]*

overcoat ein Mantel (*m*)

overcooked verkocht *[fairkocнt]*

overdrive der Schnellgang *[shnellgang]*

overexposed überbelichtet *[oober-belicнtet]*

overheat: it's overheating (*car*) es läuft heiß *[ess loyft hyce]*

overland auf dem Landweg *[owff daym lantvayk]*

overlook: overlooking the Rhine mit Blick auf den Rhein *[owff]*

overnight über Nacht *[oober nacнt]*

oversleep: I overslept ich habe mich verschlafen *[icн hahb-uh micн fair-shlahfen]*

overtake überholen *[ooberhohlen]*

overweight zu schwer *[tsoo shvair]*

owe: how much do I owe you? was bin ich Ihnen schuldig? *[vass bin icн eenen shooldicн]*

own: my own ... mein eigener ... *[myne 'eye'gener]*; **are you on your own?** sind Sie allein hier? *[zint zee alyne heer]*; **I'm on my own** ich bin allein hier

owner der Besitzer

oyster eine Auster *[owsster]*

P

pack: a pack of cigarettes eine Schachtel Zigaretten *[ine-uh shacнtel]*; **I'll go and pack** ich gehe packen *[icн gay-uh]*

package das Paket *[packayt]*

package holiday, package tour eine Pauschalreise *[powshahlryze-uh]*

packed lunch ein Mittagessen *(nt)* zum Mitnehmen *[mittahkessen tsoom mitnaymen]*

packed out: the place was packed out es war dort gerammelt voll *[ess vahr dort gerammelt foll]*

packet *(parcel)* das Paket *[packayt]*; **a packet of cigarettes** eine Schachtel Zigaretten *[ine-uh shacнtel]*

paddle das Paddel

padlock ein Vorhängeschloß *[forheng-uh-shloss]*

page *(of book)* die Seite *[zyte-uh]*; **could you page him?** können Sie ihn ausrufen lassen? *[kurnen zee een owssrōōfen]*

pain der Schmerz *[shmairts]*; **I have a pain here** ich habe hier Schmerzen *[icн hahb-uh heer]*

painful schmerzhaft *[shmairts-haft]*

painkillers ein Schmerzmittel *(nt)* *[shmairtsmittel]*

paint *(noun)* die Farbe *[farb-uh]*; **I'm going to do some painting** *(pictures)* ich werde ein bißchen malen *[icн vaird-uh ine bisscнen mahlen]*

paintbrush der Pinsel *[pinzel]*

painting das Bild *[bilt]*

pair: a pair of ... ein Paar ... *[pahr]*

pajamas ein Schlafanzug *(m)* *[shlahfantsōōk]*

Pakistan Pakistan

Pakistani *(adj)* pakistanisch *[pakistahnish]*; *(man)* der Pakistaner *[pakistahner]*; *(woman)* die Pakistanerin

pal der Kumpel *[koompel]*

palace der Palast

pale blaß *[blass]*; **pale blue** zartblau *[tsartblow]*

palpitations Herzklopfen *[hairtsklopfen]*

pancake ein Pfannkuchen *(m)* *[pfannkōōcнen]*

panic: don't panic! keine Panik! *[kyne-uh pahnik]*

panties ein Höschen *(nt)* *[hursscнen]*

pants *(trousers)* eine Hose *[hohz-uh]*; *(underpants)* eine Unterhose *[oonter—]*

panty girdle ein Miederhöschen *(nt)* *[meederhursscнen]*

pantyhose eine Strumpfhose *[shtroompfhohz-uh]*

paper das Papier *[pappeer]*; *(newspaper)* eine Zeitung *[tsytoong]*; **a piece of paper** ein Stück *(nt)* Papier *[ine shtœck pappeer]*

paper handkerchiefs die Papiertaschentücher *[pappeertashentœcнer]*

paraffin das Paraffin

parallel: parallel to ... parallel zu ... *[parralayl tsōō]*

paralytic *(drunk)* blau *[blow]*

parasol *(over table)* ein Sonnenschirm *(m)* *[zonnensheerm]*

parcel das Paket *[packayt]*

pardon (me)? *(didn't understand)* bitte? *[bitt-uh]*

parents: my parents meine Eltern *[myne-uh eltern]*

parents-in-law die Schwiegereltern *[shveegereltern]*

park der Park; **where can I park?** wo kann ich parken? *[vo kan icн parken]*; **there's nowhere to park** man kann nirgends parken *[man kan neergents]*

parka ein Parka *(m)*

parking lights das Parklicht *[parklicнt]*

parking lot ein Parkplatz *(m)* *[parkplats]*

parking place: there's a parking place! da ist ein Parkplatz! *[ine parkplats]*

part ein Teil *(nt)* *[tyle]*

part exchange die Inzahlungnahme *[intsahloongnahm-uh]*

partner der Partner; *(woman)* die Partnerin

party *(group)* die Gruppe *[groopp-uh]*;

(*celebration*) die Fete [*fayt-uh*]; **let's have a party** wir sollten eine Party machen [*veer zollten ine-uh partee machen*]

pass (*mountain*) der Paß [*pas*]; (*overtake*) überholen [*ooberhohlen*]; **he passed out** er ist umgekippt [*oomgekippt*]; **he made a pass at me** er hat bei mir einen Annäherungsversuch gemacht [*air hat by meer ine-en an-nayeroongs-fairzooch gemacht*]

passable (*road*) befahrbar

passenger der Passagier [*passajeer*]

passport der Paß [*pas*]

past: in the past in der Vergangenheit [*in dair fairgangenhyte*]; **just past the bank** kurz hinter der Bank; *see page 118*

pastry der Teig [*tyke*]; (*cake*) ein Teilchen (*nt*) [*tylchen*]

patch: could you put a patch on this? könnten Sie das flicken? [*kurnten zee*]

pâté die Pastete [*passtayt-uh*]

path der Weg [*vayk*]

patient: be patient haben Sie Geduld [*hahben zee gedoolt*]

patio die Terrasse [*terrass-uh*]

pattern (*on cloth etc*) das Muster [*mooster*]; **a dress pattern** ein Schnittmuster [*shnittmooster*]

paunch der Bauch [*bowch*]

pavement (*sidewalk*) der Bürgersteig [*boorgershtyke*]

pay bezahlen [*betsahlen*]; **can I pay, please?** kann ich bezahlen, bitte? [*bitt-uh*]; **it's already paid for** es ist schon bezahlt [*shohn betsahlt*]; **I'll pay for this** das bezahle ich

pay phone ein Münzfernsprecher (*m*) [*moontsfairnshprecher*]

peace and quiet Ruhe [*roo-uh*]

peach ein Pfirsich (*m*) [*pfeerzich*]

peanuts die Erdnüsse [*airtnooss-uh*]

pear eine Birne [*beern-uh*]

peas die Erbsen [*airpsen*]

pearl die Perle [*pairl-uh*]

peculiar (*taste, custom etc*) eigenartig ['*eye'-genartich*]

pedal das Pedal [*pedahl*]

pedalo ein Tretboot (*nt*) [*traytboht*]

pedestrian der Fußgänger [*foossgenger*]

pedestrian crossing der Fußgängerüberweg [*foossgenger-oobervayk*]

pedestrian precinct die Fußgängerzone [*foossgengertsohn-uh*]

pee: I need to go for a pee ich muß mal pinkeln gehen [*ich mooss mahl pinkeln gayen*]

peeping Tom ein Spanner (*m*) [*shpanner*]

peg (*for washing*) die Wäscheklammer [*vesh-uh-klammer*]; (*for tent*) der Hering [*hairing*]

pen ein Kugelschreiber (*m*) [*koogelshryber*]; **do you have a pen?** haben Sie einen Stift? [*hahben zee ine-en shtift*]

pencil ein Bleistift (*m*) [*bly-shtift*]

pen friend der Brieffreund [*breef-froynt*]

penicillin das Penizillin [*penitsilleen*]

penknife ein Taschenmesser (*nt*) [*tashen-messer*]

pen pal der Brieffreund [*breef-froynt*]

pensioner der Rentner

people die Leute [*loyt-uh*]; **a lot of people** viele Leute [*feel-uh*]; **German people** die Deutschen [*dee doytshen*]

pepper (*spice*) der Pfeffer; **green/red pepper** eine grüne/rote Paprikaschote [*ine-uh groon-uh/roht-uh paprikashoht-uh*]

peppermint (*sweet*) ein Pfefferminz (*nt*) [*—mints*]

per: per night pro Nacht; **how much per hour?** was kostet es pro Stunde? [*vass*]

per cent Prozent [*protsent*]

perfect perfekt [*pairfekt*]

perfume das Parfüm [*parfoom*]

perhaps vielleicht [*feelychte*]

period (*of time*) die Zeit [*tsyte*]; (*woman's*) die Periode [*pairee-ohd-uh*]

perm eine Dauerwelle [*dowervell-uh*]

permit die Genehmigung [*genaymigoong*]

person eine Person [*pairzohn*]

pessimistic pessimistisch [*pessimistish*]

petrol das Benzin [*bentseen*]

petrol can der Reservekanister [*rezairv-uh-kanister*]

petrol station eine Tankstelle [*tankshtell-uh*]

petrol tank der Tank

pharmacy eine Apotheke [*appotayk-uh*]

phone *see* **telephone**

photogenic fotogen [*fotogayn*]

photograph ein Foto (*nt*); **would you take a photograph of us?** könnten Sie ein Bild von uns machen? [*kurnten zee ine bilt fon oonss machen*]

photographer der Fotograf [*fotograhf*]

phrase: a useful phrase ein nützlicher Ausdruck *[ine nœotslicher owssdroock]*

phrasebook ein Sprachführer *(m)* *[shprahchfœrer]*

pianist ein Klavierspieler *[klaveershpeeler]*

piano ein Klavier *(nt)* *[klaveer]*

pickpocket ein Taschendieb *(m)* *[tashendeep]*

pick up: when can I pick them up? wann kann ich sie abholen? *[van kan ich zee ap-hohlen]*; **will you come and pick me up?** können Sie mich abholen? *[kurnen zee]*

picnic ein Picknick *(nt)*

picture ein Bild *(nt)* *[bilt]*

pie *(meat)* eine Pastete *[pastayt-uh]*; *(fruit)* ein Obstkuchen *(m)* *[ohpst-kōōchen]*

piece ein Stück *(nt)* *[shtœck]*; **a piece of …** ein Stück …

pig ein Schwein *(nt)* *[shvyne]*

pigeon eine Taube *[towb-uh]*

piles *(med)* Hämorrhoiden *[hemorreeden]*

pile-up ein Massenzusammenstoß *(m)* *[massen-tsōōzammen-shtohss]*

pill eine Pille *[pill-uh]*; **I'm on the pill** ich nehme die Pille *[ich naym-uh dee]*

pillarbox ein Briefkasten *(m)* *[breefkasten]*

pillow ein Kissen *(nt)*

pillow case ein Kissenbezug *(m)* *[kissenbetsōōk]*

pin eine Nadel *[nahdel]*

pineapple eine Ananas *[ananas]*

pineapple juice ein Ananassaft *(m)* *[ananas-zaft]*

pink rosa *[rohza]*

pint *see page 121*

pipe das Rohr; *(smoking)* eine Pfeife *[pfyfe-uh]*

pipe cleaners die Pfeifenreiniger *[pfyfenryniger]*

pipe tobacco der Pfeifentabak *[pfyfentabak]*

pity: it's a pity es ist schade *[shahd-uh]*

pizza eine Pizza

place: is this place taken? ist dieser Platz besetzt? *[deezer plats bezetst]*; **would you keep my place for me?** könnten Sie mir den Platz freihalten? *[kurnten zee meer dayn plats fryhalten]*; **at my place** bei mir *[by meer]*

place mat ein Set

plain *(food)* einfach *[ine-fach]*; *(not patterned)* uni *[œnee]*

plane das Flugzeug *[flōōktsoyk]*

plant eine Pflanze *[pflants-uh]*

plaster cast ein Gipsverband *(m)* *[gipssfairbant]*

plastic das Plastik

plastic bag eine Plastiktüte *[plastiktœt-uh]*

plate ein Teller *(m)*

platform der Bahnsteig *[bahnshtyke]*; **which platform, please?** welches Gleis, bitte? *[velches glyce bitt-uh]*

play *(verb)* spielen *[shpeelen]*; *(in theatre)* das Stück *[shtœck]*

playboy ein Playboy *(m)*

playground ein Spielplatz *(m)* *[shpeelplats]*

pleasant angenehm *[angenaym]*

please: could you please …? könnten Sie bitte … *[kurnten zee bitt-uh]*; **yes please** ja bitte *[yah]*

plenty: plenty of … viel … *[feel]*; **that's plenty, thanks** das ist genug, danke *[genōōk dank-uh]*

pleurisy die Brustfellentzündung *[broost-fell-entsœndoong]*

pliers eine Zange *[tsang-uh]*

plonk der Wein *[vyne]*

plug *(elec)* ein Stecker *(m)* *[shtecker]*; *(car)* eine Zündkerze *[tsœntkairts-uh]*; *(bathroom)* der Stöpsel *[shturpsel]*

plughole der Abfluß *[apflooss]*

plum eine Pflaume *[pflowm-uh]*

plumber ein Klempner *(m)*

plus plus *[plooss]*

p.m.: at 4 p.m. um 4 Uhr nachmittags *[nachmittahks]*; **at 9 p.m.** um 9 Uhr abends *[ahbents]*

pneumonia eine Lungenentzündung *[loongen-entsœndoong]*

poached eggs verlorene Eier *[fairlohren-uh 'eye'-er]*

pocket die Tasche *[tash-uh]*; **in my pocket** in meiner Tasche *[myner]*

pocketbook *(woman's bag)* eine Handtasche *[hant-tash-uh]*

pocketknife ein Taschenmesser *[tashenmesser]*

podiatrist der Fußpfleger *[fōōss-pflayger]*

point: could you point to it? könnten Sie darauf zeigen? *[kurnten zee darowff tsygen]*; **four point six** vier Komma sechs;

there's no point es hat keinen Sinn *[ess hat kynen zin]*

points *(car)* die Unterbrecherkontakte *[oonterbreCHer-kontakt-uh]*

poisonous giftig *[gifticH]*

police die Polizei *[polits-'eye']*; **call the police!** rufen Sie die Polizei! *[rōōfen zee dee]*

policeman der Polizist *[politsist]*

police station die Polizeiwache *[polits-'eye'-vacH-uh]*

polish die Creme *[kraym-uh]*; **will you polish my shoes?** können Sie meine Schuhe putzen? *[kurnen zee myne-uh shōō-uh pootsen]*

polite höflich *[hurflicH]*

politician der Politiker *[poleetiker]*

politics die Politik *[politteek]*

polluted verschmutzt *[fairshmootst]*

pond ein Teich *(m)* *[tycHe]*

pony ein Pony *(nt)* *[ponnee]*

pool *(swimming)* ein Becken *(nt)*; *(game)* Poolbillard *[pōōlbillyart]*

pool table der Billardtisch *[billyart-tish]*

poor *(not rich)* arm; *(quality etc)* schlecht *[shlecHt]*; **poor old Wolfgang!** der arme Wolfgang! *[dair arm-uh volfgang]*

pope der Papst *[pahpst]*

pop music die Popmusik *[popmōōzeek]*

pop singer der Popsänger *[popzenger]*

popular beliebt *[beleept]*

population die Bevölkerung *[befurlke-roong]*

pork das Schweinefleisch *[shvyne-uh-flysh]*

port *(for boats)* der Hafen *[hahfen]*; *(drink)* ein Portwein *(m)* *[portvyne]*

porter *(hotel)* der Portier *[portyay]*; *(for luggage)* der Gepäckträger *[gepeck-trayger]*

portrait das Porträt *[portray]*

Portugal Portugal *[portōōgahl]*

poser *(phoney person)* ein Angeber *(m)* *[an-gayber]*

posh vornehm *[fornaym]*

possibility die Möglichkeit *[murglicHkyte]*

possible möglich *[murglicH]*; **is it possible to …?** ist es möglich, zu …?; **as … as possible** so … wie möglich *[zo … vee]*

post *(mail)* die Post *[posst]*; **could you post this for me?** könnten Sie das für mich aufgeben? *[kurnten zee dass foor micH owfigayben]*

postbox ein Briefkasten *(m)* *[breefkas-sten]*

postcard eine Postkarte *[posstkart-uh]*

poster ein Plakat *(nt)* *[plakaht]*

poste restante postlagernd *[posst-lahgernt]*

post office das Postamt *[posstamt]*

pot ein Topf *(m)*; **a pot of tea** eine Kanne Tee *[ine-uh kann-uh tay]*; **pots and pans** das Kochgeschirr *[kocHgesheer]*

potato die Kartoffel

potato chips die Chips *[ships]*

potato salad der Kartoffelsalat *[kartoffel-zalaht]*

pottery die Töpferei *[turpfer-'eye']*; *(items)* Töpferwaren *[—vahren]*

pound *(money, weight)* das Pfund *[pfoont]*; *see page 120*

pour: it's pouring down es regnet in Strömen *[ess raygnet in shtrurmen]*

powder *(for face)* der Puder *[pōōder]*

powdered milk das Milchpulver *[milcHpoolver]*

power cut ein Stromausfall *(m)* *[shtrohmowss-fal]*

power point eine Steckdose *[shteckdohz-uh]*

power station das Kraftwerk *[kraftvairk]*

practise, practice: I need to practise ich brauche Übung *[icH browcH-uh ooboong]*

pram der Kinderwagen *[kindervahgen]*

prawn cocktail ein Krabbencocktail *(m)*

prawns die Garnelen *[garnaylen]*

prefer: I prefer white wine ich mag lieber Weißwein *[icH mahk leeber]*

preferably: preferably not tomorrow wenn möglich, nicht morgen *[ven murglicH]*

pregnant schwanger *[shvanger]*

prescription ein Rezept *(nt)* *[raytsept]*

present: at present zur Zeit *[tsōōr tsyte]*; **here's a present for you** hier ist ein Geschenk für Sie *[ine geshenk foor zee]*

president der Präsident *[prezeedent]*

press: could you press these? könnten Sie das für mich bügeln? *[kurnten zee dass foor micH boogeln]*

pretty hübsch *[hoopsh]*; **it's pretty expensive** es ist ganz schön teuer *[gants shurn toyer]*

price der Preis *[pryce]*

priest ein Geistlicher (*m*) [*gystlicher*]

prime minister der Premierminister [*premyayminister*]

print (*picture*) ein Abzug (*m*) [*aptsook*]

printed matter die Drucksache [*droock-zach-uh*]

priority (*in driving*) die Vorfahrt [*forfart*]

prison das Gefängnis [*gefengniss*]

private privat [*privaht*]; **private bath** ein eigenes Bad (*nt*) [*ine 'eye-geness baht*]

prize der Preis [*pryce*]

probably wahrscheinlich [*vahrshyne-lich*]

problem das Problem [*problaym*]; **I have a problem** ich habe ein Problem [*ich hahb-uh ine*]; **no problem** kein Problem [*kyne*]

product das Produkt [*prodookt*]

program(me) das Programm

promise: I promise ich verspreche es [*fairshprech-uh*]; **is that a promise?** ganz bestimmt? [*gants beshtimmt*]

pronounce: how do you pronounce this word? wie spricht man dieses Wort aus? [*vee shpricht man deezess vort owss*]

properly: it's not repaired properly es ist nicht richtig repariert worden [*nicht richtich repareert vorden*]

prostitute eine Prostituierte [*prostitoo-eert-uh*]

protect schützen [*shootsen*]

protection factor der Lichtschutzfaktor [*lichtshootsfaktor*]

protein remover (*for contact lenses*) der Protein-Entferner [*pro-te-een-entfairner*]

Protestant protestantisch [*protestantish*]

proud stolz [*shtolts*]

prunes die Backpflaumen [*backpflowmen*]

public (*adj*) öffentlich [*urfentlich*]

public convenience eine öffentliche Toilette [*urfentlich-uh twalett-uh*]

public holiday ein gesetzlicher Feiertag [*gezetslicher fy-er-tahk*]

pudding (*dessert*) der Nachtisch [*nachtish*]

pull (*verb*) ziehen [*tsee-en*]; **he pulled out without indicating** er ist ohne zu blinken ausgeschert [*air ist ohn-uh tsoo blinken owssgeshairt*]

pullover ein Pullover (*m*) [*poolohfer*]

pump eine Pumpe [*poomp-uh*]

punctual pünktlich [*poonktlich*]

puncture eine Reifenpanne [*ryfenpan-uh*]

pure rein [*ryne*]

purple lila [*leela*]

purse das Portemonnaie [*portmonay*]; (*handbag*) die Handtasche [*hant-tash-uh*]

push (*verb*) schieben [*sheeben*]; **don't push in!** (*into queue*) drängeln Sie sich nicht vor! [*drengeln zee zich nicht for*]

push-chair ein Sportwagen (*m*) [*shport-vahgen*]

put: where did you put it? wo haben Sie es hingetan? [*vo hahben zee ess hinge-tahn*]; **where can I put it?** wo kann ich es lassen? [*vo kan ich ess lassen*]; **could you put the lights on?** könnten Sie das Licht anmachen? [*kurnten zee dass licht anmachen*]; **will you put the light out?** könnten Sie das Licht ausmachen? [*owssmachen*]; **you've put the price up** Sie haben den Preis erhöht [*zee hahben dayn pryce airhurt*]; **could you put us up for the night?** könnten Sie uns für eine Nacht unterbringen? [*oonss foor ine-uh nacht oonterbringen*]

pyjamas ein Schlafanzug (*m*) [*shlahf-antsook*]

Q

quality die Qualität [*kvalitayt*]; **poor quality** schlechte Qualität [*shlecht-uh*]; **good quality** gute Qualität [*goot-uh*]

quarantine die Quarantäne [*kvarran-tayn-uh*]

quart see page 121

quarter ein Viertel (*nt*) [*feertel*]; **a quarter of an hour** eine Viertelstunde [*feer-*

telshtoond-uh]; see page 118
quay der Kai [ky]
quayside: on the quayside am Kai [ky]
question eine Frage [frahg-uh]; **out of the question** das kommt nicht in Frage
queue die Schlange [shlang-uh]; **there was a big queue** dort war eine lange Schlange [dort vahr ine-uh lang-uh]
quick schnell [shnell]; **that was quick** das war schnell [dass vahr]; **which is the quickest way?** wie komme ich am

schnellsten dorthin? [vee komm-uh ich am shnellsten dort-hin]
quickly schnell [shnell]
quiet (place, hotel) ruhig [rooich]; **be quiet** seien Sie still [zy-en zee shtill]
quinine das Chinin [chineen]
quite: quite a lot eine ganze Menge [ine-uh gants-uh meng-uh]; **it's quite different** es ist ganz anders [gants anderss]; **I'm not quite sure** ich bin nicht ganz sicher [nicht gants zicher]

R

rabbit ein Kaninchen (nt) [kaneenchen]
rabies die Tollwut [tol-voot]
race (horses, cars) das Rennen; **I'll race you there** wir laufen dorthin um die Wette [veer lowfen dort-hin oom dee vett-uh]
racket (tennis etc) der Schläger [shlayger]
radiator (car) der Kühler [kooler]; (in room) der Heizkörper [hytes-kurper]
radio das Radio [rahdee-o]; **on the radio** im Radio
rag (cleaning) ein Lappen (m)
rail: by rail mit der Bahn [dair]
railroad, railway die Eisenbahn ['eye'zenbahn]
railroad crossing ein Bahnübergang (m) [bahnoobergang]
rain der Regen [raygen]; **in the rain** im Regen; **it's raining** es regnet [ess raygnet]
rain boots die Gummistiefel [goomee-shteefel]
raincoat ein Regenmantel (m) [raygen-mantel]
rape die Vergewaltigung [fairgeval-tigoong]
rare selten [zelten]; (steak) englisch [english]
rash (on skin) der Ausschlag [owss-shlahk]
raspberries die Himbeeren [himbairen]
rat eine Ratte [ratt-uh]
rate (for changing money) der Wechselkurs [veckselkoorss]; **what's the rate for the pound?** wie steht der Kurs für das Pfund? [vee shtayt dair koorss foor]; **what**

are your rates? was sind Ihre Preise? [vass zint eer-uh pryze-uh]
rather: it's rather late es ist ziemlich spät [tseemlich shpayt]; **I'd rather have fish** ich möchte lieber Fisch [ich murcht-uh leeber]
raw roh
razor ein Rasiermesser (nt) [razzeer-messer]; (electric) ein Rasierapparat (m) [razzeerapparaht]
razor blades die Rasierklingen [razzeer-klingen]
reach: within easy reach leicht erreichbar [lycht air-rychbar]
read lesen [layzen]; **I can't read it** ich kann das nicht lesen
ready: when will it be ready? wann ist es fertig? [van ist ess fairtich]; **I'll go and get ready** ich mache mich jetzt fertig [ich mach-uh mich yetst]; **I'm not ready yet** ich bin noch nicht fertig [noch nicht]
real echt [echt]
really wirklich [veerklich]; **I really must go** ich muß wirklich gehen [ich mooss ... gayen]
realtor der Grundstücksmakler [groontshtocksmahkler]
rear: at the rear hinten
rear wheels die Hinterräder [hinter-rayder]
rearview mirror der Rückspiegel [rock-shpeegel]
reason: the reason is that ... der Grund ist, daß ... [dair groont ist dass]

reasonable (*price, arrangement*) vernünftig *[fairnoonstich]*; (*quite good*) ganz gut *[gants gōōt]*

receipt eine Quittung *[kvittoong]*

recently kürzlich *[koortslich]*

reception (*hotel*) der Empfang; (*for guests*) ein Empfang

reception desk die Rezeption *[retseptsyohn]*

receptionist (*in hotel*) (*man*) der Empfangschef *[—shef]*; (*woman*) die Empfangsdame *[—dahm-uh]*

recipe ein Rezept (*nt*) *[retsept]*; **can you give me the recipe for this?** können Sie mir das Rezept dafür geben? *[kurnen zee meer ... dafoor gayben]*

recognize erkennen *[airkennen]*; **I didn't recognize it** ich habe es nicht erkannt *[ich hahb-uh ess nicht airkannt]*

recommend: could you recommend ...? könnten Sie ... empfehlen *[kurnten zee ... empfaylen]*

record (*music*) eine Schallplatte *[shallplat-uh]*

record player ein Plattenspieler (*m*) *[plattenshpeeler]*

red rot *[roht]*

red wine der Rotwein *[rohtvyne]*

reduction (*in price*) die Ermäßigung *[airmayssigoong]*

refreshing erfrischend *[airfrishent]*

refrigerator der Kühlschrank *[koolshrank]*

refund: do I get a refund? kann ich das Geld zurückbekommen? *[kan ich dass gelt tsoorookbekommen]*

region das Gebiet *[gebeet]*

registered: by registered mail per Einschreiben *[pair ine-shryben]*

registration number (*of car*) das Kennzeichen *[kentsychen]*

relative: my relatives meine Verwandten *[myne-uh fairvanten]*

relaxing: it's very relaxing es ist sehr entspannend *[zair entshpannent]*

reliable zuverlässig *[tsoofairlessich]*

religion die Religion *[relig-yohn]*

remains (*of old city etc*) die Ruinen *[rōō-eenen]*

remember: I don't remember ich kann mich nicht erinnern *[ich kan mich nicht airinnern]*; **do you remember?** erinnern Sie sich? *[zee zich]*

remote (*village etc*) abgelegen *[apgelaygen]*

rent (*for room etc*) die Miete *[meet-uh]*; **I'd like to rent a bike/car** ich möchte ein Fahrrad/Auto leihen *[ich murcht-uh ine fahraht/owto ly-en]*

rental car ein Mietauto *[meetowto]*

repair reparieren *[repareeren]*; **can you repair this?** können Sie das reparieren? *[kurnen zee dass]*

repeat wiederholen *[veederhohlen]*; **would you repeat that?** können Sie das noch einmal wiederholen? *[kurnen zee dass noch ine-mahl]*

representative (*of company*) ein Vertreter (*m*) *[fairtrayter]*

rescue retten

reservation eine Reservierung *[rezairveeroong]*; **I have a reservation** ich habe eine Reservierung *[ich hahb-uh]*

reserve reservieren *[rezairveeren]*; **I reserved a room in the name of ...** für mich ist ein Zimmer unter dem Namen ... reserviert *[foor mich ist ine tsimmer oonter daym nahmen ... rezairveert]*; **can I reserve a table for tonight?** kann ich für heute abend einen Tisch reservieren? *[kan ich foor hoyt-uh ahbent ine-en tish]*

rest: I need a rest (*holiday etc*) ich brauche Erholung *[browch-uh airhohloong]*; **the rest of the group** der Rest der Gruppe

restaurant ein Restaurant (*nt*) *[restorong]*

rest room die Toilette *[twalett-uh]*

retired: I'm retired ich bin im Ruhestand *[ich bin im rōō-uh-shtant]*

return: a return to Stuttgart eine Rückfahrkarte nach Stuttgart *[ine-uh roockfahrkart-uh nach]*; **I'll return it tomorrow** ich bringe es morgen zurück *[ich bring-uh ess morgen tsoorook]*

returnable (*deposit*) rückzahlbar *[roocktsahlbar]*

reverse charge call ein R-Gespräch (*nt*) *[air-geshpraych]*

reverse gear der Rückwärtsgang *[roockvairtsgang]*

revolting ekelhaft *[aykelhaft]*

rheumatism das Rheuma *[royma]*

Rhine der Rhein *[ryne]*

rib die Rippe *[rip-uh]*; **a cracked rib** eine angebrochene Rippe *[angebrochen-uh]*

ribbon (*for hair*) ein Band (*nt*) *[bant]*

rice der Reis *[ryce]*

rich (*person*) reich *[rycHe]*; **it's too rich** (*food*) es ist zu schwer *[tsoo shvair]*

ride: can you give me a ride into town? können Sie mich in die Stadt mitnehmen? *[kurnen zee micH in dee shtatt mitnaymen]*; **thanks for the ride** danke fürs Mitnehmen *[dank-uh foorss]*

ridiculous: that's ridiculous das ist lächerlich *[dass ist lecHerlicH]*

right (*correct*) richtig *[ricHticH]*; (*not left*) rechts *[recHts]*; **you're right** Sie haben recht *[zee hahben recHt]*; **you were right** Sie hatten recht; **that's right** das stimmt *[dass shtimmt]*; **that can't be right** das kann nicht stimmen; **right!** (*ok*) okay!; **is this the right road for ...?** bin ich hier auf der Straße nach ...? *[bin icH heer owff dair shtrahss-uh nacH]*; **on the right** rechts *[recHts]*; **turn right** biegen Sie rechts ab *[beegen zee ... ap]*; **not right now** nicht gleich *[nicHt glycHe]*

righthand drive mit Rechtssteuerung *[recHts-shtoyeroong]*

ring (*on finger*) ein Ring (*m*); (*on cooker*) die Platte *[platt-uh]*; **I'll ring you** ich werde Sie anrufen *[icH vaird-uh zee anroofen]*

ring road die Ringstraße *[ringshtrahss-uh]*

ripe reif *[ryfe]*

rip-off: it's a rip-off das ist Wucher *[dass ist voocHer]*; **rip-off prices** Wucherpreise *[voocHerpryze-uh]*

risky riskant *[riskant]*; **it's too risky** das ist zu riskant

river der Fluß *[flooss]*; **by the river** am Fluß

road die Straße *[shtrahss-uh]*; **is this the road to ...?** ist dies die Straße nach ...? *[ist deess dee ... nacH]*; **further down the road** weiter die Straße entlang *[vyter]*

road accident ein Verkehrsunfall (*m*) *[fairkairss-oonfal]*

road hog ein Verkehrsrowdy (*m*) *[fairkairss-rowdee]*

road map eine Straßenkarte *[shtrahssen-kart-uh]*

roadside: by the roadside am Straßenrand *[shtrahssenrant]*

roadsign das Verkehrszeichen *[fairkairs-tsycHen]*

roadwork(s) die Straßenbauarbeiten *[shtrahssenbow-arbyten]*

roast beef das Roastbeef

rob: I've been robbed ich bin bestohlen worden *[icH bin beshtohlen vorden]*

robe (*housecoat*) ein Hausmantel (*m*) *[howssmantel]*

rock (*stone*) ein Fels (*m*) *[felss]*; **on the rocks** (*with ice*) mit Eis *[mit ice]*

rock climbing Felsklettern

rocky felsig *[felzicH]*

roll (*bread*) ein Brötchen (*nt*) *[brurtcHen]*

Roman Catholic (römisch-)katholisch *[(rurmish-)kattohlish]*

romance eine Romanze *[romants-uh]*

Rome: when in Rome ... andere Länder, andere Sitten *[ander-uh lender ander-uh zitten]*

roof das Dach *[dacH]*; **on the roof** auf dem Dach *[owff daym]*

roof rack (*on car*) der Dachgepäckträger *[dacHgepeck-trayger]*

room das Zimmer *[tsimmer]*; **do you have a room?** haben Sie ein Zimmer frei? *[hahben zee ine tsimmer fry]*; **a room for two people** ein Zimmer für zwei *[foor]*; **a room for three nights** ein Zimmer für drei Nächte *[necHt-uh]*; **a room with bathroom** ein Zimmer mit Bad *[baht]*; **in my room** in meinem Zimmer *[in my-nem]*; **there's no room** da ist kein Platz *[kyne plats]*

room service der Zimmerservice *[tsimmer'service']*

rope ein Seil (*nt*) *[zyle]*

rose eine Rose *[rohz-uh]*

rosé (*wine*) der Rosewein *[rohzay-vyne]*

rotary ein Kreisverkehr (*m*) *[kryce-fair-kair]*

rough (*sea, crossing*) stürmisch *[shtoor-mish]*; **the engine sounds a bit rough** der Motor hört sich nicht besonders gut an *[dair motohr hurt zicH nicHt bezonders goot an]*; **I've been sleeping rough** ich habe im Freien übernachtet *[icH hahb-uh im fry-en oobernacHtet]*

roughly (*approx*) ungefähr *[oongefair]*

roulette das Roulette

round (*adj*) rund *[roont]*; **it's my round** das ist meine Runde *[myne-uh roond-uh]*

roundabout ein Kreisverkehr (*m*) *[kryce-fairkair]*

round-trip: a round-trip ticket to ...

eine Rückfahrkarte nach ... [*ine-uh* r**oo**ckfarkart-uh na*CH*]

route die Strecke [*shtreck-uh*]; **what's the best route?** welches ist der beste Weg? [*velCHess ist dair best-uh vayk*]

rowboat, rowing boat ein Ruderboot (*nt*) [*r**oo**derboht*]

rubber das Gummi [*g**oo**mee*]; (*eraser*) ein Radiergummi (*m*) [*raddeer—*]

rubber band ein Gummiband (*nt*) [*g**oo**mee-bant*]

rubbish (*waste*) der Abfall [*apfal*]; (*poor quality items*) der Mist; **rubbish!** Quatsch! [*kvatsh*]

rucksack ein Rucksack (*m*) [*r**oo**ckzack*]

rude unhöflich [*oonhurflich*]; **he was very rude** er war sehr unhöflich [*air vahr zair*]

rug ein Teppich (*m*) [*teppiCH*]

ruins die Ruinen [*r**oo**-eenen*]

rum der Rum [*roomm*]

rum and coke ein Rum mit Cola [*roomm mit kola*]

run (*person*) rennen; **I go running every morning** ich mache jeden Morgen einen Dauerlauf [*ich maCH-uh yayden morgen ine-en dowerlowff*]; **quick, run!** los, laufen Sie! [*lohss, lowfen zee*]; **how often do the buses run?** wie oft fahren die Busse? [*vee oft fahren dee booss-uh*]; **he's been run over** er ist überfahren worden [*air ist ooberfahren vorden*]; **I've run out of gas/petrol** mir ist das Benzin ausgegangen [*meer ist dass bentseen owssgegangen*]

rupture (*med*) ein Bruch (*m*) [*brooCH*]

rush hour die Rush-hour

Russia Rußland [*rooslant*]

rusty: my German's rather rusty ich bin mit meinem Deutsch ziemlich aus der Übung gekommen [*mynem doytsh tseemlich owss dair ooboong*]

S

saccharine das Sacharin [*zacHareen*]

sad traurig [*trowriCH*]

saddle der Sattel [*zattel*]

safe sicher [*ziCHer*]; **will it be safe here?** ist es hier sicher?; **is it safe to drink?** kann man es unbesorgt trinken? [*ess oonbezorkt*]; **is it a safe beach for swimming?** kann man an diesem Strand ohne Gefahr schwimmen? [*an deezem shtrant ohn-uh gefahr shvimmen*]; **could you put this in your safe?** könnten Sie das in Ihren Safe legen? [*kurnten zee dass in eeren sayff laygen*]

safety pin eine Sicherheitsnadel [*ziCHer-hytes-nahdel*]

sail das Segel [*zaygel*]; **can we go sailing?** können wir segeln gehen? [*kurnen veer zaygeln gayen*]

sailor (*navy*) ein Seemann (*m*) [*zayman*]; (*sport*) ein Segler (*m*) [*zaygler*]

salad der Salat [*zalaht*]

salad cream die Mayonnaise [*my-ohnayz-uh*]

salad dressing die Salatsoße [*zalaht-*

zohss-uh]

sale: is it for sale? kann man es kaufen? [*ess kowfen*]; **it's not for sale** es ist nicht verkäuflich [*fairkoyflich*]

sales clerk der Verkäufer [*fairkoyfer*]

salmon der Lachs [*lacks*]

salt das Salz [*zalts*]

salty: it's too salty es ist zu salzig [*tsoo zaltsich*]

same gleicher [*glycHer*]; **the same colour as this** dieselbe Farbe wie diese [*deezelb-uh farb-uh vee deez-uh*]; **the same again, please** dasselbe nochmal, bitte [*dasselb-uh nocHmahl bitt-uh*]; **have a good day — same to you** einen schönen Tag — gleichfalls [*glycHe-falss*]; **it's all the same to me** das ist mir ganz egal [*meer gants aygahl*]; **thanks all the same** trotzdem vielen Dank [*trotsdaym*]

sand der Sand [*zant*]

sandal eine Sandale [*zandahl-uh*]; **a pair of sandals** ein Paar (*nt*) Sandalen

sandwich ein belegtes Brot [*belayktess broht*]; **a ham sandwich** ein Schinken-

brot (*nt*)
sandy: sandy beach ein Sandstrand (*m*) *[zant-shtrant]*
sanitary napkin, sanitary towel eine Damenbinde *[dahmenbind-uh]*
sarcastic sarkastisch *[zarkasstish]*
sardines die Sardinen *[zardeenen]*
satisfactory zufriedenstellend *[tsōō-freedenshtellent]*; **this is not satisfactory** damit bin ich nicht zufrieden *[nicht tsōōfreeden]*
Saturday der Samstag *[zamstahk]*
sauce die Soße *[zohss-uh]*
saucepan ein Kochtopf (*m*) *[kochtopf]*
saucer eine Untertasse *[oontertass-uh]*
sauna eine Sauna *[zowna]*
sausage eine Wurst *[vōōrst]*
sauté potatoes die Bratkartoffeln *[braht-kartoffeln]*
save (*life*) retten
savo(u)ry pikant *[pikant]*
say: how do you say ... in German? was heißt ... auf deutsch? *[vass hyste ... owff doytsh]*; **what did you say?** was haben Sie gesagt? *[hahben zee gezahkt]*; **what did he say?** was hat er gesagt?; **you can say that again** das kann man wohl sagen *[dass kan man vohl zahgen]*; **I wouldn't say no** ich würde nicht nein sagen *[ich voord-uh nicht nyne zahgen]*
scald: he's scalded himself er hat sich verbrüht *[fairbrōōt]*
scarf ein Schal (*m*) *[shahl]*; (*head*) ein Kopftuch (*nt*) *[kopftōōch]*
scarlet scharlach *[sharlach]*
scenery die Landschaft *[lantshafft]*
scent (*perfume*) der Duft *[dooft]*
schedule (*for trains etc*) der Fahrplan *[fahrplahn]*
scheduled flight ein Linienflug (*m*) *[leenee-enflōōk]*
school die Schule *[shōōl-uh]*; (*university*) die Universität *[ooneevairzitayt]*; **I'm still at school** ich gehe noch zur Schule
science die Naturwissenschaft *[nattōōr-vissenshafft]*
scissors: a pair of scissors eine Schere *[ine-uh shair-uh]*
scooter ein Roller (*m*) *[rol-er]*
scorching: it's really scorching es ist brütend heiß *[brōōt-ent hyce]*
score: what's the score? wie steht's? *[vee shtayts]*

scotch (*whisky*) ein Scotch (*m*)
Scotch tape (*tm*) der Tesafilm (*tm*) *[tayza-film]*
Scotland Schottland *[shotlant]*
Scottish schottisch *[shottish]*
scrambled eggs die Rühreier *[rōōr-'eye'er]*
scratch der Kratzer *[kratser]*; **it's only a scratch** es ist nur ein Kratzer
scream schreien *[shry-en]*
screw eine Schraube *[shrowb-uh]*
screwdriver ein Schraubenzieher (*m*) *[shrowbentsee-er]*
scrubbing brush (*for hands*) eine Handbürste *[hantboorst-uh]*
scruffy vergammelt *[fairgammelt]*
scuba diving Sporttauchen *[shport-towchen]*
sea das Meer *[mair]*; **by the sea** am Meer
sea air die Meeresluft *[mairesslooft]*
seafood die Meeresfrüchte *[mairess-frōōcht-uh]*
seafood restaurant ein Fischrestaurant (*nt*) *[fishrestorong]*
seafront der Strand *[shtrant]*; **on the seafront** am Strand
seagull eine Möwe *[murv-uh]*
search suchen *[zōōchen]*; **I searched everywhere** ich habe überall gesucht *[hahb-uh ooberal gezōōcht]*
search party die Suchmannschaft *[zōōchmanshafft]*
seashell eine Muschel *[mooshel]*
seasick: I feel seasick ich bin seekrank *[zaykrank]*; **I get seasick** ich werde leicht seekrank *[lychte]*
seaside: by the seaside am Meer *[mair]*; **let's go to the seaside** wollen wir ans Meer fahren?
season die Jahreszeit *[yahress-tsyte]*; **in the high season** in der Hochsaison *[hochzayzong]*; **in the low season** außerhalb der Saison *[owsserhalp dair]*
seasoning ein Gewürz (*nt*) *[gevoorts]*
seat ein Sitzplatz *[zitsplats]*; **is this anyone's seat?** sitzt hier jemand? *[zitst heer yaymant]*
seat belt der Sicherheitsgurt *[zicherhytes-gōōrt]*; **do you have to wear a seatbelt?** muß man sich anschnallen? *[anshnal-en]*
seaweed der Tang
secluded abgelegen *[apgelaygen]*
second (*adj*) zweiter *[tsvyter]*; (*time*) eine

Sekunde *[zekoond-uh]*; **just a second!**
Moment mal! *[moment mahl]*; **can I
have a second helping?** kann ich einen
Nachschlag bekommen? *[nachshlahk]*
second class (*travel*) zweite Klasse
[tsvyte-uh klass-uh]
second-hand gebraucht *[gebrowcht]*
secret (*adj*) geheim *[gehyme]*
security check die Sicherheitskontrolle
[zicherhytes-kontroll-uh]
sedative ein Beruhigungsmittel (*nt*)
[beroo-igoongsmittel]
see sehen *[zayen]*; **I didn't see it** ich habe
es nicht gesehen *[ich hahb-uh ess nicht
gezayen]*; **have you seen my husband?**
haben Sie meinen Mann gesehen? *[hah-
ben zee]*; **I saw him this morning** ich
habe ihn heute morgen gesehen; **can I
see the manager?** kann ich den Geschäftsführer sprechen? *[kan ich dayn
gesheftsfœrer shprechen]*; **see you tonight!** bis heute abend! *[biss hoyt-uh
ahbent]*; **can I see?** kann ich mal sehen?;
oh, I see ach so *[zo]*; **will you see to it?**
können Sie sich darum kümmern? *[kur-
nen zee zich daroom kœmern]*
seldom selten *[zelten]*
self-catering apartment ein Apparte-
ment für Selbstversorger *[appartemong
fœr zelpstfairzorger]*
self-service Selbstbedienung *[zelpst-
bedeenoong]*
sell verkaufen *[fairkowfen]*; **do you sell
...?** haben Sie ...? *[hahben zee]*; **will you
sell it to me?** würden Sie es mir verkaufen?
sellotape (*tm*) der Tesafilm (*tm*) *[tayza-
film]*
send senden *[zenden]*; **I want to send
this to England** ich möchte dies nach
England senden *[ich murcht-uh]*; **I'll
have to send this food back** ich muß
dieses Essen zurückgehen lassen *[ich
mooss deezess essen tsoorœckgayen
lassen]*
senior: Mr Jones senior Herr Jones
senior *[zaynyohr]*
senior citizen der Rentner; (*woman*) die
Rentnerin
sensational sensationell *[zenzatsyohnel]*
sense: I have no sense of direction ich
habe keinen Orientierungssinn
[orienteeroongs-zin]; **it doesn't make**

sense es ergibt keinen Sinn *[ess airgipt
kynen zin]*
sensible vernünftig *[fairnœnftich]*
sensitive empfindlich *[emp-fintlich]*
sentimental sentimental *[zentimentahl]*
separate getrennt; **can we have separate
bills?** können wir getrennt bezahlen?
[kurnen veer getrent betsahlen]
separated: I'm separated ich lebe
getrennt *[ich layb-uh]*
separately getrennt
September der September *[zeptember]*
septic vereitert *[fair'eye'tert]*
serious ernst *[airnst]*; **I'm serious** ich
meine das ernst *[ich myne-uh]*; **you
can't be serious!** das kann nicht Ihr
Ernst sein! *[eer airnst zyne]*; **is it serious, doctor?** ist es ernst, Herr Doktor?
seriously: seriously ill ernsthaft krank
[airnst-haft]
service: the service was excellent der
Service war ausgezeichnet; **could we
have some service, please!** Bedienung!
[bedeenoong]; (*church*) der Gottesdienst
[gottess-deenst]; **the car needs a service**
das Auto muß zur Inspektion *[tsoor
inshpekts-yohn]*
service charge die Bedienung
[bedeenoong]
service station eine Tankstelle mit
Werkstatt *[tankshtell-uh mit vairkshtatt]*
serviette eine Serviette *[zairvee-ett-uh]*
set: it's time we were setting off wir
sollten uns auf den Weg machen *[veer
zollten oonss owff dayn vayk machen]*
set menu die Tageskarte *[tahgess-kart-
uh]*
settle up: can we settle up now? können
wir jetzt bezahlen? *[kurnen veer yetst
betsahlen]*
several mehrere *[mairer-uh]*
sew: could you sew this back on? können
Sie das wieder annähen? *[kurnen zee dass
veeder an-nayen]*
sex (*activity*) der Sex
sexist sexistisch *[secksistish]*
sexy sexy
shade: in the shade im Schatten
shadow der Schatten *[shatten]*
shake: to shake hands sich die Hand
geben *[zich dee hant gayben]*
shallow seicht *[zycht]*
shame: what a shame! wie schade! *[vee*

shahd-uh]

shampoo das Shampoo; **can I have a
shampoo and set?** können Sie mir die
Haare waschen und legen? *[dee hahr-uh
vashen oont laygen]*

shandy, shandy-gaff ein Bier *(nt)* mit
Limonade *[beer mit limonahd-uh]*

share *(room, table)* teilen *[tylen]*; **let's
share the cost** teilen wir uns die Kosten

sharp *(knife, taste)* scharf *[sharf]*; *(pain)*
heftig *[heftich]*

shattered: I'm shattered *(very tired)* ich
bin todmüde *[tohtmood-uh]*

shave: I need a shave ich muß mich
rasieren *[ich mooss mich razzeeren]*;
can you give me a shave? können Sie
mich rasieren?

shaver ein Rasierapparat *(m)* *[razzeer-
apparaht]*

shaving brush ein Rasierpinsel *(m)*
[razzeerpinzel]

shaving foam die Rasiercreme *[razzeer-
kraym-uh]*

shaving point eine Steckdose für Rasier-
rapparate *[shteckdohz-uh foor razzeer-
apparaht-uh]*

shaving soap die Rasierseife *[razzeer-
zyfe-uh]*

she sie *[zee]*; **is she staying here?** wohnt
sie hier?; *see page 111*

sheep ein Schaf *(nt)* *[shahf]*

sheet ein Bettlaken *(nt)* *[betlahken]*

shelf ein Brett *(nt)*

shell *(seashell)* eine Muschel *[mooshel]*

shellfish die Meeresfrüchte *[mairess-
frocht-uh]*

sherry ein Sherry *(m)*

shingles *(med)* eine Gürtelrose *[goortel-
rohz-uh]*

ship ein Schiff *(nt)* *[shiff]*; **by ship** mit dem
Schiff

shirt das Hemd *[hemt]*

shit Scheiße *[shyce-uh]*

shock *(surprise)* ein Schock *(m)* *[shock]*; **I
got an electric shock from the ...** ich
habe einen elektrischen Schlag von ...
bekommen *[ich hahb-uh ine-en elek-
trishen shlahk]*

shock-absorber der Stoßdämpfer
[shtohss-dempfer]

shocking schockierend *[shockeerent]*

shoelaces die Schnürsenkel *[shnoor-
zenkel]*

shoe polish die Schuhcreme *[shookraym-
uh]*

shoes die Schuhe *[shoo-uh]*; **a pair of
shoes** ein Paar *(nt)* Schuhe

shop ein Geschäft *(nt)* *[gesheft]*

shopping: I'm going shopping ich gehe
einkaufen *[ich gay-uh ine-kowfen]*

shop window ein Schaufenster *(nt)*
[showfenster]

shore das Ufer *[oofer]*

short *(person)* klein *[klyne]*; *(time)* kurz
[koorts]; **it's only a short distance** es ist
nur eine kurze Strecke *[noor ine-uh
koorts-uh shtreck-uh]*

**short-change: you've short-changed
me** Sie haben mir zu wenig herausgege-
ben *[zee hahben meer tsoo vaynich
herowssgegayben]*

short circuit ein Kurzschluß *(m)* *[koorts-
shlooss]*

shortcut eine Abkürzung *[apkoortsoong]*

shorts die Shorts; *(underwear)* eine Unterhose *[oonterhohz-uh]*

should: what should I do? was soll ich
machen? *[vass zoll ich machen]*; **he
shouldn't be long** er kommt sicher bald
[air komt zicher balt]; **you should have
told me** das hätten Sie mir sagen sollen
[hetten zee]

shoulder die Schulter *[shoolter]*

shoulder blade das Schulterblatt *[shool-
terblatt]*

shout schreien *[shry-en]*

show: could you show me? könnten Sie
mir das zeigen? *[kurnten zee meer dass
tsygen]*; **does it show?** sieht man es?
[zeet man ess]; **we'd like to go to a show**
wir möchten ins Theater gehen *[veer
murchten inss tayahter]*

shower *(in bathroom)* eine Dusche *[doosh-
uh]*; **with shower** mit Dusche

shower cap eine Duschhaube *[doosh-
howb-uh]*

show-off: don't be a show-off geben Sie
nicht so an *[gayben zee nicht zo an]*

shrimps die Garnelen *[garnaylen]*

shrink: it's shrunk es ist eingelaufen
[ine-gelowfen]

shut schließen *[shleessen]*; **when do you
shut?** wann machen Sie zu? *[van machen
zee tsoo]*; **when do they shut?** wann
machen sie zu?; **it was shut** es war geschlossen *[ess vahr geshlossen]*; **I've**

shut myself out ich habe mich ausgesperrt *[ICH hahb-uh mICH owssgeshpairt]*; **shut up!** halten Sie den Mund! *[hal-ten zee dayn moont]*

shutter (*phot*) der Verschluß *[fairshlooss]*; (*on window*) der Fensterladen *[fensterlahden]*

shutter release der Auslöser *[owsslurzer]*

shy schüchtern *[shoochtern]*

sick krank; **I think I'm going to be sick** (*vomit*) ich glaube, ich muß mich übergeben *[ICH glowb-uh ICH mooss mICH oobergayben]*

side die Seite *[zyte-uh]*; **at the side of the road** am Straßenrand *[shtrahssenrant]*; **the other side of town** das andere Ende der Stadt *[dass ander-uh end-uh dair shtatt]*

side lights das Standlicht *[shtantlICHt]*

side salad eine Salatbeilage *[zalahtbylahg-uh]*

side street eine Seitenstraße *[zytenshtrahss-uh]*

sidewalk der Bürgersteig *[boorgershtyke]*

sidewalk café ein Straßencafé (*nt*) *[shtrahssenkaffay]*

sight: the sights of ... die Sehenswürdigkeiten von ... *[zayensvoordICH-kyten]*

sightseeing: sightseeing tour eine Rundfahrt *[roontfahrt]*; **we're going sightseeing** wir machen eine Rundfahrt

sign (*roadsign*) ein Verkehrszeichen (*nt*) *[fairkairss-tsyCHen]*; (*notice*) ein Schild (*nt*) *[shilt]*; **where do I sign?** wo muß ich unterschreiben? *[vo mooss ICH oontershryben]*

signal: he didn't give a signal er hat kein Zeichen gegeben *[kyne tsyCHen gegayben]*

signature die Unterschrift *[oontershrift]*

signpost ein Wegweiser (*m*) *[vayk-vyzer]*

silence die Ruhe *[roo-uh]*

silencer der Auspufftopf *[owsspooftopf]*

silk die Seide *[zyde-uh]*

silly albern *[al-bairn]*; **that's silly** das ist lächerlich *[leCHerlICH]*

silver das Silber *[zilber]*

silver foil die Alufolie *[aloofohlee-uh]*

similar ähnlich *[aynlICH]*

simple einfach *[ine-faCH]*

since: since yesterday seit gestern *[zyte]*; **since we got here** seit wir hier sind

sincere ehrlich *[airlICH]*

sing singen *[zingen]*

singer der Sänger *[zenger]*

single: a single room ein Einzelzimmer *[ine-tseltsimmer]*; **a single to ...** eine einfache Fahrt nach ... *[ine-uh inefaCH-uh fahrt naCH]*; **I'm single** ich bin ledig *[ICH bin laydICH]*

sink (*kitchen*) das Spülbecken *[shpoolbecken]*; **it sank** es ist versunken *[fairzoonken]*

sir mein Herr *[myne hair]*; **excuse me, sir** entschuldigen Sie bitte

sirloin ein Filet (*nt*) *[fillay]*

sister: my sister meine Schwester *[myne-uh shvester]*

sister-in-law: my sister-in-law meine Schwägerin *[myne-uh shvaygerin]*

sit: may I sit here? kann ich mich hier hinsetzen? *[kan ICH mICH heer hinzetsen]*; **is anyone sitting here?** sitzt hier jemand? *[zitst heer yaymant]*

site (*campsite etc*) ein Platz (*m*) *[plats]*

sitting: the second sitting for lunch die zweite Mittagessenzeit *[mittahkessentsyte]*

situation eine Situation *[zitoo-atsyohn]*

size die Größe *[grurss-uh]*

sketch eine Skizze *[skits-uh]*

ski ein Ski (*m*) *[shee]*; (*verb*) Ski fahren; **a pair of skis** ein Paar (*nt*) Skier *[shee-er]*

ski boots die Skistiefel *[shee-shteefel]*

skid: I skidded ich bin ausgerutscht *[owssgerootsht]*

skiing das Skifahren *[sheefahren]*; **we're going skiing** wir gehen Skilaufen *[sheelowfen]*

ski instructor der Skilehrer *[sheelairer]*

ski-lift der Skilift *[sheelift]*

skin die Haut *[howt]*

skinny dünn *[doon]*

ski-pants eine Skihose *[shee-hohz-uh]*

ski-pass der Skipaß *[sheepas]*

ski pole der Skistock *[sheeshtock]*

skirt ein Rock (*m*)

ski run die Skipiste *[shee-pist-uh]*

ski slope die Piste *[pist-uh]*

ski wax Skiwachs *[sheevacks]*

skull der Schädel *[shaydel]*

sky der Himmel

sleep: I can't sleep ich kann nicht schlafen *[ICH kan nICHt shlahfen]*; **did you sleep well?** haben Sie gut geschlafen?

[hahben zee gōōt geshlahfen]; **I need a good sleep** ich muß mich mal richtig ausschlafen *[owss-shlahfen]*

sleeper (*rail*) ein Schlafwagen (*m*) *[shlahfvahgen]*

sleeping bag ein Schlafsack (*m*) *[shlahfzack]*

sleeping car ein Schlafwagen (*m*) *[shlahfvahgen]*

sleeping pill eine Schlaftablette *[shlahf-tablett-uh]*

sleepy schläfrig *[shlayfrich]*; **I'm feeling sleepy** ich bin müde *[ich bin mood-uh]*

sleet der Schneeregen *[shnayraygen]*

sleeve der Ärmel *[airmel]*

slice eine Scheibe *[shybe-uh]*

slide (*phot*) ein Dia (*nt*) *[dee-a]*

slim (*adj*) schlank *[shlank]*; **I'm slimming** ich mache eine Schlankheitskur *[ich mach-uh ine-uh shlankhytes-kōōr]*

slip (*under dress*) ein Unterrock (*m*) *[oonterrock]*; **I slipped** (*on pavement etc*) ich bin ausgerutscht *[owss-gerootsht]*

slipped disc ein Bandscheibenschaden (*m*) *[bantshyben-shahden]*

slippery rutschig *[rootshich]*

slow langsam *[langzam]*; **slow down** etwas langsamer bitte *[etvass]*

slowly langsam *[langzam]*; **could you say it slowly?** könnten Sie das etwas langsamer sagen? *[kurnten zee dass etvass langzamer zahgen]*

small klein *[klyne]*

small change das Kleingeld *[klyne-gelt]*

smallpox die Pocken

smart (*clothes*) schick *[shick]*

smashing toll *[tol]*

smell: there's a funny smell es riecht komisch *[ess reecht kohmish]*; **what a lovely smell** was für ein herrlicher Duft *[vass foor ine hairlicher dooft]*; **it smells** es stinkt *[shtinkt]*

smile lächeln *[lecheln]*

smoke der Rauch *[rowch]*; **do you smoke?** rauchen Sie? *[rowchen zee]*; **do you mind if I smoke?** macht es Ihnen etwas aus, wenn ich rauche? *[macht ess een-en etvass owss ven ich rowch-uh]*; **I don't smoke** ich bin Nichtraucher *[nichtrowcher]*

smooth glatt

smoothy ein Lackaffe (*m*) *[lackaff-uh]*

snack: I'd just like a snack ich möchte

nur eine Kleinigkeit *[ich murcht-uh noor ine-uh klynichkyte]*

snackbar eine Imbißstube *[imbiss-shtōōb-uh]*

snake eine Schlange *[shlang-uh]*

sneakers die Freizeitschuhe *[frytsyte-shōō-uh]*

snob ein Snob (*m*)

snow der Schnee *[shnay]*

so: it's so hot es ist so heiß *[zo hyce]*; **not so fast** nicht so schnell; **it wasn't — it was so!** war es nicht — war es doch! *[doch]*; **so am I** ich auch *[ich owch]*; **so do I** ich auch; **how was it? — so-so** wie war's? — so la la

soaked: I'm soaked ich bin völlig durchnäßt *[furlich doorchnesst]*

soaking solution (*for contact lenses*) die Aufbewahrungslösung *[owffbevahr-oongs-lurzoong]*

soap die Seife *[zyfe-uh]*

soap-powder das Waschpulver *[vash-poolver]*

sober nüchtern *[noochtern]*

soccer Fußball *[fōōssbal]*

sock ein Socken (*m*) *[zocken]*

socket (*elec*) eine Steckdose *[shteckdohz-uh]*

soda (water) ein Mineralwasser (*nt*) *[minerahlvasser]*

sofa ein Sofa (*nt*) *[zofa]*

soft weich *[vyche]*

soft drink ein alkoholfreies Getränk (*nt*) *[alkohohlfry-ess getrenk]*

soft lenses weiche Kontaktlinsen *[vyche-uh]*

soldier der Soldat *[zoldaht]*

sole (*of shoe*) die Sohle *[zohl-uh]*; **could you put new soles on these?** könnten Sie diese Schuhe neu besohlen? *[kurnten zee deez-uh shōō-uh noy bezohlen]*

solid fest

solid fuel (*for camping stove*) fester Brennstoff (*m*) *[fester brennshtoff]*

some: may I have some water? kann ich etwas Wasser haben? *[etvass vasser]*; **do you have some matches?** haben Sie Streichhölzer?; **that's some drink!** das ist vielleicht ein Getränk! *[feelychte ine getrenk]*; **some of them** einige von ihnen *[ine-ig-uh fon eenen]*; **can I have some?** (*of those*) kann ich ein paar davon haben? *[ine pahr]*; (*of that*) kann ich etwas davon haben? *[etvass daffon]*

somebody, someone jemand *[yaymant]*

something etwas *[etvass]*; **something to drink** etwas zu trinken

sometime irgendwann *[eergentvan]*

sometimes manchmal *[mancHmahl]*

somewhere irgendwo *[eergentvo]*

son: my son mein Sohn *[myne zohn]*

song ein Lied (*nt*) *[leet]*

son-in-law: my son-in-law mein Schwiegersohn *[myne shveegerzohn]*

soon bald *[balt]*; **I'll be back soon** ich bin bald zurück *[icH bin balt tsoorŏock]*; **as soon as you can** sobald Sie können *[zobalt zee kurnen]*

sore: it's sore es tut weh *[ess tŏŏt vay]*

sore throat die Halsschmerzen *[halsshmairtsen]*

sorry: (I'm) sorry (es) tut mir leid *[tŏŏt meer lyte]*; **sorry?** (*pardon*) bitte? *[bittuh]*

sort: what sort of ...? welche Art von ...? *[velcH-uh art fon]*; **a different sort of ...** eine andere Art ... *[ander-uh]*; **will you sort it out?** können Sie das regeln? *[kurnen zee dass raygeln]*

soup die Suppe *[zoop-uh]*

sour (*taste, apple*) sauer *[zower]*

south der Süden *[zŏŏden]*; **to the south** nach Süden

South Africa Südafrika *[zŏŏtafrika]*

South African (*adj*) südafrikanisch *[zŏŏtafrikahnish]*; (*man*) der Südafrikaner; (*woman*) die Südafrikanerin

southeast der Südosten *[zŏŏtosten]*; **to the southeast** nach Südosten

South Germany Süddeutschland *[zŏŏtdoytshland]*

southwest der Südwesten *[zŏŏtvesten]*; **to the southwest** nach Südwesten

souvenir ein Souvenir (*nt*)

spa der Kurort *[kŏŏrort]*

space heater ein Heizgerät (*nt*) *[hytesgerayt]*

spade ein Spaten (*m*) *[shpahten]*

Spain Spanien *[shpahnee-en]*

Spanish spanisch *[shpahnish]*

spanner ein Schraubenschlüssel (*m*) *[shrowbenshlŏssel]*

spare part ein Ersatzteil (*nt*) *[airzats-tyle]*

spare tyre/tire ein Ersatzreifen (*m*) *[airzatsryfen]*

spark(ing) plug eine Zündkerze *[tsŏontkairts-uh]*

speak: do you speak English? sprechen Sie Englisch? *[shprecHen zee eng-lish]*; **I don't speak ...** ich spreche kein ... *[icH shprecH-uh kyne]*; **can I speak to ...?** kann ich ... sprechen?; **speaking** (*telec*) am Apparat *[apparaht]*

special speziell *[shpetsee-el]*; **nothing special** nichts Besonderes *[nicHts bezonderess]*

specialist ein Fachmann (*m*) *[facHman]*; (*doctor*) der Spezialist *[shpetzee-alist]*

special(i)ty (*in restaurant*) die Spezialität *[shpetsee-alitayt]*; **the special(i)ty of the house** die Spezialität des Hauses

spectacles eine Brille *[brill-uh]*

speed die Geschwindigkeit *[geshvindicHkyte]*; **he was speeding** er ist zu schnell gefahren *[air ist tsŏŏ shnell]*

speedboat ein Rennboot (*nt*) *[renboht]*

speed limit die Geschwindigkeitsbeschränkung *[geshvindicHkytesbeshrenkoong]*

speedometer der Tachometer *[tacHomayter]*

spell: how do you spell it? wie schreibt man das? *[vee shrypte man dass]*

spend: I've spent all my money ich habe mein ganzes Geld ausgegeben *[myne gantsess gelt owssgegayben]*

spice ein Gewürz (*nt*) *[gevŏorts]*

spicy: it's very spicy es ist stark gewürzt *[ess ist shtarrk gevŏortst]*

spider eine Spinne *[shpin-uh]*

spin-dryer die Schleuder *[shloyder]*

splendid herrlich *[hairlicH]*

splint (*for broken limb*) eine Schiene *[sheen-uh]*

splinter ein Splitter (*m*) *[shplitter]*

splitting: I've got a splitting headache ich habe rasende Kopfschmerzen *[rahzend-uh kopfshmairtsen]*

spoke (*in wheel*) eine Speiche *[shpycHe-uh]*

sponge ein Schwamm *[shvam]*

spoon ein Löffel *[lurfel]*

sport der Sport *[shport]*

sport(s) jacket ein Sakko (*nt*) *[zakko]*

spot: will they do it on the spot? wird das sofort erledigt? *[veert dass zofort airlaydicHt]*; (*on skin*) ein Pickel (*m*)

sprain: I've sprained my ankle ich habe mir den Fuß verstaucht *[icH hahb-uh* meer dayn *fooss* fairsht*ow*cHt]

spray (*for hair*) das Spray *[shpray]*

spring (*season*) der Frühling *[fr**oo**ling]*; (*of seat etc*) die Feder *[f**ay**der]*

square (*in town*) ein Platz *[plats]*; **ten square metres** zehn Quadratmeter *[kvadr**ah**tmayter]*

squash (*sport*) Squash

stain (*on clothes*) ein Fleck (*m*)

stairs die Treppe *[tr**e**pp-uh]*

stale (*bread*) alt

stall: the engine keeps stalling der Motor geht dauernd aus *[dair mot**oh**r gayt d**ow**ernt owss]*

stalls das Parkett

stamp eine Briefmarke *[br**ee**fmark-uh]*; **a stamp for a letter for England please** eine Marke für einen Brief nach England bitte *[**ine**-uh m**a**rk-uh f**oo**r **ine**-en breef]*

stand: I can't stand … ich kann … nicht ausstehen *[ni*cht* **ow**ss-shtayen]*

standard (*adj*) normal *[norm**ah**l]*

standby ticket ein Standby-Ticket

star ein Stern (*m*) *[shtairn]*

start: when does the film start? wann fängt der Film an? *[van fenkt]*; **the car won't start** das Auto springt nicht an *[shprinkt ni*cht* an]*

starter (*car*) der Anlasser; (*food*) die Vorspeise *[f**o**rshpyze-uh]*

starving: I'm starving ich sterbe vor Hunger *[i*cH* sht**ai**rb-uh for h**oo**nger]*

state (*in country*) ein Land (*nt*) *[lant]*; **the States** (*USA*) die Vereinigten Staaten *[dee fair'**eye**'ni*cH*ten sht**ah**ten]*

station (*for trains*) der Bahnhof *[b**ah**n-hohf]*

statue eine Statue *[sht**ah**t**oo**-uh]*

stay: we enjoyed our stay unser Aufenthalt hat uns gefallen *[**ow**fenthalt]*; **where are you staying?** wo wohnen Sie? *[vo v**oh**nen zee]*; **I'm staying at …** ich wohne in … *[v**oh**n-uh]*; **I'd like to stay another week** ich möchte gern eine Woche länger bleiben *[i*cH* m**u**r*cH*t-uh gairn **ine**-uh v**o***cH*-uh lenger bl**y**ben]*; **I'm staying in tonight** ich bleibe heute abend zu Hause *[ts**oo** h**ow**z-uh]*

steak ein Steak *[shtayk]*

steal: my bag has been stolen meine Tasche ist gestohlen worden *[gesht**oh**len v**o**rden]*

steep (*hill*) steil *[shtyle]*

steering (*car*) die Lenkung *[l**e**nkoong]*

steering wheel das Lenkrad *[l**e**nkraht]*

stein ein Bierkrug *[b**ee**rkr**oo**k]*; (*in South Germany*) eine Maß *[mahss]*

stereo eine Stereoanlage *[sht**ay**ray-o-anl**ah**g-uh]*

sterling das Pfund Sterling *[pfoont]*

stew ein Eintopf (*m*) *[**ine**-topf]*

steward (*on plane*) der Steward

stewardess die Stewardess

sticking plaster das Heftpflaster

sticky klebrig *[kl**ay**bri*cH*]*

sticky tape ein Klebeband (*nt*) *[kl**ay**b-uh-bant]*

still: I'm still waiting ich warte immer noch *[**immer** no*cH*]*; **will you still be open?** haben Sie dann noch auf? *[owff]*; **it's still not right** es ist immer noch nicht richtig; **that's still better** das ist noch besser

sting: a bee sting ein Bienenstich *[b**ee**nensti*cH*]*; **I've been stung** ich bin gestochen worden *[gesht**o***cH*en v**o**rden]*

stink der Gestank *[gesht**a**nk]*

stockings die Strümpfe *[shtr**oo**mpf-uh]*

stolen: my wallet's been stolen mir ist die Brieftasche gestohlen worden *[gesht**oh**len v**o**rden]*

stomach der Magen *[m**ah**gen]*; **do you have something for an upset stomach?** haben Sie etwas gegen Magenverstimmung? *[g**ay**gen m**ah**gen-fairshtimmoong]*

stomach-ache die Magenschmerzen *[m**ah**gen-shm**ai**rtsen]*

stone (*rock*) ein Stein *[shtyne]*; *see page 120*

stop (*bus stop*) eine Haltestelle *[h**a**l-tuh-shtell-uh]*; **which is the stop for …?** welches ist die Haltestelle für …? *[v**e**l*cH*ess]*; **please stop here** (*to taxi-driver*) bitte halten Sie hier *[h**a**l-ten zee heer]*; **do you stop near …?** halten Sie in der Nähe von …?; **stop doing that!** hören Sie auf damit! *[h**u**ren zee owff dam**i**t]*

stopover eine Zwischenstation *[tsv**i**shen-shtats-yohn]*

store ein Geschäft (*nt*) *[gesh**e**ft]*

stor(e)y (*building*) eine Etage *[ayt**ah**j-uh]*

storm ein Sturm (*m*) *[shtoorm]*

story (*tale*) eine Geschichte *[gesh**i***cH*t-uh]*

stove der Herd *[hairt]*

straight (*road etc*) gerade *[ger**ah**d-uh]*; **it's straight ahead** es ist geradeaus *[ess ist* *gerahd-uh-owss]*; **straight away** sofort *[zofort]*; **a straight whisky** ein Whisky pur *[poor]*

straighten: can you straighten things out? können Sie die Sache in Ordnung bringen? *[dee zacн-uh in ordnoong]*

stranded: I'm stranded ich sitze auf dem trockenen *[icн zits-uh owff daym]*

strange (*odd*) seltsam *[zetzam]*; (*unknown*) fremd *[fremt]*

stranger: I'm a stranger here ich bin hier fremd *[heer fremt]*

strap (*on watch*) ein Band (*nt*) *[bant]*; (*on suitcase*) ein Riemen (*m*) *[reemen]*; (*on dress*) ein Träger (*m*) *[trayger]*

strawberry eine Erdbeere *[airtbair-uh]*

streak: could you put streaks in? (*in hair*) können Sie mir Strähnen hereinmachen? *[kurnen zee meer shtraynen hairyne-macнen]*

stream ein Bach (*m*) *[bacн]*

street eine Straße *[shtrahss-uh]*; **on the street** auf der Straße

street café ein Straßencafé (*nt*) *[shtrahssen-kaffay]*

streetcar eine Straßenbahn *[shtrahssen-bahn]*

streetmap ein Stadtplan (*m*) *[shtatt-plahn]*

strep throat eine Halsentzündung *[halss-entsoondoong]*

strike: they're on strike sie streiken *[zee shtryken]*

string eine Schnur *[shnoor]*

striped (*shirt etc*) gestreift *[geshtryft]*

striptease der Striptease

stroke: he's had a stroke er hat einen Schlaganfall gehabt *[air hat ine-en shlahkanfal gehahpt]*

stroll: let's go for a stroll machen wir einen Spaziergang *[macнen veer ine-en spatseergang]*

stroller (*for babies*) ein Sportwagen (*m*) *[shportvahgen]*

strong (*person, drink*) stark *[shtark]*; (*taste*) kräftig *[krefticн]*

stroppy pampig *[pampicн]*

stuck: the key's stuck der Schlüssel steckt fest *[shteckt fest]*

student ein Student *[shtoodent]*; (*woman*) eine Studentin

stupid dumm *[doomm]*

sty (*in eye*) ein Gerstenkorn (*nt*) *[gairsten-*

korn]

subtitles Untertitel *[oonterteetel]*

suburb eine Vorstadt *[forshtatt]*

subway die U-Bahn *[oo-bahn]*

successful: was it successful? war es erfolgreich? *[vahr ess airfolkrycнe]*

suddenly plötzlich *[plurtslicн]*

sue: I intend to sue ich werde Sie verklagen *[icн vaird-uh zee fairklahgen]*

suede das Wildleder *[villt-layder]*

sugar der Zucker *[tsoocker]*

suggest: what do you suggest? was schlagen Sie vor? *[vass shlahgen zee for]*

suit ein Anzug (*m*) *[antsook]*; **it doesn't suit me** (*colour etc*) es steht mir nicht *[ess shtayt meer nicнt]*; **it suits you** es steht Ihnen *[eenen]*; **that suits me fine** (*plan etc*) das ist mir recht *[dass ist meer recнt]*

suitable (*time, place*) geeignet *[ge-'eye'gnet]*

suitcase ein Koffer (*m*)

sulk: he's sulking er ist beleidigt *[be-lydicнt]*

sultry (*weather*) schwül *[shvool]*

summer der Sommer *[zommer]*; **in the summer** im Sommer

sun die Sonne *[zonn-uh]*; **in the sun** in der Sonne; **out of the sun** im Schatten *[shatten]*; **I've had too much sun** ich habe zuviel Sonne abbekommen *[hahb-uh tsoofeel zonn-uh apbekommen]*

sunbathe sonnenbaden *[zonnenbahden]*

sunblock die Sun-Block-Creme *[—kraym-uh]*

sunburn ein Sonnenbrand (*m*) *[zonnen-brant]*

Sunday der Sonntag *[zontahk]*

sunglasses eine Sonnenbrille *[zonnen-brill-uh]*

sun lounger (*recliner*) ein Ruhesessel (*m*) *[roo-uh-zessel]*

sunny: if it's sunny bei Sonnenschein *[by zonnenshyne]*

sunrise der Sonnenaufgang *[zonnenowff-gang]*

sun roof (*in car*) das Schiebedach *[sheeb-uh-dacн]*

sunset der Sonnenuntergang *[zonnen-oontergang]*

sunshade (*over table*) ein Sonnenschirm (*m*) *[zonnensheerm]*

sunshine der Sonnenschein *[zonnen-shyne]*

sunstroke ein Sonnenstich (*m*) *[zonnen-shtich]*

suntan die Sonnenbräune *[zonnenbroyn-uh]*

suntan lotion, suntan oil das Sonnenöl *[zonnenurl]*

suntanned braungebrannt *[brown-gebrannt]*

super (*time, meal etc*) phantastisch *[fantastish]*; **super!** Klasse! *[klass-uh]*

superb großartig *[grohss-artich]*

supermarket ein Supermarkt (*m*) *[zoopermarkt]*

supper das Abendessen *[ahbentessen]*

supplement (*extra charge*) ein Zuschlag (*m*) *[tsoo̅shlahk]*

suppose: I suppose so ich glaube schon *[ich glowb-uh shohn]*

suppository das Zäpfchen *[tsepfchen]*

sure: I'm sure ich bin sicher *[ich bin zicher]*; **are you sure?** sind Sie sicher?; **he's sure** er ist sicher; **sure!** klar!

surname der Nachname *[nachnahm-uh]*

surprise eine Überraschung *[oober-rashoong]*

surprising: that's not surprising das ist nicht verwunderlich *[fairvoonderlich]*

suspension (*on car*) die Federung *[fayder-oong]*

swallow schlucken *[shloocken]*

swearword ein Kraftausdruck (*m*) *[kraftowssdroock]*

sweat schwitzen *[shvitsen]*; **covered in sweat** schweißgebadet *[shvyce-gebahdet]*

sweater ein Pullover (*m*) *[poolohver]*

sweet (*taste*) süß *[zooss]*; (*dessert*) der Nach-tisch *[nachtish]*

Sweden Schweden *[schvayden]*

sweets die Süßigkeiten *[zoosichkyten]*

swelling eine Schwellung *[shvelloong]*

sweltering glühend heiß *[gloo-ent hyce]*

swerve: I had to swerve ich mußte ausweichen *[ich moost-uh owssvychen]*

swim: I'm going for a swim ich gehe schwimmen *[ich gay-uh shvimmen]*; **do you want to go for a swim?** möchten Sie schwimmen gehen? *[murchten zee]*; **I can't swim** ich kann nicht schwimmen

swimming Schwimmen *[shvimmen]*; **I like swimming** ich schwimme gern *[ich shvimm-uh gairn]*

swimming costume ein Badeanzug (*m*) *[bahd-uh-antsoo̅k]*

swimming pool ein Schwimmbad (*nt*) *[shvimbaht]*

swimming trunks eine Badehose *[bahd-uh-hohz-uh]*

Swiss schweizerisch *[shvytes-erish]*; (*man*) der Schweizer *[shvytes-er]*; (*woman*) die Schweizerin *[shvytes-erin]*

switch ein Schalter (*m*) *[shallter]*; **could you switch it on?** könnten Sie es anschalten? *[kurnten zee ess anshallten]*; **could you switch it off?** könnten Sie es ausschalten? *[owss-shallten]*

Switzerland die Schweiz *[shvytes]*

swollen geschwollen *[geshvollen]*

swollen glands geschwollene Drüsen *[geshvollen-uh droozen]*

sympathy das Verständnis *[fairshtent-niss]*

synagogue eine Synagoge *[zinagohg-uh]*

synthetic synthetisch *[zintaytish]*

T

table der Tisch *[tish]*; **a table for two** einen Tisch für zwei Personen *[pairzoh-nen]*; **at our usual table** an unserem normalen Tisch *[normahlen]*

tablecloth ein Tischtuch (*nt*) *[tishtoo̅ch]*

table tennis Tischtennis *[tishtennis]*

table wine der Tafelwein *[tahfelvyne]*

tactful taktvoll *[taktfol]*

tailback ein Rückstau (*m*) *[roockshtow]*

tailor der Schneider *[shnyder]*

take nehmen *[naymen]*; **will you take this to room 12?** könnten Sie das auf Zimmer 12 bringen? *[kurnten zee dass owff]*; **will you take me to the airport?** können Sie mich zum Flughafen bringen?; **do you take credit cards?** akzeptieren Sie Kreditkarten? *[aktsepteeren zee]*; **OK, I'll take it** okay, ich nehme es *[icн naym-uh ess]*; **how long does it take?** wie lange dauert es? *[vee lang-uh dowert ess]*; **it took 2 hours** es dauerte 2 Stunden *[dowert-uh]*; **is this seat taken?** ist dieser Platz besetzt? *[deezer plats bezetst]*; **to take away** *(food)* zum Mitnehmen *[tsoom mitnaymen]*; **will you take this back, it's broken** können Sie das zurücknehmen, es ist kaputt *[tsoorœcknaymen]*; **could you take it in at the side?** *(dress)* können Sie es an den Seiten enger machen? *[eng-er macнen]*; **when does the plane take off?** wann startet das Flugzeug? *[van shtartet dass flooktsoyk]*; **can you take a little off the top?** können Sie oben etwas beischneiden? *[ohben etvass byshnyden]*

talcum powder der Körperpuder *[kurperpooder]*

talk sprechen *[shprecнen]*

tall groß *[grohss]*

tampax *(tm)* ein Tampon *(m)*

tampons die Tampons

tan die Bräune *[broyn-uh]*

tank *(of car)* der Tank

tap der Wasserhahn *[vasserhahn]*

tape *(for cassette)* das Band *[bant]*; *(sticky)* das Klebeband *[klayb-uh-bant]*

tape measure ein Maßband *[mahssbant]*

tape recorder ein Kassettenrecorder

taste der Geschmack *[geshmack]*; **can I taste it?** kann ich es probieren? *[kan icн ess probeeren]*; **it has a peculiar taste** es hat einen eigenartigen Geschmack; **it tastes very nice** es schmeckt sehr gut *[ess shmeckt zair goot]*; **it tastes revolting** es schmeckt scheußlich *[shoysslicн]*

taxi das Taxi; **will you get me a taxi?** können Sie mir ein Taxi bestellen? *[kurnen zee meer ine taxi beshtellen]*

taxi-driver der Taxifahrer

taxi rank, taxi stand ein Taxistand *(m)* *[—shtant]*

tea *(drink)* der Tee *[tay]*; **tea for two please** Tee für zwei Personen bitte *[fœr tsvye pairzohnen bitt-uh]*; **could I have a cup of tea?** kann ich eine Tasse Tee bekommen? *[ine-uh tass-uh tay]*

teabag ein Teebeutel *(m)* *[tayboytel]*

teach: could you teach me? könnten Sie es mir beibringen? *[kurnten zee ess meer*

bybringen]*; **could you teach me German?** könnten Sie mir Deutschunterricht geben? *[doytshoonterricнt gayben]*

teacher ein Lehrer *[lairer]*; *(woman)* eine Lehrerin

team das Team

teapot eine Teekanne *[taykan-uh]*

tea towel ein Geschirrtuch *(nt)* *[gesheertoocн]*

teenager ein Teenager *(m)*

teetotal(l)er ein Nichttrinker *(m)* *[nicнt—]*

telegram ein Telegramm *(nt)*; **I want to send a telegram** ich möchte ein Telegramm senden *[zenden]*

telephone das Telefon *[telefohn]*; **can I make a telephone call?** kann ich das Telefon benutzen? *[benootsen]*; **could you talk to him for me on the telephone?** könnten Sie vielleicht mit ihm sprechen? *[kurnten zee feelycнt mit eem shprecнen]*

telephone box eine Telefonzelle *[telefohntsell-uh]*

telephone directory das Telefonbuch *[telefohnboocн]*

telephone number die Telefonnummer *[telefohn-noomer]*; **what's your telephone number?** was ist Ihre Telefonnummer?

telephoto lens das Teleobjektiv *[tele-obyekteef]*

television das Fernsehen *[fairnzayen]*; **I'd like to watch television** ich möchte gern fernsehen *[murcнt-uh gairn]*; **is the match on television?** wird das Spiel im Fernsehen übertragen? *[œbertrahgen]*

telex: I want to send a telex ich möchte ein Telex schicken *[ine taylex shicken]*

tell: could you tell him ...? können Sie ihm sagen ...? *[kurnen zee eem zahgen]*

temperature *(weather etc)* die Temperatur *[temperatoor]*; **he has a temperature** er hat Fieber *[air hat feeber]*

temporary vorübergehend *[forœbergayent]*

tenant *(of apartment)* der Mieter *[meeter]*

tennis Tennis

tennis ball ein Tennisball *(m)* *[—bal]*

tennis court ein Tennisplatz *(m)* *[—plats]*

tennis racket ein Tennisschläger *(m)* *[—shlayger]*

tent ein Zelt (*nt*) *[tselt]*

term (*school*) das Halbjahr *[halp-yar]*

terminus die Endstation *[ent-shtats-yohn]*

terrace die Terrasse *[terrass-uh]*; **on the terrace** auf der Terrasse

terrible furchtbar *[foorcHtbar]*

terrific sagenhaft *[zahgenhaft]*

testicle der Hoden *[hohden]*

than als *[alss]*; **smaller than** kleiner als

thanks, thank you danke *[dank-uh]*; **thank you very much** vielen Dank *[feelen dank]*; **thank you for everything** vielen Dank für alles *[foor al-ess]*; **no thanks** nein danke *[nyne dank-uh]*

that: that woman diese Frau *[deez-uh frow]*; **that man** dieser Mann *[deezer man]*; **that house** dieses Haus *[deezess howss]*; **I hope that ...** ich hoffe, daß ... *[dass]*; **that's very strange** das ist sehr seltsam; **that's it** (*that's right*) genau *[genow]*; **is it that expensive?** ist es so teuer? *[zo toyer]*

the (*singular*) der/die/das *[dair/dee/dass]*; (*plural*) die *[dee]*; *see page 107*

theatre, theater das Theater *[tayahter]*

their ihr/ihre *[eer/eer-uh]*; *see page 110*

theirs ihrer *[eer-er]*; *see page 112*

them sie *[zee]*; **for them** für sie *[foor zee]*; **with them** mit ihnen *[een-en]*; *see page 111*

then dann

there dort; **over there** dort drüben *[drooben]*; **up there** da oben; **there is/are ...** es gibt ... *[es gipt]*; **there you are** (*giving something*) bitte *[bitt-uh]*

thermal spring eine Thermalquelle *[tair-mahlkvell-uh]*

thermometer ein Thermometer (*nt*) *[tair-momayter]*

thermos flask eine Thermosflasche *[tair-moss-flash-uh]*

thermostat der Thermostat *[tairmostaht]*

these diese *[deez-uh]*; **can I have these?** kann ich diese hier haben?

they sie *[zee]*; **are they ready?** sind sie fertig? *[zint zee fairticH]*; *see page 111*

thick dick; (*stupid*) blöd *[blurt]*

thief ein Dieb (*m*) *[deep]*

thigh der Schenkel *[shenkel]*

thin dünn *[doon]*

thing ein Ding (*nt*); **have you seen my things?** haben Sie meine Sachen ge-

sehen? *[hahben zee myne-uh zacHen gezayen]*; **first thing in the morning** als erstes am Morgen *[alss airstess]*

think denken; **what do you think?** was meinen Sie? *[vass mynen zee]*; **I think so** ich glaube ja *[icH glowb-uh yah]*; **I don't think so** ich glaube nicht; **I'll think about it** ich werde darüber nachdenken *[icH vaird-uh daroober nacHdenken]*

third party (*insurance*) eine Haftpflichtversicherung *[haftpflicHt-fairzicHeroong]*

thirsty: I'm thirsty ich habe Durst *[doorst]*

this: this hotel dieses Hotel *[deezess]*; **this street** diese Straße *[deez-uh shtrahss-uh]*; **this man** dieser Mann *[deezer]*; **this is my wife** das ist meine Frau *[dass ist myne-uh frow]*; **this is my favo(u)rite café** dies ist mein Lieblingscafé *[deess]*; **is this yours?** gehört dies Ihnen? *[gehurt deess eenen]*; **this is ...** (*on phone*) hier spricht ... *[heer shpricHt]*

those diese da *[deez-uh da]*; **not these, those** nicht diese hier, diese da

thread der Faden *[fahden]*

throat der Hals *[halss]*

throat lozenges die Halstabletten

throttle (*motorbike*) der Gashebel *[gahss-haybel]*; (*boat*) die Drossel

through durch *[doorcH]*; **does it go through Cologne?** geht es über Köln? *[gayt ess oober kurln]*; **Monday through Friday** Montag bis Freitag *[biss]*; **straight through the city centre** mitten durch das Stadtzentrum *[mitten]*

through train ein durchgehender Zug (*m*) *[doorcHgayender tsook]*

throw werfen *[vairfen]*; **don't throw it away** werfen Sie es nicht weg *[vairfen zee ess nicHt veck]*; **I'm going to throw up** ich muß mich übergeben *[icH mooss micH oobergayben]*

thumb der Daumen *[dowmen]*

thumbtack eine Heftzwecke *[heftsveck-uh]*

thunder der Donner

thunderstorm ein Gewitter (*nt*) *[gevitter]*

Thursday der Donnerstag *[donnerstahk]*

ticket (*train, bus, boat*) eine Fahrkarte *[fahrkart-uh]*; (*plane*) ein Ticket (*nt*); (*cinema*) eine Eintrittskarte *[ine-tritts-*

kart-uh]; (*cloakroom*) eine Garderoben-marke *[garderohbenmark-uh]*

ticket office der Fahrkartenschalter *[fahrkartenshallter]*

tide: at low tide bei Ebbe *[by ebb-uh]*; **at high tide** bei Flut *[by flōōt]*

tie (*necktie*) eine Krawatte *[kravatt-uh]*

tight (*clothes*) eng; **the waist is too tight** es ist in der Taille zu eng *[tsōō]*

tights eine Strumpfhose *[shtroompf-hohz-uh]*

time die Zeit *[tsyte]*; **what's the time?** wie spät ist es? *[vee shpayt ist ess]*; **at what time do you close?** wann schließen Sie? *[van shleessen zee]*; **there's not much time** die Zeit ist knapp; **for the time being** vorläufig *[forloyfich]*; **from time to time** von Zeit zu Zeit; **right on time** genau rechtzeitig *[genow rechtsytich]*; **this time** diesmal *[deessmahl]*; **last time** letztes Mal *[letstess]*; **next time** nächstes Mal *[naychstess]*; **four times** viermal *[feermahl]*; **have a good time!** viel Spaß *[feel shpahss]*; *see page 118*

timetable der Fahrplan *[fahrplahn]*

tin (*can*) eine Dose *[dohz-uh]*

tin-opener ein Dosenöffner (*m*) *[dohzen-urfner]*

tint (*hair*) tönen *[turnen]*

tiny winzig *[vintsich]*

tip das Trinkgeld *[trinkgelt]*; **does that include the tip?** ist das einschließlich Trinkgeld? *[ine-shleesslich]*

tire (*for car*) ein Reifen (*m*) *[ryfen]*

tired müde *[mœd-uh]*; **I'm tired** ich bin müde

tiring anstrengend *[anshtrengent]*

tissues die Papiertücher *[pappeertœcher]*

to: to Düsseldorf/England nach Düsseldorf/England *[nach]*; **to the airport** zum Flughafen *[tsoom]*; **here's to you!** (*toast*) auf Ihr Wohl! *[owff eer vohl]*; *see page 118*

toast ein Toast (*m*); (*drinking*) ein Toast (*m*)

tobacco der Tabak *[tabak]*

tobacconist, tobacco store ein Tabakladen (*m*) *[tabaklahden]*

today heute *[hoyt-uh]*; **today week** heute in einer Woche *[in ine-er voch-uh]*

toe der Zeh *[tsay]*

toffee ein Karamelbonbon (*m*) *[karamaylbonbon]*

together zusammen *[tsōōzammen]*; **we're**

together wir sind zusammen; **can we pay together?** können wir zusammen bezahlen?

toilet die Toilette *[tvallett-uh]*; **where's the toilet?** wo ist die Toilette? *[vo]*; **I want to go to the toilet** ich muß auf die Toilette *[owff dee]*; **she's in the toilet** sie ist in der Toilette

toilet paper das Toilettenpapier *[tvallettenpappeer]*

toilet water das Toilettenwasser *[tvallettenvasser]*

toll: motorway toll die Autobahngebühr *[owto-bahngebœr]*

tomato eine Tomate *[tomaht-uh]*

tomato juice ein Tomatensaft (*m*) *[tomahtenzaft]*

tomato ketchup der Tomatenketchup *[tomahten—]*

tomorrow morgen; **tomorrow morning** morgen früh *[frœ]*; **tomorrow afternoon** morgen nachmittag *[nachmittahk]*; **tomorrow evening** morgen abend *[ah-bent]*; **the day after tomorrow** übermorgen *[œbermorgen]*; *see you tomorrow* bis morgen

ton die Tonne *[tonn-uh]*; *see page 120*

toner die Gesichtslotion *[gezichts-lohts-yohn]*

tongue die Zunge *[tsoong-uh]*

tonic (water) das Tonic

tonight heute abend *[hoyt-uh ahbent]*; **not tonight** nicht heute abend

tonsillitis eine Mandelentzündung *[man-delentsœndoong]*

tonsils die Mandeln

too zu *[tsōō]*; (*also*) auch *[owch]*; **too much** zuviel *[tsōōfeel]*; **me too** ich auch; **I'm not feeling too good** ich fühle mich nicht sehr wohl *[ich fœl-uh mich nicht zair vohl]*

tooth ein Zahn (*m*) *[tsahn]*

toothache die Zahnschmerzen *[tsahnshmairtsen]*

toothbrush eine Zahnbürste *[tsahn-bœrst-uh]*

toothpaste die Zahnpasta *[tsahnpasta]*

top: on top of ... oben auf ... *[oben owff]*; **on top of the car** oben auf dem Auto; **on the top floor** im obersten Stock; **at the top** oben; **at the top of the hill** oben am Berg; **top quality** Spitzenqualität *[shpit-senkvalitayt]*; **bikini top** das Bikini-

Oberteil *[—obertyle]*

topless oben ohne *[oben ohn-uh]*; **topless beach** ein Oben-ohne-Strand *(m)* *[—shtrant]*

torch eine Taschenlampe *[tashenlamp-uh]*

total die Endsumme *[entzoom-uh]*

touch berühren *[beroaren]*; **let's keep in touch** wir sollten in Verbindung bleiben *[veer zollten in fairbindoong blyben]*

tough *(meat)* zäh *[tsay]*; **tough luck!** Pech! *[peсн]*

tour eine Reise *[ryze-uh]*; **is there a tour of ...?** gibt es eine Führung durch ...? *[ine-uh faoroong doorсн]*

tour guide ein Reiseführer *(m)* *[ryze-uh-faorer]*

tourist ein Tourist *[toorist]*

tourist office ein Fremdenverkehrsbüro *(nt)* *[fremdenfairkairsboaro]*

touristy: somewhere not so touristy wo nicht so viele Touristen sind *[vo niснt zo feel-uh tooristen zint]*

tour operator ein Reiseveranstalter *(m)* *[ryze-uh-fairanshtaller]*

tow: can you give me a tow? können Sie mich abschleppen? *[kurnen zee miсн apshleppen]*

toward(s) nach *[naсн]*; **toward(s) Bremen** in Richtung Bremen *[riснtoong]*

towel ein Handtuch *(nt)* *[hant-tooсн]*

town die Stadt *[shtatt]*; **in town** in der Stadt; **which bus goes into town?** welcher Bus fährt in die Stadt? *[fairt in dee]*; **we're staying just out of town** wir wohnen am Stadtrand *[am shtattrant]*

town hall das Rathaus *[raht-howss]*

tow rope ein Abschleppseil *(nt)* *[apshlepp-zyle]*

toy ein Spielzeug *(nt)* *[shpeeltsoyk]*

track suit ein Trainingsanzug *(m)* *[—antsook]*

traditional traditionell *[tradits-yohnel]*; **a traditional German meal** ein typisch deutsches Essen *[taopish doytshess]*

traffic der Verkehr *[fairkair]*

traffic circle ein Kreisverkehr *(m)* *[kryce-fairkair]*

traffic cop ein Verkehrspolizist *(m)* *[fair-kairspolitsist]*

traffic jam ein Verkehrsstau *(m)* *[fair-kairss-shtow]*

traffic light(s) die Ampel

trailer *(for carrying tent etc)* ein Anhänger *(m)* *[anhenger]*; *(caravan)* ein Wohnwagen *[vohnvahgen]*

train ein Zug *(m)* *[tsook]*; **when's the next train to ...?** wann fährt der nächste Zug nach ...? *[van fairt]*; **by train** mit dem Zug

trainers *(shoes)* die Turnschuhe *[toornshoo-uh]*

train station der Bahnhof *[bahnhohf]*

tram eine Straßenbahn *[shtrahssenbahn]*

tramp *(person)* ein Landstreicher *(m)* *[lantshtryсner]*

tranquillizers das Beruhigungsmittel *[beroo-igoongsmittel]*

transatlantic transatlantisch

transformer ein Transformator *(m)* *[—ahtor]*

transistor *(radio)* ein Transistorradio *(nt)* *[tranzistor-rahdee-o]*

translate übersetzen *[aoberzetsen]*; **could you translate that?** könnten Sie das übersetzen? *[kurnten zee]*

translation die Übersetzung *[aoberzet-soong]*

transit desk der Transitschalter *[tranzeetshallter]*

transmission *(of car)* das Getriebe *[getreeb-uh]*

travel reisen *[ryzen]*; **we're travel(l)ing around** wir machen eine Rundreise *[veer maсnen ine-uh roontryze-uh]*

travel agent ein Reisebüro *(nt)* *[ryze-uh-baoro]*

travel(l)er der Reisende *[ryzend-uh]*

traveller's cheque, traveler's check ein Reisescheck *(m)* *[ryze-uh-sheck]*

tray ein Tablett *(nt)*

tree ein Baum *(m)* *[bowm]*

tremendous fantastisch *[—tish]*

trendy schick *[shick]*

tricky *(difficult)* schwierig *[shveeriсн]*

trim: just a trim please nur etwas beischneiden, bitte *[noor etvass byshnyden]*

trip ein Ausflug *(m)* *[owssflook]*; **I'd like to go on a trip to ...** ich möchte gern eine Reise nach ... machen *[iсн murсnt-uh gairn ine-uh ryze-uh naсн ... maсnen]*; **have a good trip!** gute Reise!

tripod ein Stativ *(nt)* *[shtateef]*

trouble die Schwierigkeiten *[shveeriсн-kyten]*; **I'm having trouble with ...** ich habe Schwierigkeiten mit ...;

sorry to trouble you es tut mir leid, Sie zu belästigen *[ess tōōt meer lyte zee tsōō belestigen]*
trousers eine Hose *[hohz-uh]*
trouser suit ein Hosenanzug *(m)* *[hohzen-antsōōk]*
trout eine Forelle *[forel-uh]*
truck ein Lastwagen *(m)* *[lasstvahgen]*
truck driver ein Lastwagenfahrer *(m)* *[lasstvahgenfahrer]*
true wahr *[vahr]*; **that's not true** das stimmt nicht *[dass shtimmt nicht]*
trunk *(of car)* der Kofferraum *[kofferrowm]*
trunks *(swimming)* eine Badehose *[bahduh-hohz-uh]*
truth die Wahrheit *[vahrhyte]*; **it's the truth** das ist die Wahrheit
try versuchen *[fairzōōchen]*; **please try** bitte versuchen Sie es; **will you try for me?** könnten Sie es versuchen? *[kurnten zee]*; **I've never tried it** *(food, sport)* ich habe es noch nie probiert *[ich hahb-uh ess noch nee probeert]*; **can I have a try?** kann ich es versuchen?; **may I try it on?** kann ich es anprobieren? *[anprobeeren]*
T-shirt ein T-shirt *(nt)*
tube *(for tyre)* ein Schlauch *(m)* *[shlowch]*
Tuesday der Dienstag *[deenstahk]*
tuition: I'd like tuition ich möchte gern Unterricht nehmen *[ich murcht-uh gairn oonterricht naymen]*
tulip eine Tulpe *[toolp-uh]*
tuna fish der Thunfisch *[tōōnfish]*
tune die Melodie *[melodee]*

tunnel ein Tunnel *(m)* *[toonel]*
Turk *(man)* der Türke *[toork-uh]*; *(woman)* die Türkin *[toorkin]*
Turkey die Türkei *[toor-ky]*
Turkish türkisch *[toorkish]*
turn: it's my turn next ich bin als nächster dran *[ich bin als naychster dran]*; **turn left** biegen Sie links ab *[beegen zee links ap]*; **where do we turn off?** wo müssen wir abbiegen? *[apbeegen]*; **can you turn the lights on?** können Sie das Licht anmachen? *[kurnen zee dass licht anmachen]*; **can you turn the lights off?** können Sie das Licht ausmachen? *[owssmachen]*; **he didn't turn up** er ist nicht gekommen
turning *(in road)* eine Abzweigung *[aptsvygoong]*
TV das Fernsehen *[fairnzayen]*
tweezers eine Pinzette *[pintsett-uh]*
twice zweimal *[tsvymahl]*; **twice as much** zweimal soviel *[tsvymahl zofeel]*
twin beds zwei Einzelbetten *[tsvy ine-tselbetten]*
twins die Zwillinge *[tsvilling-uh]*
twist: I've twisted my ankle ich habe mir den Fuß vertreten *[ich hahb-uh meer dayn fōōss fairtrayten]*
type die Art; **a different type of ...** eine andere Art von ...
typewriter eine Schreibmaschine *[shrype-masheen-uh]*
typical typisch *[toopish]*
tyre ein Reifen *(m)* *[ryfen]*
Tyrol Tirol *[tirohl]*
Tyrolean Tiroler *[tirohler]*

U

ugly häßlich *[hesslich]*
ulcer ein Geschwür *[geshvoor]*
Ulster Ulster
umbrella ein Schirm *(m)* *[sheerm]*
uncle: my uncle mein Onkel
uncomfortable unbequem *[oonbekvaym]*
unconscious bewußtlos *[bevoostlohss]*
under unter *[oonter]*; **under age** minder-

jährig *[minnder-yairich]*
underdone *(food)* nicht gar *[nicht gahr]*; *(meat)* nicht durchgebraten *[doorchgebrahten]*
underground *(railway)* die U-Bahn *[ōō-bahn]*
underpants eine Unterhose *[oonterhohz-uh]*
undershirt ein Unterhemd *(nt)* *[oonter-

hemt]

understand: I don't understand das
verstehe ich nicht *[dass fairsht**ay**-uh ich
nicht]*; **I understand** ich verstehe; **do
you understand?** verstehen Sie?
*[fairsht**ay**en zee]*

underwear die Unterwäsche *[**oo**nter-
vesh-uh]*

undo *(clothes)* aufmachen *[**ow**ffmachen]*

uneatable: it's uneatable es ist un-
genießbar *[ess ist **oo**ngen**ee**ssbar]*

unemployed arbeitslos *[**a**rbytes-lohss]*

unfair: that's unfair das ist ungerecht
*[dass ist **oo**ngerecht]*

unfortunately leider *[**ly**der]*

unfriendly unfreundlich *[**oo**nfroyntlich]*

unhappy unglücklich *[**oo**nglœcklich]*

unhealthy ungesund *[**oo**ngezoont]*

United States die Vereinigten Staaten
*[fair'**eye**'nichten sht**ah**ten]*; **in the United States** in den USA *[dayn **ōō**-ess-ah]*

university eine Universität *[**oo**nivairzi-
t**ay**t]*

unlimited mileage ohne Kilometerbe-
schränkung *[**oh**n-uh kilom**ay**ter-
beshrenkoong]*

unlock aufschließen *[**ow**ffshleessen]*; **the
door was unlocked** die Tür war nicht
verschlossen *[nicht fairshl**o**ssen]*

unpack auspacken *[**ow**sspacken]*

unpleasant unangenehm *[**oo**nan-
genaym]*

untie aufmachen *[**ow**ffmachen]*

until bis *[biss]*; **until we meet again** bis
wir uns wiedersehen *[veer oonss v**ee**der-

zayen]*; **not until Wednesday** erst
Mittwoch *[airst]*

unusual ungewöhnlich *[**oo**ngevurnlich]*

up oben; **further up the road** weiter die
Straße entlang *[v**y**teer dee shtr**ah**ss-uh]*;
up there da oben; **he's not up yet** er ist
noch nicht auf *[noch nicht owff]*; **what's
up?** was ist los? *[vass ist lohss]*

upmarket *(restaurant, bar)* anspruchsvoll
*[**a**nshpr**oo**chsfoll]*

upset stomach eine Magenverstimmung
*[m**ah**genfairshtimmoong]*

upside down verkehrt herum *[fairk**ai**rt
hair**oo**m]*

upstairs oben; **I'm going upstairs** ich
gehe nach oben *[ich g**ay**-uh nach **o**ben]*

urgent dringend *[dringent]*; **it's very urgent** es ist sehr dringend

urinary tract infection eine Harn-
traktinfektion *[h**a**rntraktinfekts-y**oh**n]*

us uns *[oonss]*; **with us** mit uns; **for us** für
uns; **it's us** wir sind es *[veer zint]*; *see
page 111*

use: may I use …? kann ich … benutzen?
*[ben**oo**tsen]*

used: I used to swim a lot ich bin früher
viel geschwommen *[ich bin fr**œ**-er feel
geshv**o**mmen]*; **when I get used to …**
wenn ich mich an … gewöhnt habe *[ven
ich mich … gev**u**rnt h**ah**b-uh]*

useful nützlich *[n**œ**tslich]*

usual üblich *[**œ**blich]*; **as usual** wie gewöhnlich *[vee gew**u**rnlich]*

usually gewöhnlich *[gev**u**rnlich]*

U-turn eine Wende *[v**e**nd-uh]*

V

vacancy: do you have any vacancies?
(hotel) haben Sie Zimmer frei? *[h**ah**ben
zee tsimmer fry]*

vacation die Ferien *[f**ai**ree-en]*; **we're
here on vacation** wir sind auf Urlaub
hier *[veer zint owff **ōō**rlowp heer]*

vaccination die Impfung *[**i**mpfoong]*

vacuum cleaner ein Staubsauger *(m)*
*[sht**ow**p-zowger]*

vacuum flask eine Thermosflasche

*[t**ai**rmoss-flash-uh]*

vagina die Vagina *[v**ah**geena]*

valid gültig *[g**œ**ltich]*; **how long is it
valid for?** wie lange ist es gültig? *[vee]*

valley das Tal *[tahl]*

valuable *(adj)* wertvoll *[v**ai**rtfol]*; **can I
leave my valuables here?** kann ich mei-
ne Wertsachen hierlassen? *[ich m**y**ne-uh
v**ai**rtzachen h**ee**rlassen]*

value der Wert *[vairt]*

van der Lieferwagen *[leefervahgen]*; (*for camping etc*) der Kleinbus *[klyne-booss]*

vanilla die Vanille *[vaneel-yuh]*; **vanilla ice-cream** ein Vanilleeis (*nt*) *[—ice]*

varicose veins die Krampfadern *[krampf-ahdern]*

variety show eine Varietévorführung *[vahree-etay-forfooroong]*

vary: it varies es ist unterschiedlich *[ess ist oontersheetlich]*

vase eine Vase *[vahz-uh]*

vaudeville das Varieté *[vahree-etay]*

VD eine Geschlechtskrankheit *[geshlechts-krankhyte]*

veal das Kalbfleisch *[kalpflyshe]*

vegetable(s) das Gemüse *[gemooz-uh]*

vegetarian vegetarisch *[vegetahrish]*; **I'm a vegetarian** ich bin Vegetarier

velvet der Samt *[zamt]*

vending machine ein Automat *[owtomaht]*

ventilator ein Ventilator (*m*) *[ventilahtor]*

very sehr *[zair]*; **just a very little German** nur ein ganz kleines bißchen Deutsch *[noor ine gants klyness bisschen doytsh]*; **just a very little for me** nur eine Kleinigkeit für mich *[klynichkyte]*; **I like it very much** ich mag es sehr gern *[ich mahk ess zair gairn]*

vest ein Unterhemd (*nt*) *[oonterhemt]*; (*waistcoat*) eine Weste *[vest-uh]*

via über *[oober]*

video (*recorder*) ein Videorecorder (*m*); (*cassette*) ein Videokassette *[—kasett-uh]*

Vienna Wien *[veen]*

Viennese Wiener *[veener]*

view der Blick; **what a superb view!** was für eine herrliche Aussicht! *[vass foor ineuh hairlich-uh owss-zicht]*

viewfinder der Sucher *[zoocher]*

villa eine Villa

village ein Dorf (*nt*)

vine eine Rebe *[rayb-uh]*

vinegar der Essig *[essich]*

vine-growing area ein Weinbaugebiet (*nt*) *[vyne-bowgebeet]*

vineyard ein Weinberg (*m*) *[vyne-bairk]*

vintage der Jahrgang *[yahrgang]*; **vintage wine** ein edler Wein (*m*) *[ine aydler vyne]*

visa ein Visum (*nt*) *[veezoom]*

visibility die Sichtbarkeit *[zichtbarkyte]*

visit besuchen *[bezoochen]*; **I'd like to visit …** ich möchte … besuchen; **come and visit us** kommen Sie auf einen Besuch bei uns vorbei *[zee owff ine-en bezooch by oonss for-by]*

vital: it's vital that … es ist unbedingt notwendig, daß … *[oonbedinkt nohtvendich]*

vitamins die Vitamine *[vitameen-uh]*

vodka ein Wodka (*m*) *[vodka]*

voice die Stimme *[shtimm-uh]*

voltage die Spannung *[shpannoong]*

vomit erbrechen *[airbrechen]*

W

wafer (*ice-cream*) eine Eiswaffel *[ice-vaffel]*

waist die Taille *[tal-yuh]*

waistcoat eine Weste *[vest-uh]*

wait warten *[varten]*; **wait for me** warten Sie auf mich *[zee owff mich]*; **don't wait for me** warten Sie nicht auf mich; **it was worth waiting for** es hat sich gelohnt, darauf zu warten; **I'll wait till my wife comes** ich warte, bis meine Frau kommt *[vart-uh biss]*; **I'll wait a little longer** ich warte noch etwas; **can you do it while I wait?** kann ich darauf warten?

[darowff]

waiter der Ober; **waiter!** Herr Ober! *[hair ober]*

waiting room der Wartesaal *[vart-uhzahl]*

waitress die Kellnerin; **waitress!** Fräulein! *[froylyne]*

wake: will you wake me up at 6.30? können Sie mich um 6.30 Uhr wecken? *[kurnen zee mich … vecken]*

Wales Wales

walk: let's walk there wir können zu Fuß

dorthin gehen *[tsoo fooss dort-hin gayen]*; **is it possible to walk there?** kann man zu Fuß dorthin gehen?; **I'll walk back** ich gehe zurück *[ich gay-uh tsoorock]*; **is it a long walk?** geht man lange dorthin? *[gayt man lang-uh]*; **it's only a short walk** es ist nicht weit zu gehen *[nicht vyte]*; **I'm going out for a walk** ich gehe spazieren *[shpatseeren]*; **let's take a walk around town** gehen wir ein bißchen in der Stadt spazieren *[ine bisschen]*

walking: I want to do some walking ich möchte ein bißchen wandern *[ich murcht-uh ine bisschen van-dern]*

walking boots die Wanderstiefel *[van-dershteefel]*

walking stick ein Spazierstock (*m*) *[shpatseershtock]*

walkman (*tm*) ein Walkman (*m*)

wall die Wand *[vant]*; (*external*) die Mauer *[mower]*

wallet die Brieftasche *[breeftash-uh]*

wander: I like just wandering around ich wandere gern einfach so durch die Gegend *[ich vander-uh gairn ine-fach zo doorch dee gaygent]*

want: I want a ... ich möchte ein(e) ... *[ich murcht-uh]*; **I don't want any wine** ich möchte keinen Wein; **I want to go home** ich will nach Hause *[vill]*; **but I want to** ich möchte es aber; **I don't want to** ich will nicht *[nicht]*; **he wants to ...** er will ...; **what do you want?** was wollen Sie? *[vass vollen zee]*

war der Krieg *[kreek]*

ward (*in hospital*) die Station *[shtatsee-ohn]*

warm warm *[vahrm]*; **it's so warm today** es ist so warm heute; **I'm so warm** mir ist so warm *[meer]*

warning die Warnung *[vahrnoong]*

was: it was ... es war ... *[ess vahr]*; *see page 114*

wash waschen *[vashen]*; **I need a wash** ich muß mich waschen; **can you wash the car?** können Sie mein Auto waschen? *[kurnen zee]*; **can you wash these?** können Sie die für mich waschen?; **it'll wash off** (*stain*) das läßt sich herauswaschen *[lest zich herowss-vashen]*

washcloth ein Waschlappen (*m*) *[vash-lappen]*

washer (*for bolt*) eine Dichtung *[dichtoong]*

washhand basin ein Handwaschbecken (*nt*) *[hantvash-becken]*

washing (*clothes*) die Wäsche *[vesh-uh]*; **where can I hang my washing?** wo kann ich meine Wäsche aufhängen? *[vesh-uh owff-hengen]*; **can you do my washing for me?** kann ich meine Wäsche bei Ihnen waschen lassen? *[... by eenen ...]*

washing machine eine Waschmaschine *[vashmasheen-uh]*

washing powder das Waschpulver *[vashpoolver]*

washing-up: I'll do the washing-up ich mache den Abwasch *[ich mach-uh dayn apvash]*

washing-up liquid das Spülmittel *[shpoolmittel]*

wasp eine Wespe *[vesp-uh]*

wasteful: that's wasteful das ist verschwenderisch *[fairshvenderish]*

wastepaper basket ein Papierkorb (*m*) *[pappeerkorp]*

watch (*wrist-*) eine Armbanduhr *[armbant-oor]*; **will you watch my things for me?** könnten Sie auf meine Sachen aufpassen? *[kurnten zee owff myne-uh zachen owffpassen]*; **I'll just watch** ich sehe nur zu *[ich zay-uh noor tsoo]*; **watch out!** passen Sie auf! *[passen zee owff]*

watch strap das Uhrarmband *[oor-armbant]*

water das Wasser *[vasser]*; **may I have some water?** kann ich etwas Wasser haben?

watercolo(u)r (*painting*) ein Aquarell (*nt*) *[akvarel]*

waterproof wasserfest *[vasserfest]*

waterski: I'd like to learn to waterski ich möchte gern Wasserskilaufen lernen *[vasseershee-lowfen]*

waterskiing Wasserskilaufen *[vasser-shee-lowfen]*

water sports der Wassersport *[vasser-shport]*

water wings die Schwimmflügel *[shvim-floogel]*

wave (*sea*) eine Welle *[vell-uh]*

way: which way is it? welche Richtung ist es? *[velch-uh richtoong ist ess]*; **it's this**

way es ist hier entlang *[heer entlang]*; **it's that way** es ist dort entlang; **could you tell me the way to …?** könnten Sie mir sagen, wie ich nach … komme? *[kurnten zee meer zahgen vee ich nach … komm-uh]*; **is it on the way to Munich?** liegt es auf dem Weg nach München? *[owff daym vayk nach]*; **you're blocking the way** Sie versperren den Weg *[zee fair-shperren dayn]*; **is it a long way to …?** ist es weit bis nach …? *[vyte]*; **would you show me the way to do it?** könnten Sie mir zeigen, wie man das macht? *[tsy-gen vee man dass macht]*; **do it this way** Sie müssen es so machen *[zee mœssen ess zo machen]*; **no way!** auf keinen Fall! *[owff kynen fal]*

we wir *[veer]*; *see page 111*

weak schwach *[shvach]*

wealthy reich *[ryche]*

weather das Wetter *[vetter]*; **what foul weather!** was für ein mieses Wetter! *[meezess]*; **what beautiful weather!** wie schön das Wetter ist! *[vee shurn]*

weather forecast der Wetterbericht *[vetter-bericht]*

wedding die Hochzeit *[hochtsyte]*

wedding anniversary der Hochzeitstag *[hochtsytes-tahk]*

wedding ring der Ehering *[ay-uh-ring]*

Wednesday der Mittwoch *[mittvoch]*

week eine Woche *[voch-uh]*; **a week (from) today** heute in einer Woche *[hoyt-uh in ine-er]*; **a week (from) tomorrow** morgen in einer Woche; **Monday week** Montag in einer Woche

weekend: at/on the weekend am Wochenende *[vochen-end-uh]*

weight das Gewicht *[gevicht]*; **I want to lose weight** ich möchte gern abnehmen *[ich murcht-uh gairn apnaymen]*

weight limit das zugelassene Höchstgewicht *[tsoogelassen-uh hurchst-gevicht]*

weird (*thing to happen*) unheimlich *[oon-hyme-lich]*; (*person, taste*) seltsam *[zeltzam]*

welcome: welcome to … willkommen in … *[villkommen in]*; **you're welcome** bitte sehr *[bitt-uh zair]*

well: I don't feel well ich fühle mich nicht wohl *[ich fool-uh mich nicht vohl]*; **I haven't been very well** mir ging es in letzter Zeit nicht sehr gut *[meer ging ess in letster tsyte nicht zair goot]*; **she's not well** sie fühlt sich nicht wohl *[zee]*; **how are you? — very well, thanks** wie geht's Ihnen? — sehr gut, danke *[zair goot dank-uh]*; **you speak English very well** Sie sprechen sehr gut Englisch *[zee shprechen zair goot eng-lish]*; **me as well** ich auch *[ich owch]*; **well done!** gut gemacht! *[goot gemacht]*; **well, …** nun, … *[noon]*; **well well!** na so was! *[nah zo vass]*

well-done (*steak*) gut durchgebraten *[goot doorchgebrahten]*

wellingtons die Gummistiefel *[goommee-shteefel]*

Welsh walisisch *[val-eezish]*

were *see page 114*

west der Westen *[vesten]*; **to the west** nach Westen *[nach]*

West Indian westindisch *[vestindish]*; (*man*) der Westindier *[vestindee-er]*; (*woman*) die Westindierin

West Indies Westindien *[vestindee-en]*

wet naß *[nass]*; **it's all wet** es ist ganz naß *[gants]*; **it's been wet all week** es regnet schon die ganze Woche *[ess raygnet shohn dee gants-uh voch-uh]*

wet suit ein Taucheranzug (*m*) *[towcher-antsook]*

what? was? *[vass]*; **what's that?** was ist das?; **I don't know what to do** ich weiß nicht, was ich tun soll; **what a view!** was für ein Blick! *[vass fœr ine]*

wheel das Rad *[raht]*

wheelchair ein Rollstuhl (*m*) *[rol-shtool]*

when? wann? *[van]*; **when we get back** wenn wir zurückkommen *[ven veer tsoo-rœck-kommen]*; **when I was in Berlin** als ich in Berlin war *[alss]*

where? wo? *[vo]*; **where is …?** wo ist …?; **I don't know where he is** ich weiß nicht, wo er ist; **that's where I left it** da habe ich es liegenlassen *[da hahb-uh ich ess leegen-lassen]*; **where are you going?** wohin gehen Sie? *[vohin gayen zee]*; **where are you from?** woher kommen Sie? *[vohair]*

which: which bus? welcher Bus? *[velcher booss]*; **which house?** welches Haus? *[velchess howss]*; **which town?** welche Stadt? *[velch-uh shtatt]*; **I forget which it was** ich habe vergessen, welcher es war; **the one which …** derjenige, der

... [**dair**yaynig-uh]

while: while I'm here während ich hier bin [**vai**rent icH heer]

whipped cream die Schlagsahne [shl**ah**kzahn-uh]

whisky ein Whisky (m)

whisper flüstern [fl**œ**stern]

white weiß [**vy**ce]

white wine der Weißwein [**vy**ce-vyne]

Whitsun Pfingsten

who? wer? [**vair**]; **who was that?** wer war das? [vair vahr dass]; **the man who ...** der Mann, der ... [**dair**]; **the woman who ...** die Frau, die ... [**dee**]; **the girl who ...** das Mädchen, das ...

whole: the whole week die ganze Woche [dee g**a**nts-uh v**o**cH-uh]; **two whole days** zwei volle Tage [f**o**ll-uh t**ah**g-uh]; **the whole lot** das Ganze

whooping cough der Keuchhusten [k**oy**cH-h**ōō**sten]

whose: whose is this? wem gehört das? [vaym geh**u**rt dass]

why? warum? [vahr**oo**m]; **why not?** warum nicht? [n**i**cHt]; **that's why it's not working** deshalb funktioniert es nicht [dess-h**a**lp]

wide breit [**bry**te]

wide-angle lens ein Weitwinkelobjektiv (nt) [**vy**te-vinkel-obyekt**ee**f]

widow eine Witwe [v**i**t-vuh]

widower ein Witwer (m) [v**i**tver]

wife: my wife meine Frau [**my**ne-uh frow]

wig eine Perücke [pair**œ**ck-uh]

will: will you give this to him? würden Sie ihm das geben [v**œ**rden zee]; see page 117

win gewinnen [gev**i**nnen]; **who won?** wer hat gewonnen? [vair hat gev**o**nnen]

wind der Wind [vint]

window ein Fenster (nt); (of shop) das Schaufenster [sh**o**wfenster]; **near the window** am Fenster; **in the window** (of shop) im Schaufenster

window seat ein Fensterplatz (m)

windscreen, windshield die Windschutzscheibe [v**i**ntshoots-shybe-uh]

windscreen wipers, windshield wipers die Scheibenwischer [sh**y**ben-visher]

windsurf: I'd like to windsurf ich möchte gern windsurfen [v**i**ntsurfen]

windsurfing das Windsurfen [v**i**ntsurfen]

windy: it's so windy es ist so windig [ess ist zo v**i**ndicH]

wine der Wein [vyne]; **can we have some more wine?** können wir noch etwas Wein haben? [k**u**rnen veer]

wine glass das Weinglas [v**y**ne-glahss]

wine list die Weinkarte [v**y**ne-kart-uh]

wine-tasting eine Weinprobe [v**y**ne-prohb-uh]

wing ein Flügel (m) [fl**œ**gel]; (of car) der Kotflügel [k**oh**tflœgel]

wing mirror der Außenspiegel [**ow**ssenshpeegel]

winter der Winter [v**i**nter]; **in the winter** im Winter

winter holiday der Winterurlaub [v**i**nter**ōō**rlowp]

winter sports der Wintersport [v**i**ntershport]

wire die Draht; (elec) die Leitung [**ly**toong]

wireless ein Radio (nt) [r**ah**dee-o]

wiring (in house) die elektrischen Leitungen [dee el**e**ktrishen l**y**toongen]

wish: wishing you were here ich wünschte, Sie wären hier [icH v**œ**nsht-uh zee vairen heer]; **best wishes** mit besten Wünschen [v**œ**nshen]

with mit; **I'm staying with ...** ich wohne bei ... [icH v**oh**n-uh by]

without ohne [**oh**n-uh]

witness ein Zeuge [ts**oy**g-uh]; (woman) eine Zeugin [ts**oy**gin]; **will you be a witness for me?** würden Sie für mich als Zeuge zur Verfügung stehen? [v**œ**rden zee f**œr** micH alss ... ts**ōō**r fairf**œ**gong sht**ay**en]

witty (person) geistreich [g**y**ste-rycHe]

wobble: it wobbles (wheel etc) es wackelt [ess v**a**ckelt]

woman die Frau [frow]; **women** Frauen [fr**o**wen]

wonderful herrlich [**hair**licH]

won't: it won't start es startet nicht [ess sht**a**rtet n**i**cHt]; see page 117

wood (material) das Holz [holts]

woods (forest) ein Wald (m) [valt]

wool die Wolle [v**o**ll-uh]

word ein Wort (nt) [vort]; **you have my word** Sie haben mein Wort [zee h**ah**bben]

work arbeiten [**ar**byten]; **how does it**

work? wie funktioniert es? *[vee foonk-tsee-oneert ess]*; **it's not working** es funktioniert nicht; **I work in an office** ich arbeite in einem Büro *[ich arbyte-uh]*; **do you have any work for me?** haben Sie einen Job für mich? *[hahben zee ine-en job foor mich]*; **when do you finish work?** wann haben Sie Feierabend? *[fy-er-ahbent]*

world die Welt *[velt]*

worn-out *(person)* erschöpft *[airshurpft]*; *(clothes, shoes)* abgetragen *[apgetrahgen]*

worry: I'm worried about her ich mache mir Sorgen um sie *[ich mach-uh meer zorgen oom zee]*; **don't worry** machen Sie sich keine Sorgen *[kyne-uh]*

worse: it's worse es ist schlimmer *[ess ist shlimmer]*; **it's getting worse** es wird schlimmer *[veert]*

worst schlimmster *[shlimmster]*

worth: it's not worth 50 es ist keine 50 wert *[ess ist kyne-uh ... vairt]*; **it's worth more than that** es ist mehr wert als das *[mair vairt alss dass]*; **is it worth a visit?** lohnt sich ein Besuch dort? *[lohnt zich ine bezooch dort]*

would: would you give this to ...? könnten Sie dies ... geben? *[kurnten zee]*; **what would you do?** was würden Sie machen? *[vass voorden zee machen]*

wrap: could you wrap it up? können Sie es einpacken? *[kurnen zee ess inepacken]*

wrapping die Verpackung *[fairpackoong]*

wrapping paper das Packpapier *[packpappeer]*

wrench *(tool)* ein Schraubenschlüssel *(m)* *[shrowbenshloosel]*

wrist das Handgelenk *[hantgelenk]*

write schreiben *[shryben]*; **could you write it down?** könnten Sie es aufschreiben? *[kurnten zee ess owffshryben]*; **how do you write it?** wie schreibt man das? *[vee shrypte man dass]*; **I'll write to you** ich werde Ihnen schreiben; **I wrote to you last month** ich habe Ihnen letzten Monat geschrieben *[ich hahb-uh eenen letsten mohnat geshreeben]*

write-off: the car's a write-off der Wagen hat Totalschaden *[dair vahgen hat totahl-shahden]*

writer der Schriftsteller *[shriftshteller]*; *(woman)* die Schriftstellerin

writing paper das Schreibpapier *[shrype-pappeer]*

wrong: you're wrong Sie haben unrecht *[zee hahben oonrecht]*; **the bill's wrong** in der Rechnung ist ein Fehler *[in dair rechnoong ist ine fayler]*; **sorry, wrong number** tut mir leid, falsch verbunden *[toot meer lyte falsh fairboonden]*; **I'm on the wrong train** ich bin im falschen Zug *[im falshen tsook]*; **I went to the wrong room** ich bin in das falsche Zimmer gegangen; **that's the wrong key** das ist der falsche Schlüssel; **there's something wrong with ...** mit ... stimmt etwas nicht *[shtimmt etvass nicht]*; **what's wrong?** was ist los? *[vass ist lohss]*; **what's wrong with it?** was stimmt daran nicht? *[dahran nicht]*

die Röntgenaufnahme *[rurntgen-owffnahm-uh]*

Y

yacht eine Jacht *[yacнt]*
yacht club der Segelklub *[zaygel-kloob]*
yard: in the yard im Garten; *see page 119*
year ein Jahr *[yahr]*
yellow gelb *[gelp]*
yellow pages die Gelben Seiten *[zyten]*
yes ja *[yah]*; (*answering negative question*) doch *[docн]*
yesterday gestern; **yesterday morning** gestern morgen; **yesterday afternoon** gestern nachmittag; **the day before yesterday** vorgestern *[forgestern]*
yet: has it arrived yet? ist es schon angekommen? *[shohn]*; **not yet** noch nicht *[nocн nicнt]*
yobbo der Rowdy
yog(h)urt ein Joghurt (*m*) *[yohgoort]*
you Sie *[zee]*; (*sing. familiar*) du *[doo]*; (*pl. familiar*) ihr *[eer]*; **for you** für Sie/dich/

euch *[oycн]*; **with you** mit Ihnen/dir/ euch *[eenen, deer]*; *see page 111*
young jung *[yoong]*
young people die jungen Leute *[dee yoongen loyt-uh]*
your Ihr *[eer]*; (*sing. familiar*) dein *[dyne]*; (*pl. familiar*) euer *[oy-yer]*; **is this your camera?** ist dies Ihre Kamera?; *see page 110*
yours Ihrer *[eerer]*; (*sing. familiar*) deiner *[dyne-er]*; (*pl. familiar*) eurer *[oyrer]*; *see page 112*
youth hostel eine Jugendherberge *[yoo-gent-hairbairg-uh]*; **we're youth hostel-(l)ing** wir übernachten in Jugendherbergen *[veer oobernacнten in yoogent-hairbairgen]*
Yugoslavia Jugoslawien *[yoogoslahvee-en]*

Z

zero null *[nool]*; **it's below zero** es ist unter null *[oonter]*
zip, zipper der Reißverschluß *[rycefairshlooss]*; **could you put a new zip on?** könnten Sie einen neuen Reißver-

schluß anbringen? *[kurnten zee ine-en noyen]*
zoo ein Zoo (*m*) *[tso]*
zoom lens ein Zoomobjektiv (*nt*) *[zoom-obyekteef]*

German – English

A

Aal *[ahl]* eel
Aalsuppe *[ahlzoop-uh]* eel soup
Ab from, down
Abbiegen turn off
Abblendlicht dipped/dimmed headlights
Abendessen dinner
Abendkasse box office, tickets at the door
Abf. (Abfahrt) dept, departure
Abfahrt departures
Abfall litter
Abfertigung check-in
Abgefüllt in ... bottled in ...
Abgezähltes Geld please tender exact fare, no change given
Abhebung collection
Absender sender
Absolutes Halteverbot waiting strictly prohibited
Absolutes Parkverbot parking strictly prohibited
Absolutes Rauchverbot smoking strictly prohibited
Abtei abbey
Abteil compartment
Abteilung department
Abwärts down
Achtung! Straßenbahn beware of tram/streetcar
ADAC (Allgemeiner Deutscher Automobil-Club) German motoring organization
Adresse address
Alle Kassen all health insurance schemes accepted
Alle Rechte vorbehalten all rights reserved
Alle Richtungen all directions
Alpen Alps
Altenheim old people's home
a.M. (am Main) on the Main
Am Spieß *[am shpeess]* on the spit
Ananas pineapple
Andenken souvenirs
Anfassen der Waren verboten do not touch

Angeln verboten no fishing
Ank. (Ankunft) arr, arrival
Ankauf we buy ...
Ankunft arrivals
Ankunftshalle arrivals (area)
Anlieger frei residents only
Anmeldung reception
Anrufbares Telefon incoming calls may be received on this phone
Anschluß an ... connects with ...
Anschrift address
Antiquitäten antiques
Anzahlung deposit
AOK (Allgemeine Ortskrankenkasse) German health insurance organization
Äpfel *[epfel]* apples
Äpfel im Schlafrock *[shlahfrock]* baked apples in pastry
Apfelkompott stewed apples
Apfelmus *[apfelmōōss]* apple purée
Apfelsaft *[apfelzaft]* apple juice
Apfelsinen *[apfelzeenen]* oranges
Apfelstrudel *[apfel-shtrōōdel]* apple strudel
Apfeltasche *[apfeltash-uh]* apple turnover
Apfelwein *[apfelvyne]* cider
Apotheke chemist's, pharmacy
Äppelwoi *[eppelvoy]* cider
Aprikosen *[aprikohzen]* apricots
a.R. (am Rhein) on the Rhine
ARD (Arbeitsgemeinschaft der Rundfunkanstalten Deutschlands) first German television channel
Arme Ritter *[arm-uh]* bread soaked in milk and egg then fried, French toast
Arschloch! *[arshlocʜ]* bastard!
Artischocken *[artishocken]* artichokes
Arzt doctor
Ärztlicher Notdienst emergency medical service
Aspik aspic
Auberginen *[ohbairjeenen]* aubergines, eggplants

Auf up, open
Auf eigene Gefahr at own risk
Aufenthaltsraum lounge
Auflauf *[owfflowff]* (baked) pudding or omelet(te)
Aufschnitt *[owffshnitt]* sliced cold cuts
Aufwärts up
Aufzug lift, elevator
Augenarzt optician; ophthalmologist
Augenoptiker ophthalmic optician
Aus off, out
Ausfahrt exit
Ausfahrt freihalten keep exit clear
Ausfahrt freilassen keep exit clear
Ausgang exit, way out
Ausgenommen except
Auskunft information
Ausland abroad, overseas, international
Ausländisches Erzeugnis foreign produce
Ausländische Währungen foreign currencies
Auslandsgespräch international call
Auslese wine made from the ripest bunch-

es of grapes, belongs to the top German wine category
Außer Betrieb out of order
Äußerlich (anzuwenden) for external use
Außer samstags/sonntags except for Saturdays/Sundays
Aussichtspunkt viewpoint
Austern *[owstern]* oysters
Ausverkauf sale
Ausverkauft sold out
Ausweis identification
Auszahlungen withdrawals
Autobahn motorway, highway
Autobahndreieck junction, intersection
Autobahnkreuz junction, intersection
Autobahnraststätte motorway/highway service station
Autofähre car-ferry
Automat vending machine
Autoreparaturen auto repairs
Autovermietung car hire, car rental
Autowäsche car wash
Autozubehör auto accessories

B

Babyartikel babywear, items for babies
Bäcker baker
Backobst *[backohpst]* dried fruit
Backpflaumen *[backpflowmen]* prunes
Bad bathroom
Baden verboten no bathing
Badezimmerartikel bathroom furniture and fittings
Badezimmerbedarf for the bathroom
Bahnhof station
Bahnhofsmission charity offering help to travel(l)ers
Bahnhofspolizei railway/railroad police
Bahnkilometer kilometres/kilometers by rail
Bahnsteig platform, track
Bahnsteigkarte platform ticket
Bahnübergang level/grade crossing
Baiser *[bezzay]* meringue
Balkansalat *[bal-kahn-zalaht]* cabbage and pepper salad

Balkon balcony, circle
Bananen *[banahnen]* bananas
Bandnudeln *[bantnoōdeln]* ribbon noodles
Basilikum *[bazilikoom]* basil
Bauernauflauf *[bowernowfflowff]* bacon and potato omelet(te)
Bauernfrühstück *[bowernfrœshtœk]* bacon and potato omelet(te)
Bauernomelett *[bowernomlet]* bacon and potato omelet(te)
Baumwolle cotton
Baustelle building site
Bayern Bavaria
Bechamelkartoffeln *[beshamelkartoffeln]* sliced potatoes in creamy sauce
Bedienung *[bedeenoong]* service
Bedienung inbegriffen service included
Bedienungsanleitung instructions for use
Beerdigungsunternehmen undertaker,

mortician

Beerenauslese wine from specially selected single grapes, belongs to the top German wine category

Beginn der Vorstellung um ... performance begins at ...

Bei Frost Glatteisgefahr road liable to ice over in cold conditions

Beilagen [bylahgen] side dishes

Bei Nichtgefallen Geld zurück money back if not satisfied

Bei Versagen Knopf drücken press button to get money back

Bekanntmachung notice, bulletin

Bekleidung clothing

Belegt occupied, busy, engaged

Beleuchtungsartikel lamps and lighting

Benzin petrol, gas

Bergfahrt up

Berliner (Ballen) [bairleener (bal-en)] jam doughnut

Berühren der Waren verboten do not touch

Besetzt occupied, busy, engaged

Besetztzeichen engaged/busy tone

Bestandteile ingredients

Bestattungen funeral directors

Besteck cutlery, flatware

Besuchszeiten visiting times

Betreten auf eigene Gefahr enter at own risk

Betreten der Baustelle verboten no admission to building site

Betreten des Rasens nicht gestattet keep off the grass

Betriebsbereit ready for use

Betriebsferien holidays, vacation

Betteln und Hausieren verboten no beggars, no hawkers

Betten beds

Bettwäsche bed linen

Be- und Entladen erlaubt loading and off-loading permitted

Bezahlung mit Kreditkarten möglich credit cards welcome

Bf. (Bahnhof) station

BH (Büstenhalter) bra

Bier [beer] beer

Biersuppe [beerzoop-uh] beer soup

Billigpreise reduced prices

Bindemittel starch

Bio-Laden health food shop/store

Biologisch abbaubar bio-degradable

Birnen [beernen] pears

Biskuit [biskweet] sponge

Biskuitrolle [biskweetrol-uh] Swiss roll

Bismarckheringe [bismark-hairing-uh] filleted pickled herring

Bitte [bittuh] please, can I help you?, you're welcome

Bitte anschnallen please fasten your seatbelts

Bitte einordnen get in lane

Bitte einzeln eintreten please enter one at a time

Bitte klingeln please ring

Bitte klopfen please knock

Bitte nicht stören please do not disturb

Bitte schließen please close the door

Bitte warten please wait

Blätterteig [blettertyke] puff pastry

Blau [blow] au bleu, boiled

Blaukraut [blowkrowt] red cabbage

Bleifrei lead-free

Blumen flowers

Blumenkohl [bloomenkohl] cauliflower

Blumenkohlsuppe [bloomenkohlzoop-uh] cauliflower soup

Blutig [blootich] rare

Blutwurst [blootvoorst] blood sausage

Bockwurst [bockvoorst] large frankfurter

Bodensee Lake Constance

Bohnen beans

Bohneneintopf [bohnen-ine-topf] bean stew

Bohnensalat [bohnenzalaht] bean salad

Bohnensuppe [bohnenzoop-uh] bean soup

Bootsverleih boats for hire/rent

Bordkarte boarding pass

Botschaft embassy

Bouillon [booyon] clear soup

Bouletten [booletten] meat balls

Bowle [bohl-uh] punch

Branchenverzeichnis yellow pages

Braten [brahten] roast meat

Bratensoße [brahtenzohss-uh] gravy

Bratheringe [braht-hairing-uh] (pickled) fried herring (served cold)

Bratkartoffeln [brahtkartoffeln] fried potatoes

Bratwurst [brahtvoorst] grilled pork sausage

Brauereiabfüllung bottled in the brewery

BRD (Bundesrepublik Deutschland)

FRG, Federal Republic of Germany
Brennbar combustible
Brief letter
Briefkasten letter box, mail box
Briefmarke stamp
Brillen spectacles, eye glasses
Brot *[broht]* bread
Brötchen *[brurtcHen]* roll
Brotsuppe *[brohtzoop-uh]* bread soup
Brücke bridge
Brühwurst *[broovoorst]* large frankfurter
Brust *[broost]* breast
Bücherei library
Bücher und Zeitschriften books and magazines
Buchhandlung bookshop, bookstore

Bückling *[bookling]* smoked red herring
Bühne stage
Bundesrepublik Deutschland Federal Republic of Germany
Bundesstraße major road
Bunte Platte *[boont-uh plat-uh]* mixed salad (with meat)
Burg castle
Burgundersoße *[boorgoonder-zohss-uh]* Burgundy wine sauce
Büroartikel office supplies
Bushaltestelle bus stop
Buttercremetorte *[bootterkraym-tort-uh]* cream cake
Buttermilch *[boottermilcH]* buttermilk
bzw. (beziehungsweise) or

C

Café café, serving mainly cakes, coffee and tea etc
Campingbedarf camping equipment
Champignons *[shampinyongs]* mushrooms
Champignonsauce *[shampinyong-zohss-uh]* mushroom sauce
Chemische Reinigung dry-cleaner
Chicoree *[shikoray]* chicory

Chinakohl *[sheena-kohl]* Chinese cabbage
Chinarestaurant Chinese restaurant
Chips *[ships]* crisps, potato chips
Coiffeur hairdresser
Cordon bleu veal cordon bleu
Currywurst mit Pommes frites *['curry'-voorst mit pom frit]* curried pork sausage with chips

D

Damen ladies, ladies' rest room
Damen(be)kleidung ladies' wear
Damenmoden ladies' fashions
Damenunterwäsche lingerie
Danke *[dank-uh]* thank you
DB (Deutsche Bundesbahn) German Federal Railways/Railroad
DDR (Deutsche Demokratische Republik) GDR, German Democratic Republic, East Germany
Defekt out of order
Der Bundesgesundheitsminister:

Rauchen gefährdet Ihre Gesundheit government warning: smoking can damage your health
Der Kunde ist König the customer is always right
Deutsches Beefsteak *[doytshess 'beef-steak']* mince meat, ground beef
Deutsches Erzeugnis made in Germany
Deutschland Germany
d.h. (das heißt) i.e.
Dicke Bohnen *[dick-uh]* broad beans
Dienstag Tuesday

Dillsoße *[dillzohss-uh]* dill sauce
DJH (Deutsche Jugendherberge)
youth hostel
DM (Deutsche Mark) DM, German
mark
Diskothek discotheque
Dom cathedral
Donnerstag Thursday
Doppelzimmer double room
DR (Deutsche Reichsbahn) East German Railways/Railroad
Dragees sugar-coated tablets
Dreimal täglich einzunehmen to be
taken three times a day
DRK (Deutsches Rotes Kreuz) German Red Cross
Drogerie chemist's, drugstore
Drücken push
Durchfahrt verboten no thoroughfare
Durchgang passage
Durchgebraten *[doorcнgebrahten]*
well-done
Durchgehend geöffnet open all day/
night
Durchwachsen *[doorcнvacksen]* with
fat
Durchwachsener Speck *[doorcн-
vacksener shpeck]* streaky bacon
Dusche shower
D-Zug express train

E

EG (Europäische Gemeinschaft)
EEC, European Economic Community
Eier *['eye'-er]* eggs
Eierauflauf *['eye'-er-owfllowff]* omelet(te)
Eierkuchen *['eye'-er-kōōcнen]* pancakes
Eierpfannkuchen *['eye'-er-pfann-
kōōcнen]* pancakes
Eierspeise *['eye'-er-shpyze-uh]* egg dish
Ein in, on
Einbahnstraße one-way street
Einfache Fahrt single/one-way journey
Einfahrt freihalten keep entrance clear
Einfahrt freilassen keep entrance clear
Eingang entrance, way in
Eingelegt *[ine-gelaykt]* pickled
Eingelegte Bratheringe *[ine-gelaykt-
uh braht-hairing-uh]* pickled herrings
Eingetragenes Warenzeichen registered trademark
Einheitspreis flat rate
Einkaufskorb shopping basket
Einkaufswagen trolley, shopping cart
Einlaß admission
Einmarkstück one mark coin
Einreiben rub in
Einschreibsendungen registered letters
and parcels
Einstieg vorn/hinten enter at the front/
rear
Eintopf *[ine-topf]* stew
Eintopfgericht *[ine-topfgericнt]* stew
Eintritt frei admission free
Eintrittskarte ticket
Eintrittspreise admission
**Ein Umtausch gegen bar ist nicht
möglich** goods cannot be exchanged
for cash
Einzahlungen deposits
Einzelpreis price (per item)
Einzelzimmer single room
Eis *[ice]* ice, ice cream
Eisbecher *[ice-becher]* ice cream sundae
Eisbein *[ice-byne]* knuckles of pork
Eiscafé ice-cream parlo(u)r, also serving
drinks
Eisenwarenhandlung ironmonger,
hardware store
Eisschokolade *[ice-shokolahd-uh]* iced
chocolate drink
Eissplittertorte *[ice-shplittertort-uh]*
cake with fine chips of ice in it
Eisstadion ice rink
Eiswein wine made from grapes picked
after a frost, belongs to the top German
wine category
Elektriker electrician
Elektroartikel electrical goods
Elektrogeräte electrical equipment
Eltern haften für ihre Kinder parents

are responsible for their children
Empfang reception
Empfänger addressee
Ende der Autobahn end of motorway/highway
Ende der Vorfahrtsstraße end of priority
Endiviensalat *[endeevee-en-zalaht]* endive salad
Endstation terminus
Englisch *[eng-lish]* *(of meat)* rare
Entenbraten *[entenbrahten]* roast duck
Entgrätet *[entgraytet]* boned, filleted
Enthält ... contains ...
Entschuldigen Sie bitte *[entshooldigen zee bittuh]* excuse me
Entschuldigung *[entshooldigoong]* sorry, excuse me
Erbsen *[airpsen]* peas
Erbsensuppe *[airpsenzoop-uh]* pea soup

Erdbeertorte *[airtbairtort-uh]* strawberry cake
Erdgeschoß *(UK)* ground floor, *(USA)* first floor
Ergibt die doppelte/dreifache Menge makes twice/three times the amount
Erholungsgebiet recreational area
Ermäßigte Preise reduced prices
Ermäßigungen reductions, concessions
Ersatzteile spare parts
Erste Hilfe first aid
Erste Klasse first class
Erst gurten, dann starten clunk click every trip, seatbelts on
Erwachsene adults
Essig *[essiCH]* vinegar
Etage floor
Euroscheck(karte) Eurocheque card
Ev. (evangelisch) Protestant
Explosionsgefahr danger of explosion

F

Facharzt für ... ... specialist *(doctor)*
Fahrausweis ticket
Fahrausweise sind auf Verlangen vorzuzeigen tickets must be displayed on request
Fahrkarten tickets
Fahrkartenautomat ticket machine
Fahrplan timetable, schedule
Fahrpreise fares
Fahrräder bicycles
Fahrradverleih bicycle hire/rental
Fahrradweg cycle path
Falscher Hase *[fal-sher hahz-uh]* meat loaf
Familienpackung family pack
Familienprogramm family program(me)
Farben und Lacke paints
Fasan *[fazahn]* pheasant
Fasching carnival
Fasse dich kurz! keep it brief
Februar February
Federweißer new wine
Feinkost delicatessen
Feldsalat *[felt-zalaht]* lamb's lettuce

Fenchel *[fenCHel]* fennel
Ferngespräch long distance call
Fernlicht full/high beam
Fernsprecher telephone
Fernsprechzelle telephone box/booth
Festhalten hold tight
Fett fat
Fettgehalt fat content
Feuer fire
Feuergefahr fire hazard
Feuerleiter fire escape
Feuertreppe fire escape
Feuerwehr fire brigade/department
Filet *[fillay]* fillet (steak)
Fisch *[fish]* fish
Fischfilet *[fishfillay]* fish fillet
Fischfrikadellen *[fishfrikadellen]* fishcakes
Fischgerichte *[fishgeriCHt-uh]* fish dishes
Fischgeschäft fishmonger
Fischstäbchen *[fish-shtaypCHen]* fish fingers, fish sticks
Flädlesuppe *[flayd-luh-zoop-uh]* clear soup with pancake strips

Flambiert [flambeert] flambéd
Fleischbrühe [flyshe-broo-uh] stock
Fleischerei butcher
Fleischkäse [flyshe-kayz-uh] meat loaf
Fleischklößchen [flyshe-klursHen] meat ball(s)
Fleischpastete [flyshe-pastayt-uh] meat vol-au-vent
Fleischsalat [flyshe-zalaht] diced meat salad with mayonnaise
Fleisch- und Wurstwaren meats and sausages
Fleischwurst [flyshe-voorst] pork sausage
Flug flight
Fluggeschwindigkeit flight speed
Flughafen airport
Flughöhe altitude
Flugsteig gate
fl.W. (fließendes Wasser) running water
Fond [font] meat juices
Forelle [forell-uh] trout
Forelle blau [forell-uh blow] trout au bleu, boiled trout
Forelle Müllerin (Art) [forell-uh moolerin] trout with butter and lemon (breaded)
Fotoartikel photographic equipment
Fotokopien photocopies
Fr. (Frau) Mrs, Ms
Frauen women
Frauenarzt gyn(a)ecologist
Frei free, vacant
Frei von Konservierungsstoffen/ künstlichen Aromastoffen contains no preservatives/artificial flavo(u)ring
Freibad outdoor swimming pool

Freigegeben ab … Jahren suitable for those over … years of age
Freitag Friday
Freizeichen ringing tone
Freizeitzentrum leisure centre/center
Fremdenzimmer rooms to let/for rent
Friedhof cemetery
Frikadelle [frikadell-uh] rissole
Frikassee [frikassay] fricassee, stewed meat and vegetables with a thick sauce
Frisch gestrichen wet paint
Frischhaltepackung airtight pack
Friseur hairdresser
Fritiert [friteert] (deep-)fried
Frl. (Fräulein) Miss, Ms
Froschschenkel [frosh-shenkel] frogs' legs
Frostschaden frost damage
Frostschutzmittel antifreeze
Fruchtsaft [froocHtzaft] fruit juice
Frühlingsrolle [froolings-rol-uh] spring roll
Frühstück breakfast
Führungen guided tours
Fundbüro lost property, lost and found
Fünfmarkstück five mark coin
Fünfzigmarkschein fifty mark note/bill
Für Jugendliche ab … Jahren for young people over the age of …
Für Kinder ab … Jahren for children from the age of …
Fußballstadion football stadium
Fußgänger bitte andere Straßenseite benutzen pedestrians please use other side of road
Fußgängerüberweg pedestrian crossing/footbridge
Fußgängerzone pedestrian precinct

G

Gabelrollmops [gahbelrollmops] rolled-up pickled herring, rollmops
Gans [ganss] goose
Gänsebraten [genz-uh-brahten] roast goose
Gänseleber [genz-uh-layber] goose liver
Gänseleberpastete [genz-uh-layber-pastayt-uh] goose liver pâté
Garantie guarantee
Garderobe cloakroom, checkroom
Garniert [garneert] garnished
Gartenbedarf gardening department
Gasthof restaurant, inn
Gaststätte restaurant, pub

geb. (geboren) née
Gebäck *[gebeck]* pastries, cakes
Gebacken baked
Gebeizt *[gebytst]* marinated
Gebraten *[gebrahten]* fried, roast
Gebrauchsanleitung instructions for use
Gebrauchsanweisung beachten follow instructions for use
Gebrauchtwagen second-hand cars
Gebühr fee, charge, duty
Gebührenpflichtig liable to charge
Gebunden *[geboonden]* thickened
Gedeck set menu, drinks included in cover charge
Gedeckter Apfelkuchen *[gedeckter apfelkooчhen]* apple flan
Gedünstet *[gedoonstet]* steamed
Gefahr danger
Gefährliche Einmündung danger: concealed exit
Gefährliche Kurve dangerous bend
Gefährliche Strömung dangerous current
Geflügel *[gefloogel]* poultry
Geflügelleber *[gefloogel-layber]* chicken liver
Geflügelleberragout *[gefloogel-layber-ragoo]* chicken liver ragout/stew
Gefüllt *[gefoolt]* stuffed
Gefüllte Kalbsbrust *[gefoolt-uh kalpsbroost]* veal roll
Gegart cooked
Gegenanzeige contra-indications
Gegenverkehr hat Vorfahrt oncoming traffic has right of way
Gekocht *[gekoчht]* boiled
Gekochter Schinken *[gekoчhter shinken]* boiled ham
Gelbe Seiten yellow pages
Geld einwerfen insert money
Geldeinwurf insert money
Geldrückgabe coins returned
Geldwechsel bureau de change
Gelee *[jellay]* jelly
Gemischter Salat *[gemishter zalaht]* mixed salad
Gemischtes Eis *[gemishtess ice]* assorted ice creams
Gemüse *[gemooz-uh]* vegetable(s)
Gemüseplatte *[gemooz-uh plat-uh]* assorted vegetables
Gemüsereis *[gemooz-uh-ryce]* rice with vegetables

Gemüsesalat *[gemooz-uh-zalaht]* vegetable salad
Gemüsesuppe *[gemooz-uh-zoop-uh]* vegetable soup
Geöffnet open
Geöffnet von ... bis ... open from ... to ...
Gepäckaufbewahrung left luggage, baggage checkroom
Gepäckausgabe baggage claim
Gepäckkontrolle baggage check
Gepökelt *[gepurkelt]* salted, pickled
Geradeaus straight on
Geräuchert *[geroyчhert]* smoked
Geräucherte Sprotten *[geroyчhert-uh shprotten]* smoked sprats
Gericht *[geriчht]* dish
Gesamtpreis total
Geschäftszeiten hours of business
Geschenkartikel gifts
Geschirr crockery, pots and pans
Geschlossen closed
Geschlossen von ... bis ... closed from ... to ...
Geschmort *[geshmort]* braised/stewed
Geschnetzeltes *[geshnetseltess]* strips of meat in thick sauce
Geschwindigkeitsbeschränkung beachten observe speed limit
Geselchtes *[gezelчhtess]* salted and smoked meat
Gesperrt für Fahrzeuge aller Art closed to all vehicular traffic
Gespickt mit ... *[geshpickt mit]* larded with ...
Getränke *[getrenk-uh]* beverages
Getränkeautomat drinks vending machine
Gewichtsverlust durch Erhitzen weight loss through heating
Gewünschte Rufnummer wählen dial number required
Gewürze *[gevoorts-uh]* spices
Gewürzgurken *[gevoortsgoorken]* gherkins
Giftig poisonous
Giroverkehr giro transactions
Glas und Porzellan glass and china
Glatteisgefahr black ice
Gleis platform, track
Glühwein *[gloo-vyne]* mulled wine
GmbH (Gesellschaft mit beschränkter Haftung) Ltd, Inc
Goldbarsch *[goltbarsh]* type of perch

Götterspeise *[gurtershpyz-uh]* type of jelly
Gratiniert *[gratineert]* au gratin, with breadcrumbs and cheese
Gratis free
Grenze border
Grenzkontrolle border checkpoint
Grenzübergang border crossing point
Grieß *[greess]* semolina
Grießklößchen *[greessklurschen]* semolina dumplings
Grießpudding *[greesspooding]* semolina pudding
Grießsuppe *[greess-zoop-uh]* semolina soup
Grillteller mixed grill
Groschen 10 pfennig piece

Großbritannien Great Britain
Größe size
Großpackung large size
Grüne Bohnen *[groon-uh bohnen]* French beans
Grüne Nudeln *[groon-uh noodeln]* green pasta, spinach pasta
Grüner Aal *[grooner ahl]* fresh eel
Grünkohl *[groonkohl]* (curly) kale
Gruppenreisen group excursions
Gulasch *[goolash]* goulash
Gulaschsuppe *[goolash-zoop-uh]* goulash soup
Günstige Preise low prices
Gurkensalat *[goorkenzalaht]* cucumber salad
Güterzug goods train, freight train

H

H (Haltestelle) (bus) stop
Hackfleisch *[hackflyshe]* mince, ground beef
Hacksteak mince meat, ground beef
Hafenanlagen docks
Hähnchen *[haynchen]* chicken
Hähnchenkeule *[haynchenkoyl-uh]* chicken leg
Haifischflossensuppe *[hyfish-flossenzoop-uh]* shark-fin soup
Halbes Hähnchen *[halbess haynchen]* half chicken
Halbpension half board, European plan
Hallenbad indoor swimming pool
Hals-Nasen-Ohren-Arzt ear, nose and throat specialist
Halt stop
Haltbar bis ... will keep until ...
Haltbarkeitsdatum best before date
Halte deine Stadt sauber keep your city clean
Haltestelle stop
Halteverbot no waiting
Hammelbraten *[hammelbrahten]* roast mutton
Hammelfleisch *[hammelflyshe]* mutton
Hammelkeule *[hammelkoyl-uh]* leg of mutton

Hammelrücken *[hammelrooken]* saddle of mutton
Handgepäck hand baggage
Handkäs (mit Musik) *[hantkayss (mit moozeek)]* very strong smelling cheese (with a sauce)
Handschuhe gloves
Hartkäse *[hartkayz-uh]* hard cheese
Haschee *[hashay]* hash
Hasenkeule *[hahzenkoyl-uh]* haunch of hare
Hasenpfeffer *[hahzenpfeffer]* jugged hare
Hat's geschmeckt? did you enjoy your meal?
Hauptbahnhof central station
Hauptpost main post office
Hauptprogramm main feature
Hauptspeisen *[howptshpyzen]* main courses
Hausfrauenart *[howssfrowenart]* home-made-style
Haushaltgeräte household equipment
Haushaltwaren household goods
Hausmacher (Art) *[howssmacher]* home-made style
Hausmeister caretaker, janitor
Hausnummer number (of building)

Hbf. (Hauptbahnhof) central station
Hechtsuppe [hecнtzoop-uh] pike soup
Heidelbeeren [hydelbairen] bilberries, blueberries
Heilbutt [hyle-boot] halibut
Heimwerker(bedarf) do-it-yourself
Heißlufttrockner hot-air hand-dryer
Hemden shirts
Hergestellt in ... made in ...
Heringssalat [hairings-zalaht] herring salad
Heringsstipp [hairings-shtip] herring salad
Heringstopf [hairingstopf] pickled herrings
Herren gents, men's rest room
Herren(be)kleidung menswear
Herrenmoden men's fashions
Herrenunterwäsche men's underwear
Hersteller manufacturer, produced by
Herz [hairts] heart
Herzlich willkommen welcome
Herzragout [hairtsragōō] heart ragout/ stew
Heute geschlossen closed today
Hier abreißen/abschneiden tear off/ cut off here
Hier einreißen tear off here
Hier oben this way up
Hier öffnen open here
Hier sprechen speak here
Himbeeren [himbairen] raspberries
Himmel und Erde [oont aird-uh] potato and apple purée with blood/liver sausage
Hinten einsteigen entrance at rear
Hirn [heern] brains
Hirschbraten [heershbrahten] roast venison

Hirschmedaillons [heershmedahyonss] small venison fillets
HNO (Hals-Nasen-Ohren) ear, nose and throat specialist
Hochspannung high voltage
Höchstgeschwindigkeit maximum speed
Honig [hohnicн] honey
Honigkuchen [hohnicн-kōōcнen] honeycake
Honigmelone [hohnicн-melohn-uh] honeydew melon
Hoppelpoppel bacon and potato omelet(te)
Hörer abnehmen lift receiver
Hörer einhängen replace receiver
Hosen trousers, pants
Hr. (Herr) Mr
Hüfte [hœft-uh] haunch
Hühnerbrühe [hœnerbrœ-uh] chicken broth
Hühnerfrikassee [hœnerfrikassay] chicken fricassee, chicken stew with vegetables in a thick sauce
Hühnersuppe [hœnerzoop-uh] chicken soup
Hülsenfrüchte [hœlzenfrœcнt-uh] peas and beans, pulses
Hummer [hoommer] lobster
Hunde bitte anleinen dogs must be kept on the leash
Hunde sind an der Leine zu führen dogs must be kept on the leash
Hundertmarkschein hundred mark note/bill
Hupen verboten sounding horn forbidden
Hüte hats

I

i.d.T. (in der Trockenmasse) dry measure
Imbiß snacks, snackbar
Imbißstube snackbar, fast food café
Immobilienmakler estate agent, realtor
Im Notfall Scheibe einschlagen smash glass in case of emergency

Im Preis reduziert price reduced
Industriegebiet industrial zone
Inh. (Inhaber) prop, owner
Inhalt contents
Inland domestic
Inlandsgespräch inland call
Installateur plumber

Interflug East German airline   **Irland** Ireland

J

Ja *[ya]* yes
Jägerschnitzel *[yaygershnitsel]* pork with mushrooms
Januar January
Jeder Ladendiebstahl wird zur Anzeige gebracht shoplifters will be prosecuted

JH (Jugendherberge) YH, youth hostel
Joghurt *[yohgōōrt]* yoghurt
Juli July
Jugendzentrum youth centre/center
Junge Mode fashions for the young
Juni June
Juwelier jewel(l)er

K

Kabeljau *[kahbelyow]* cod
Kabinett *[—et]* light, usually dry, quality German wine
Kaffee *[kaffay]* coffee
Kaiserschmarren *[kyzershmarren]* sugared pancake with raisins
Kakao *[kakow]* cocoa
Kalbfleisch *[kalpflyshe]* veal
Kalbsbraten *[kalpsbrahten]* roast veal
Kalbsbries *[kalpsbrees]* sweetbread
Kalbsfrikassee *[kalpsfrikassay]* veal fricassee, veal stew with vegetables in a thick sauce
Kalbshaxe *[kalps-hacks-uh]* leg of veal
Kalbsmedaillons *[kalpsmedahyonss]* small veal fillets
Kalbsnierenbraten *[kalpsneeren-brahten]* roast veal with kidney
Kalbsschnitzel *[kalps-shnitsel]* veal cutlet
Kalt cold
Kalte Gerichte cold dishes
Kalte Getränke cold drinks
Kalte Platte *[kalt-uh plat-uh]* salad
Kalter Braten *[brahten]* cold meat
Kaltes Büfett *[bœffay]* cold buffet
Kaltschale *[kaltshahl-uh]* cold sweet soup
Kalt servieren serve cold

Kaninchen *[kaneenchen]* rabbit
Kaninchenbraten *[kaneenchenbrah-ten]* roast rabbit
Kännchen *[kenchen]* pot (of tea, coffee)
Kapern *[kahpern]* capers
Karamelpudding *[karamayl—]* caramel pudding
Karbonade *[karbonahd-uh]* cutlet
Karneval carnival
Karotten carrots
Karpfen carp
Karpfen blau *[blow]* carp au bleu, boiled carp
Kartoffelbrei *[kartoffel-bry]* potato purée
Kartoffelklöße *[kartoffelklurss-uh]* potato dumplings
Kartoffelknödel *[kartoffelk-nurdel]* potato dumplings
Kartoffeln potatoes
Kartoffelpuffer *[kartoffel-poofer]* potato fritters
Kartoffelpüree *[kartoffel-pœray]* potato purée
Kartoffelsalat *[kartoffel-zalaht]* potato salad
Kartoffelsuppe *[kartoffel-zoop-uh]* potato soup
Käse *[kayz-uh]* cheese

Käsegebäck *[kayz-uh-gebeck]* cheese savo(u)ries

Käsekuchen *[kayz-uh-kōōcHen]* cheesecake

Käseplatte *[kayz-uh-plat-uh]* selection of cheeses

Käse-Sahne-Torte *[kayz-uh-zahn-uh-tort-uh]* cream cheesecake

Käsesalat *[kayz-uh-zalaht]* cheese salad

Käsesoße *[kayz-uh-zohss-uh]* cheese sauce

Käsespätzle *[kayz-uh-shpetz-luh]* homemade noodles with cheese

Kasse cashdesk, cash point, box office

Kasseler Rippenspeer *[rippenshpair]* salted rib of pork

Kasserolle *[kasserol-uh]* casserole

Kassetten cassettes

Kassler smoked and braised pork chop

Kastanien *[kastahnee-en]* chestnuts

Katenleberwurst *[kahtenlayber-voorst]* smoked liver sausage

Katenrauchwurst *[kahtenrowcH-voorst]* smoked sausage

Kath. (katholisch) Catholic

Kaufhaus department store

Kaviar *[kahvee-ar]* caviar

Keine heiße Asche einfüllen do not put glowing ashes in

Kein Einstieg no entrance

Keine Selbstbedienung no self-service

Kein Trinkwasser not drinking water

Kein Verkauf an Jugendliche unter ... Jahren sales forbidden to minors under the age of ...

Kein Zutritt no entrance

Kein Zutritt für Jugendliche unter ... Jahren no admission to minors under the age of ...

Keller basement

Keramik china

Keule *[koyl-uh]* leg, *(of game)* haunch

Kieler Sprotten *[keeler shprotten]* smoked sprats

Kinder children

Kinderkleidung children's clothing

Kindermoden children's fashions

Kinderspielplatz children's playground

Kindervorstellung children's performance

Kinderwagen prams, baby carriages

Kino cinema, movie theater

Kirche church

Kirschen *[keershen]* cherries

Klare Brühe *[klahr-uh brōō-uh]* clear soup

Klasse class

Klimaanlage air-conditioning

Klimatisiert air-conditioned

Klingeln ring

Klößchensuppe *[klursscHen-zoop-uh]* clear soup with dumplings

Klöße *[klurss-uh]* dumplings

Kloster convent, monastery

Knäckebrot *[k-neck-uh-broht]* crispbread

Knacker *[k-nacker]* frankfurter(s)

Knackwurst *[k-nackvoorst]* frankfurter

Kneipe pub, bar

Knoblauch *[k-nohblowcH]* garlic

Knoblauchbrot *[k-nohblowcHbroht]* garlic bread

Knochen *[k-nocHen]* bone

Knochenschinken *[k-nocHenshinken]* ham on the bone

Knödel *[k-nurdel]* dumpling

Koffer luggage

Kognak *[konyak]* brandy

Kohl cabbage

Kohlrabi *[kohlrahbee]* kohlrabi, type of vegetable similar to a turnip

Kohlrouladen *[kohlrōōlahden]* stuffed cabbage leaves

Kohl und Pinkel cabbage, potatoes, sausage and smoked meat

Kokosnuß coconut

Köln Cologne

Kompott stewed fruit

Konditorei cake shop/store

Konfitüre *[konfitoor-uh]* jam

Königinpastete *[kurnigin-pastayt-uh]* chicken vol-au-vent/puff pastry

Königsberger Klopse *[kurnigsbairger klops-uh]* meatballs in caper sauce

Königskuchen *[kurnigskōōcHen]* type of fruitcake

Konservierungsstoffe preservatives

Konsulat consulate

Kontaktlinsen contact lenses

Konto account

Kopfsalat *[kopfzalaht]* lettuce

Kosmetik cosmetics

Kostüme ladies' suits

Kotelett *[kotlet]* chop

Krabben shrimps/prawns

Krabbencocktail prawn cocktail

Kraftbrühe *[kraftbrœ-uh]* beef tea
Krankenhaus hospital
Krankenwagen ambulance
Krapfen doughnut
Kräuter *[kroyter]* herbs
Kräuterbutter *[kroyterbootter]* herb butter
Kräuterkäse *[kroyterkayz-uh]* cheese flavo(u)red with herbs
Kräuterquark *[kroyterkvark]* curd cheese with herbs
Kräutersoße *[kroyterzohss-uh]* herb sauce
Kräutertee *[kroytertay]* herbal tea
Krautsalat *[krowtzalaht]* coleslaw
Krautwickel *[krowtvickel]* stuffed cabbage leaves
Krawatten ties, neckties

Krebs *[krayps]* crayfish
Kreditabteilung accounts department
Kredite loans
Kresse *[kress-uh]* cress
Kriechspur crawler lane
Kroketten croquettes
Kruste *[kroost-uh]* crust
Küche kitchen, cuisine
Kuchen *[kōōchen]* cake
Küchenbedarf for the kitchen
Kühl lagern keep in a cool place
Kümmel *[kœmel]* caraway
Kundendienst customer service
Kunsthalle art gallery
Kürbis *[kœrbiss]* pumpkin
Kurort spa
Kurzstrecke short journey
Kurzwaren haberdashery, notions

L

l (Liter) litre, liter
Labskaus *[lapskowss]* meat, fish and potato stew
Lachs *[lacks]* salmon
Lachsersatz *[lacks-airzats]* sliced and salted pollack (*fish*)
Lachsforelle *[lacks-forell-uh]* sea trout
Lachsschinken *[lacks-shinken]* smoked rolled fillet of ham
Lamm lamb
Lammrücken *[—rœken]* saddle of lamb
Lampen lamps
Landstraße main road, trunk road
Länge length
Langsam fahren drive slowly
Lauchsuppe *[lowchzoop-uh]* leek soup
Lebensgefahr danger
Lebensmittel foodstuffs
Leber *[layber]* liver
Leberkäse *[layber-kayz-uh]* baked pork and beef loaf
Leberklöße *[layberklurss-uh]* liver dumplings
Leberknödel *[layber-k-nurdel]* liver dumplings
Leberpastete *[layber-pastayt-uh]* liver pâté

Leberwurst *[layber-voorst]* liver sausage
Lebkuchen *[layp-kōōchen]* type of gingerbread
Lederwaren leather goods
Leicht verderblich will not keep, perishable
Leihgebühr rental
Leipziger Allerlei *[lyptsiger al-er-ly]* mixed vegetables
Licht einschalten turn on lights
Lichtspiele cinema, movie theater
Likör *[likur]* liqueur
Limonade *[limonahd-uh]* lemonade
Linie line
Linienflug scheduled flight
Linksabbieger left filter
Links halten keep left
Linseneintopf *[linzen-ine-topf]* lentil stew
Linsensuppe *[linzenzoop-uh]* lentil soup
Lkw lorry, truck
Luftdicht verpackt airtight pack
Luftdruck tyre/tire pressure, air pressure
Lufthansa West German airline
Luftkissenboot hovercraft
Luftkurort health resort
Luftpostsendungen airmail

M

Mager [mahger] lean

Mai May

Majoran [mahyo-rahn] marjoram

Makrele [makrayl-uh] mackerel

Makronen [makrohnen] macaroons

Mandeln almonds

Männer men

Man spricht Englisch English spoken

Mäntel coats

Marinade [marinahd-uh] marinade

Mariniert [marineert] marinated, pickled

Markklößchen [mark-klursснen] marrowbone dumplings

Markstück mark coin

Marmelade [marmelahd-uh] jam

Marmorkuchen [marmor-kооснen] marble cake

Maronen [marohnen] sweet chestnuts

März March

Matjes(hering) [matyess(-hairing)] young herring

Maximale Belastbarkeit maximum load

Medaillons [medahyonss] small fillets

Meeresfische [mairess-fish-uh] seafish

Meeresfrüchte [mairess-frooснt-uh] seafood

Meerrettich [mairettiсн] horseradish

Meerettichsauce [mairettiсн-zohss-uh] horseradish sauce

Mehlspeise [maylshpyze-uh] sweet dish, flummery

Mehrwertsteuer valued added tax

Melone [melohn-uh] melon

Metzger butcher

Miesmuscheln [meess-moosheln] mussels

Mietkauf lease purchase

Mietwagen car hire/rental

Milch [milсн] milk

Milchmixgetränk [milснmix-getrenk] milk shake

Milchreis [milснryce] rice pudding

Militärisches Sperrgebiet keep off: military zone

Min. (Minute) minute

Mindestens haltbar bis ... will keep at least until ...

Mineralölsteuer oil tax

Mineralwasser [minerahl-vasser] (sparkling) mineral water

Mißbrauch strafbar penalty for improper use

Mist! bugger!

Mit with

Mitbringen von Hunden ist nicht gestattet no dogs allowed

Mit Blick auf ... overlooking ...

Mitfahrzentrale agency for arranging lifts

Mittagessen lunch

Mittags geschlossen closed at lunchtime

Mittagstisch lunch menu, lunches served

Mitteilungen messages

Mittwoch Wednesday

Mit Untertiteln with subtitles

Möbel furniture

Möbliert furnished

Modeartikel fashions

Mohnkuchen [mohnkооснen] poppyseed cake

Möhren [mur-ren] carrots

Mohrenkopf [mohren—] profiterole

Mohrrüben [mohrrооben] carrots

Monatskarte monthly season ticket

Monatsraten monthly instal(l)ments

Montag Monday

Most fruit wine

Motor abstellen switch off engine

Müll abladen verboten no tipping (rubbish)

München Munich

Münzeinwurf insert coin here

Münzen coins

Münzrückgabe returned coins

Münztank coin-operated pump

Mus [mооss] puree

Muscheln [moosheln] mussels

Musikinstrumente musical instruments

Muskat(nuß)   *[mooskaht(-nooss)]*   nutmeg

MWSt. (Mehrwertsteuer) VAT, value added tax

N

Nach Art des Hauses *[nach art dess howzess]* home-made

Nach den Mahlzeiten after meals

Nach Hausfrauenart *[nach howssfrowenart]* home-made

Nachmittags geschlossen closed in the afternoons

Nach Öffnung nur beschränkt haltbar will keep for a limited period only after opening

Nachspeisen *[nachshpyzen]* desserts

Nächste Leerung next collection

Nächste Vorstellung um ... next performance at ...

Nachtclub night club

Nachtisch *[nachtish]* dessert

Nachtportier night porter

Nachtruhe von ... bis ... lights out from ... to ..., please make no noise between the hours of ... and ...

Nahverkehrszug local train

Napfkuchen *[napf-koochen]* ring-shaped fruitcake

Natürlich *[natoorlich]* natural

Naturprodukt natural produce

Nebel fog

Nein *[nyne]* no

Nettogewicht net weight

Nettoinhalt net contents

Netzkarte ticket for travel on entire network

Neuer Wein new wine

Nicht berühren do not touch

Nicht betriebsbereit not ready

Nicht bügeln do not iron

Nicht hinauslehnen do not lean out

Nicht hupen sounding horn forbidden

Nicht in der Maschine waschen do not machine wash

Nichtraucher non-smoking

Nicht schleudern do not spin-dry

Nicht stürzen fragile

Nicht zur innerlichen Anwendung for external use only

Nierenragout *[neerenragoo]* kidney ragout/stew

Norden north

Nordfriesische Inseln North Frisian Islands

Nördliche Stadtteile city north

Nordsee North Sea

Normal 2-star, regular

Notarzt emergency doctor

Notausgang emergency exit

Notausstieg emergency exit

Notbremse emergency brake

Notruf emergency services, 999

Notrufsäule emergency telephone

Nr. (Nummer) No., number

Nüchtern einzunehmen to be taken on an empty stomach

Nudeln *[noodeln]* pasta

Nudelsalat *[noodel-zalaht]* noodle salad

Nudelsuppe *[noodelzoop-uh]* noodle soup

Nur begrenzt haltbar will keep for a limited period only

Nur für Anlieger access for residents only

Nur für Bedienstete staff only

Nur für Erwachsene adults only

Nur im Notfall benutzen emergency use only

Nur mit der Hand waschen hand wash only

Nur zur äußerlichen Anwendung for external use only

Nüsse *[nooss-uh]* nuts

O

ÖBB (Österreichische Bundesbahn) Austrian Federal Railways/Railroad
Oben top
Obergeschoß top floor
Oberweite bust measurement/chest measurement
Obstsalat *[ohpst-zalaht]* fruit salad
Obst und Gemüse fruit and vegetables
Ochsenschwanzsuppe *[oksenshwants-zoop-uh]* oxtail soup
Öffnungszeiten opening hours
Ohne without
Ohne Knochen *[ohn-uh k-nocHen]* filleted
Oktoberfest Munich beer festival starting in September
Öl oil
Oliven *[oleeven]* olives

Olivenöl *[oleevenurl]* olive oil
Ölstand oil level
Ölwechsel sofort oil change done on the spot
Omelett omelet(te)
Optiker optician
Orangen *[oranjen]* oranges
Orangensaft *[oranjenzaft]* orange juice
Originalrezept original recipe
Ortsgespräch local call
Ortszeit local time
Osten east
Ostern Easter
Österreich Austria
Ostfriesische Inseln East Frisian Islands
Östliche Stadtteile city east
Ostsee Baltic

P

P (Parkplatz) car park, parking lot
Päckchen small parcels
Packung packet, packaging
Paketannahme parcels counter
Pakete parcels, packets
Palatschinken *[pallatshinken]* stuffed pancakes
Pampelmuse *[—mōōz-uh]* grapefruit
Paniert *[panneert]* with breadcrumbs
Pannenhilfe breakdown services, emergency road services
Papierhandtücher paper towels
Paprika peppers
Paprikasalat *[—zalaht]* pepper salad
Paprikaschoten *[—shohten]* peppers
Paradeiser *[paradyzer]* tomatoes
Par avion airmail
Parfümerie perfumes
Parkbucht parking space

Parkdauer parking allowed for ...
Parken nur mit Parkscheibe parking disks only
Parkett stalls
Parkhaus multi-storey car park, multi-level parking garage
Parkplatz car park, parking lot
Parkverbot no parking
Parmesankäse *[—kayz-uh]* Parmesan cheese
Paßbilder passport photographs
Paßkontrolle passport control
Pastete *[pastayt-uh]* vol-au-vent, puff-pastry
Pause interval, intermission
Pellkartoffeln potatoes boiled in their jackets
Pelze furs
Personaleingang staff entrance

Personenzug passenger train
Petersilie [*payterzeelee-uh*] parsley
Petersilienkartoffeln [*payter-
zeelee-en—*] potatoes with parsley
Pf. (Pfennig) pfennig, German unit of
currency, 100 pf=DM 1
Pfandkredit, Pfandleihe pawnbroker
Pfannkuchen [*pfankōōcHen*] pancakes
Pfd. (Pfund) lb, German pound=500g
Pfeffer pepper
Pferderennbahn race course
Pfifferlinge [*pfifferling-uh*] chanterelles,
long thin mushrooms
Pfingsten Whitsun, Pentecost
Pfirsiche [*pfeerzicH-uh*] peaches
Pflaumen [*pflowmen*] plums
Pflaumenkuchen [*pflowmenkōōcHen*]
plum tart
Pfund pound
Phonoartikel hi-fi equipment
Pichelsteiner Topf [*picHelshtyner topf*]
vegetable stew with diced beef
Pikant [*peekant*] spicy
Pikkolo quarter bottle of champagne
Pilze [*pilts-uh*] mushrooms
Pilzsoße [*pilts-zohss-uh*] mushroom
sauce
Pkw private car
Plakate ankleben verboten stick no bills
Plattenspieler record players
Platzkarte seat reservation
PLZ (Postleitzahl) post code, zip code
Pochiert [*posheert*] poached
Pökelfleisch [*purkelflyshe*] salt meat
Polizei police
Polizeipräsidium police headquarters
Polizeiwache police station
Pommes frites [*pomfrit*] French fried
potatoes
Porree [*porray*] leek

Porto postage
Porzellan porcelain
Postamt post office
Postkarte postcard
Postlagernde Sendungen poste-
restante, general delivery
Postleitzahl area code, zip code
Postsparkasse postal savings bank
Postwertzeichen postage stamp
Postwertzeichen in kl. Mengen
postage stamps in small quantities
Potthast [*pot-hast*] braised beef with
sauce
Poularde [*pōōlard-uh*] young chicken
P+R park and ride
Praktischer Arzt doctor, GP
Preise prices, tariff
Preiselbeeren [*pryzel-bairen*] cran-
berries
Preisgünstig inexpensive
Preishit star buy
Preissenkung reductions
Preiswert excellent value
Preßkopf [*presskopf*] brawn
Prinzeßbohnen [*printsess-bohnen*] un-
sliced runner beans
Privateigentum private property
Privatgrundstück private ground
Privatparkplatz private carpark/parking
lot
Privatweg private way
Programmkino arts cinema/movie
theater
Pumpernickel [*poompernickel*] black
rye bread
Püree [*pœrray*] (potato) purée
Püriert [*pœreert*] puréed
Putenschenkel [*pōōtenshenkel*] turkey
leg
Puter [*pōōter*] turkey

Q

Qualitätsware quality goods
Qualitätswein b.A. quality wine from a
special wine-growing area
Qualitätswein m.P. (mit Prädikat)
quality German wine

Quark [*kvark*] curd cheese
Quarkkuchen [*kvark-kōōcHen*] cheesecake
Quarkspeise [*kvarkshpyze-uh*] curd
cheese dish
Quittung receipt

R

Radieschen [radeesscнen] radishes
Radio und Fernsehen radio and television
Radweg kreuzt cycle path crosses road
Rahm (sour) cream
Rang row, stalls
Raststätte service area
Ratenzahlung hire purchase, installment plan
Ratenzahlung möglich credit terms
Rathaus town hall
Rattengift rat poison
Rauchen einstellen refrain from smoking
Rauchen und offenes Feuer verboten no smoking or naked lights
Rauchen verboten no smoking
Raucher smoking
Räucheraal [roycнer-ahl] smoked eel
Räucherhering [roycнer-hairing] kipper, smoked herring
Räucherspeck [roycнershpeck] smoked bacon
Rauchfleisch [rowcнflyshe] smoked meat
Räumungsverkauf closing down sale
Rechnung bill
Rechtsabbieger right filter
Rechts halten keep right
Reformhaus health food shop/store
Regenmäntel raincoats
Regenschirme umbrellas
Rehbraten [ray-brahten] roast venison
Rehkeule [ray-koyl-uh] haunch of venison
Rehrücken [rayrœken] saddle of venison
Reibekuchen [rybe-uh-kōōcнen] potato waffles
Reifendruck tyre/tire pressure
Reihe row
Reine Seide pure silk
Reine Wolle/Schurwolle pure wool
Reis [ryce] rice
Reisauflauf [ryce-owfflowff] rice pudding

Reisbrei [ryce-bry] creamed rice
Reiseandenken souvenirs
Reiseapotheke first aid kit
Reiseauskunft travel information
Reisebedarf travel requisites
Reisebüro travel agency
Reisende passengers
Reiseproviant food for the journey
Reisescheck traveller's cheque, traveler's check
Reisrand [ryce-rant] rice
Reissalat [ryce-zalaht] rice salad
Reissuppe [ryce-zoop-uh] rice soup
Reklamationen complaints
Remoulade [remōōlahd-uh] remoulade, mayonnaise with herbs, mustard and capers
Renke [renk-uh] whitefish
Rennbahn race track
Reparaturen repairs
Reservetank reserve tank
Reserviert reserved
Rettich [retticн] radish
Rettungsdienst emergency/rescue services
Rezeptpflichtig prescription required
Rhabarber [rabbarber] rhubarb
Rhein Rhine
Rheinfahrt boat trip on the Rhine
Rheinischer Sauerbraten [rynischer zowerbrahten] braised beef
Richtung direction
Rinderbraten [rinder-brahten] pot roast
Rinderfilet [rinderfillay] fillet steak
Rinderlende [—lend-uh] beef tenderloin
Rinderrouladen [—roolahden] stuffed beef rolls
Rinderschmorbraten [—shmohr-brahten] pot roast
Rinderzunge [—tsoong-uh] ox tongue
Rindfleisch [rintflyshe] beef
Rindfleischsuppe [rintflyshe-zoop-uh] beef broth
Rippchen [ripcнen] spare-rib
Risi-Pisi [rizi-pizi] rice and peas

Risotto risotto
Roh raw
Rohkostplatte *[roh-kost-plat-uh]* selection of salads
Rollmops rolled-up pickled herring, rollmops
Rollsplit loose chippings
Rolltreppe escalator
Rosa *[rohza]* rare to medium
Rosenkohl *[rohzenkohl]* Brussels sprouts
Roséwein rosé
Rosinen *[rohzeenen]* raisins
Rostbraten *[rostbrahten]* roast
Rostbratwurst *[rostbraht-voorst]* barbecued sausage
Rösti *[rurshtee]* fried potatoes and onions
Röstkartoffeln *[rurst-kartoffeln]* fried potatoes
Rotbarsch *[rohtbarsh]* type of perch
Rote Bete *[roht-uh bayt-uh]* beetroot,
red beet
Rote Grütze *[roht-uh grœts-uh]* red fruit jelly
Rotkohl *[rohtkohl]* red cabbage
Rotkraut *[rohtkrowt]* red cabbage
Rotwein *[rohtvyne]* red wine
Rückfahrkarte return/round trip ticket
Ruf call
Ruf doch mal an make that call
Rufnummer telephone number
Ruhe quiet
Ruhestörender Lärm verboten disturbance of the peace will be prosecuted
Ruhetag closed all day
Ruhige Lage peaceful, secluded spot
Rühreier *[rœr-'eye'-er]* scrambled eggs
Rührei mit Speck *[rœr-'eye' mit shpeck]* scrambled egg with bacon
Ruhrgebiet the Ruhr (industrial area)
Rundfahrt tour
Russische Eier *[roossish-uh 'eye'-er]* egg mayonnaise

S

Sachertorte *[zaCHer-tort-uh]* layered chocolate cake
Sackgasse cul-de-sac, dead end
Sahne *[zahn-uh]* cream
Sahnesoße *[zahn-uh-zohss-uh]* cream sauce
Sahnetorte *[zahn-uh-tort-uh]* cream gateau
Salate *[zalaht-uh]* salads
Salatplatte *[zalaht-plat-uh]* selection of salads
Salatsoße *[zalaht-zohss-uh]* salad dressing
Salbe ointment
Salz *[zalts]* salt
Salzburger Nockerln *[zaltsbōōrger —]* type of meringue
Salzheringe *[zalts-hairing-uh]* salted herrings
Salzkartoffeln *[zalts—]* boiled potatoes
Salzkruste *[zalts-krœst-uh]* salty crusted skin
Sammelkarte strip or book of tickets
(*cheaper than individual tickets*)
Samstag Saturday
Sandkuchen *[zantkōōcHen]* type of Madeira cake
Sauer *[zower]* sour
Sauerbraten *[zowerbrahten]* marinated potroast
Sauerkraut *[zowerkrowt]* white cabbage, finely chopped and pickled
Sauerrahm *[zower-rahm]* sour cream
S-Bahn local urban railway
SBB (Schweizerische Bundesbahn) Swiss Federal Railways/Railroad
SB-Tankstelle self-service petrol/gas station
Schallplatten records
Schals scarves
Schalter counter
Schaschlik *[shashlik]* (shish-)kebab
Schattenmorellen *[shatten-morellen]* morello cherries
Schein note, bill
Scheiße! *[shyssuh]* shit!

Schellfisch *[shellfish]* haddock

Schildkrötensuppe *[shiltkrurten-zoop-uh]* real turtle soup

Schillerlocken *[shillerlocken]* rolls of smoked haddock

Schimmelkäse *[shimmel-kayz-uh]* blue cheese

Schinken *[shinken]* ham

Schinkenröllchen *[shinken-rurlcHen]* rolled ham

Schinkenwurst *[shinkenvoorst]* ham sausage

Schirme umbrellas

Schlachtplatte *[shlacHtplat-uh]* selection of fresh sausages

Schlafanzüge pyjamas, pajamas

Schlafsaal dormitory

Schlafsack sleeping bag

Schlaftabletten sleeping pills

Schlafwagen sleeper, sleeping car

Schlafzimmerbedarf for the bedroom

Schlagsahne *[shlahk-zahn-uh]* whipped cream

Schlechte Fahrbahn road surface in poor condition

Schlei *[shly]* tench

Schleudergefahr danger of skidding

Schleuderpreise prices slashed

Schließfächer baggage lockers

Schloß castle

Schmorbraten *[shmohrbrahten]* pot roast

Schmuck jewel(le)ry

Schnecken *[shnecken]* snails

Schneiderei tailor

Schnellimbiß snackbar

Schnellzug express train

Schnittchen *[shnitcHen]* (open) sandwich

Schnittlauch *[shnit-lowcH]* chives

Schnitzel *[shnitsel]* cutlet

Schokolade *[shokolahd-uh]* chocolate

Scholle *[sholl-uh]* plaice

Schönheitspflege beauty care

Schönheitssalon beauty salon

Schottland Scotland

Schreibwaren stationery

Schritt fahren dead slow

Schuhe shoes

Schuhmacher shoemaker

Schulbedarf school items

Schule school

Schüler und Studenten school children and students

Schulterstück *[shoolter-shtook]* piece of shoulder

Schutt abladen verboten no tipping (rubbish)

Schützenfest local carnival

Schwarzbrot *[shvartsbroht]* brown rye bread

Schwarzwälder Kirschtorte *[shvarts-velder keershtort-uh]* Black Forest cherry gateau

Schwarzwurzeln *[shvarts-voortseln]* salsifies, oyster plants (*vegetable*)

Schweinebauch *[shvyne-uh-bowcH]* belly of pork

Schweinebraten *[shvyne-uh-brahten]* roast pork

Schweinefilet *[shvyne-uh-fillay]* fillet of pork

Schweinefleisch *[shvyne-uh-flyshe]* pork

Schweinekotelett *[shvyne-uh-kotlet]* pork chop

Schweineleber *[shvyne-uh-layber]* pig's liver

Schweinerippe *[shvyne-uh-ripp-uh]* cured pork chop

Schweinerollbraten *[shvyne-uh-rolbrahten]* rolled roast of pork

Schweineschnitzel *[shvyne-uh-shnitsel]* pork fillet

Schweinshaxe *[shvynss-hacks-uh]* knuckle of pork

Schweiz Switzerland

Schwimmbad swimming pool

Schwimmen verboten no swimming

Seelachs *[zaylacks]* pollack (*fish*)

Seezunge *[zay-tsoong-uh]* sole

Seife soap

Seitenstreifen nicht befahrbar soft verges, keep off

Sekt *[zekt]* sparkling wine, champagne

Selbstbedienung self-service

Selbst tanken self-service

Sellerie *[zelleree]* celery

Selleriesalat *[zelleree-zalaht]* celery salad

Semmel *[zemmel]* bread roll

Semmelknödel *[zemmelknurdel]* bread dumplings

Senf *[zenf]* mustard

Senfsahnesoße *[zenf-zahn-uh-zohss-uh]* mustard and cream sauce

Senfsoße *[zenf-zohss-uh]* mustard sauce

Serbisches Reisfleisch *[zairbishess ryce-flyshe]* diced pork, onions, tomatoes and rice

Sessellift chair-lift

Siehe ... see ...

Sitz für Schwerbehinderte seat for handicapped

Sitzplätze seats

Soleier *[zohl-'eye'-er]* pickled eggs

Sommerfahrplan summer timetable/ schedule

Sommerschlußverkauf summer clearance sale

Sonderangebot special offer

Sonderflug special flight

Sonderpreis special price

Sondervorstellung special performance

Sonnabend Saturday

Sonnenbrillen sunglasses

Sonntag Sunday

Sonntagsfahrer! *[zontahksfahrer]* learn to drive!

Sonn- und Feiertage Sundays and holidays

Soße *[zohss-uh]* sauce, gravy

Soufflé soufflé

Spanferkel *[shpahnfairkel]* sucking pig

Spareinlagen savings deposits

Spargel *[shpargel]* asparagus

Spargelcremesuppe *[shpargelkraymzoop-uh]* cream of asparagus soup

Sparguthaben savings account

Sparkasse savings bank

Spätvorstellung late performance

Spätzle *[shpets-luh]* home-made noodles

Speck *[shpeck]* bacon

Speckknödel *[shpeck-knurdel]* bacon dumplings

Specksoße *[shpeckzohss-uh]* bacon sauce

Speisekarte *[shpyze-uh-kart-uh]* menu

Speiseraum dining room

Speisewagen dining car

Sperrgebiet prohibited area

Spezialität des Hauses *[shpetsee-alitayt dess howzess]* speciality

Spiegeleier *[shpeegel-'eye'-er]* fried eggs

Spielende Kinder children at play

Spielkasino casino

Spielplatz playground

Spielwaren toys

Spießbraten *[shpeess-brahten]* joint roasted on a spit

Spinat *[shpinaht]* spinach

Spirituosen spirits

Spitzenqualität top quality

Spitzkohl *[shpitskohl]* white cabbage

Sportartikel sports goods

Sprechstunde surgery hours, consulting hours

Sprotten *[shprotten]* sprats

Sprudel(wasser) *[shproodel(-vasser)]* mineral water

Stachelbeeren *[shtacHel-bairen]* gooseberries

Stadion stadium

Stadtautobahn urban clearway

Stadthalle city hall

Stadtzentrum city centre/center

Standesamt registry office, births, marriages, deaths

Standlicht side lights, parking lights

Stangen(weiß)brot *[shtangen-(vyce)-broht]* French bread

Starkes Gefälle steep gradient

Std. (Stunde) hr, hour

Stehplätze standing room

Steinpilze *[shtyne-pilts-uh]* type of mushroom

Steinschlaggefahr danger of falling rocks

Stereoartikel stereo equipment

Stock floor

Stoffe materials, fabrics

Stollen *[shtollen]* type of fruit loaf

Störungsstelle fault repair service

Str. (Straße) street

Strammer Max *[shtrammer—]* ham and fried egg on bread

Straße street

Straßenarbeiten roadwork(s)

Straßenbahn tram, streetcar

Straßenbauarbeiten roadwork(s)

Straßenkilometer kilometres/kilometers by road

Strengstens untersagt strictly prohibited

Streuselkuchen *[shtroyzel-koocHen]* sponge cake with crumble topping

Strickwaren knitwear

Strumpfhosen stockings

Stündlich hourly

Süden south

Südliche Stadtteile city south

Sülze *[zoolts-uh]* brawn

Super 4-star, premium
Supermarkt supermarket
Suppen [*zoopen*] soups
Suppengrün [*zoopengrœn*] mixed herbs and vegetables (in soup)
Süß [*zœss*] sweet
Süßigkeiten sweets, candies
Süß-sauer [*zœss-zower*] sweet-and-sour

Süßspeisen [*zœss-shpyzen*] sweet dishes
Süßstoff sweetener, saccharin
Süßwaren confectionery
Süßwasserfische [*zœss-vasser-fish-uh*] freshwater fish
Synthetik synthetic
Szegediner Gulasch [*segedeener gōōlash*] goulash with pickled cabbage

T

Tabakwaren tobacco
Tabletten pills, tablets
Tafelwasser [*tahfel-vasser*] (still) mineral water
Tafelwein [*tahfel-vyne*] table wine
Tagesgericht [*tahgess-gericht*] dish of the day
Tageskarte [*tahgess-kart-uh*] menu of the day; day ticket
Tagessuppe [*tahgess-zoop-uh*] soup of the day
Täglich daily
Taillenweite waist measurement
Talfahrt down
Talsperre dam
Tankstelle petrol/gas station
Tanzcafé café with dancing
Tapeten wallpaper
Tatar steak tartare
Taube [*towb-uh*] pigeon
Tausend thousand
Taxistand taxi rank, taxi stand
Tee [*tay*] tea
Teigmantel [*tyke-mantel*] pastry covering
Teilzahlung möglich credit available
Telefonbuch telephone directory
Teppiche carpets

Theaterkasse box office
Thunfisch [*tōōnfish*] tuna
Tiefkühlkost frozen food
Tiefpreise rock bottom prices
Tierarzt veterinary surgeon
Tiere animals
Tierpark zoo
Tintenfisch [*tintenfish*] squid
Toiletten toilets, rest rooms
Toilettenartikel toiletries
Tollwutgefahr danger of rabies
Tomaten [*tomahten*] tomatoes
Tomatensalat [*tomahten-zalaht*] tomato salad
Tomatensuppe [*tomahten-zoop-uh*] tomato soup
Tonbandgeräte tape recorders
Topfpflanzen pot plants
Törtchen [*turtchen*] tart(s)
Torte [*tort-uh*] gateau
Treibstoff fuel
Trimm-dich-Pfad keep-fit track
Trinkhalle refreshment kiosk
Trocken dry
Tropfen drops
Tür schließen close door
TÜV (Technischer Überwachungs-Verein) MOT

U

U-Bahn underground, subway

station

Überbacken *[œberbacken]* au gratin, with breadcrumbs and cheese

Überfall attack

Übergewicht excess baggage

Überholverbot no overtaking/passing

Übernachtung mit Frühstück bed and breakfast

Überweisung transfer

Uhr o'clock

Uhren clocks

Uhrmacher watchmaker

Umgehungsstraße by-pass

Umkleidekabine changing room, dressing room

Umleitung detour, diversion

Umsteigen change

Umtausch nur gegen Quittung goods may not be exchanged without a receipt

Umweltfreundlich not harmful to the environment

Unfall accident

Unfallaufnahme casualty, accident ward

Unfallgefahr accident black spot

Ungarischer Gulasch *[oongahrisher gōōlash]* Hungarian goulash

Ungebraten *[oongebrahten]* unfried

Unmöbliert unfurnished

Unten down, bottom

Unterbodenwäsche underbody cleaning (for cars)

Unterführung underpass

Untergeschoß basement

Unterkunft accommodation(s)

Untersagt prohibited

Unterwäsche underwear

Unverkäufliches Muster not for sale, sample only

usw. (und so weiter) etc

V

Vakuumverpackt vacuum-packed

Vanille *[vaneel-uh]* vanilla

Vanillesoße *[vaneel-uh-zohss-uh]* vanilla sauce

Verboten forbidden

Verdammt (noch mal)! *[fairdamt (noch mahl)]* damn, bloody hell!

Vereinigte Staaten United States

Verengte Fahrbahn road narrows

Verengte Fahrstreifen road narrows

Verfallsdatum best before date

Vergriffen out of stock

Verkauf we sell ...

Verkauf nur gegen bar cash sales only

Verkaufsoffener Samstag shopping on Saturday afternoons

Verkehrt alle ... Minuten runs every ... minutes

Verlorene Eier *[fairlohren-uh 'eye'-er]* poached eggs

Vermittlung operator

Versicherung insurance

Verspätung delay

Verzeihung *[fairtsye-oong]* I'm sorry, excuse me

Verzogen nach ... moved to ...

Verzögerung delay

Vielen Dank *[feelen]* thanks a lot

Vielleicht *[feelycht]* maybe

Viertele *[feertel-uh]* large glass of wine

Voll belegt full, no vacancies

Vollklimatisiert fully air-conditioned

Vollkornbrot *[follkorn-broht]* dark rye bread

Vollpension full board, American plan

Vom Grill *[fom grill]* grilled

Vom Kalb *[fom kalp]* veal

Vom Rind *[fom rint]* beef

Vom Rost *[fom rost]* grilled

Vom Schwein *[fom shvyne]* pork

Vom Umtausch ausgeschlossen cannot be exchanged

Vorausbuchung unbedingt erforderlich reserved seats only

Vor dem Schlafengehen before retiring, before going to bed

Vor dem Frühstück before breakfast

Vor den Mahlzeiten before meals

Vorfahrt beachten give way, yield

Vorfahrtsstraße major road (*vehicles*

having right of way)

Vor Gebrauch schütteln shake before using

Vor Kindern schützen keep out of reach of children

Vormittags in the morning

Vorname Christian name, first name

Vorprogramm supporting program(me)

Vorsicht caution

Vorsicht bissiger Hund beware of the dog

Vorsichtig fahren drive carefully

Vorsicht Stufe! mind the step

Vorspeisen [forshpyzen] hors d'oeuvres, starters

Vorstellung performance

Vorverkauf advance booking

Vorwahl(nummer) dialling/area code

W

Waffeln [vaffeln] waffles

Wagenstandanzeiger order of carriages/cars

Wählen dial

Waldorfsalat [valdorf-zalaht] salad with celery, apples and walnuts

Wann [van] when

Warenaufzug service life/elevator

Warm hot

Warme Küche hot meals served

Wartesaal waiting room

Wartezimmer waiting room

Warum [varoom] why

Wäscherei laundry

Waschsalon launderette, laundromat

Waschstraße automatic car wash

Wasser water

Wasserdicht waterproof

Wasserlöslich soluble in water

Wassermelone [vasser-melohn-uh] water melon

Wechselkurs exchange rate

Wechselstube bureau de change

Wegen Krankheit vorübergehend geschlossen closed due to illness

Wegen Umbauarbeiten geschlossen closed for alterations

Weichkäse [vycнe-kayz-uh] soft cheese

Weihnachten Christmas

Wein [vyne] wine

Weinbergschnecken [vyne-bairk-shnecken] snails

Weinbrand [vyne-brant] brandy

Weincreme [vyne-kraym] pudding with wine

Weine und Spirituosen wines and spirits

Weinkarte wine list

Weinkeller wine cellar

Weinschaumcreme [vyne-showm-kraym] creamed pudding with wine

Weinsoße [vyne-zohss-uh] wine sauce

Weinstube wine bar

Weintrauben [vyne-trowben] grapes

Weißbrot [vyce-broht] white bread

Weißkohl [vyce-kohl] white cabbage

Weißkraut [vyce-krowt] white cabbage

Weißwein [vyce-vyne] white wine

Weißwurst [vyce-voorst] veal sausage

Wenn vom Arzt nicht anders verordnet unless otherwise prescribed by your doctor

Werkstatt auto repairs

Werkzeuge tools

Westen west

Westliche Stadtteile city west

Widerrechtlich abgestellte Fahrzeuge werden kostenpflichtig abgeschleppt illegally parked vehicles will be removed at the owner's expense

Wiener Schnitzel [veener shnitsel] veal in breadcrumbs

Wild [vilt] game

Wildschweinkeule [viltshvyne-koyl-uh] haunch of wild boar

Willkommen in ... welcome to ...

Windbeutel [vintboytel] cream puff

Winterfahrplan winter timetable/schedule

Winterschlußverkauf winter clearance sale

Wird strafrechtlich verfolgt will be

prosecuted
Wir führen ... we stock ...
Wir müssen draußen bleiben sorry, no dogs
Wir sind umgezogen we have moved
Wirsing *[veerzing]* savoy cabbage
Wo *[vo]* where
Wochenkarte weekly season ticket

Wurst *[voorst]* sausage
Würstchen *[voorstcHen]* frankfurter(s)
Wurstplatte *[voorst-plat-uh]* selection of sausages
Wurstsalat *[voorst-zalaht]* sausage salad
Wurstsülze *[voorst-zoolts-uh]* sausage brawn
würzig *[voortsicH]* spicy

Z

Zahlbar payable
Zahnarzt dentist
Zander *[tsander]* pike-perch, zander
Zapfsäule petrol/gas pump
z.B. (zum Beispiel) e.g.
ZDF (Zweites Deutsches Fernsehen) second German television channel
Zebrastreifen zebra crossing, pedestrian crosswalk
Zehnmarkschein ten mark note/bill
Zeitansage speaking clock
Zeitschriften magazines
Zeitungen newspapers
Zelten verboten no camping
Zentrum town centre/center
Zerbrechlich fragile
Ziehen pull
Zigaretten cigarettes
Zigarren cigars
Zigeunerschnitzel *[tsigoynershnitsel]* pork with peppers and relishes
Zimmer frei room(s) to let/for rent
Zimmerservice room service
Zinsen interest
Zitrone *[tsitrohn-uh]* lemon
Zitronencreme *[tsitrohnen-kraym]* lemon cream
Zoll Customs
Zollfreie Waren duty free goods
Zubehör accessories
Zucchini *[tsookeenee]* courgettes, zucchinis
Zucker *[tsooker]* sugar
Zuckererbsen *[tsooker-airbsen]* mangetout peas
Zu den Gleisen to the platforms/tracks
Zu den Zügen to the trains

Zugelassen für ... Personen carries ... persons
Zum ... to (the) ...
Zum baldigen Verbrauch bestimmt will not keep
Zum halben Preis half price
Zunge *[tsoong-uh]* tongue
Zur ... to (the) ...
Zuschlag supplement
Zuschlagpflichtig supplement payable
Zu stark herabgesetzten Preisen prices slashed
Zutaten *[tsootahten]* ingredients
Zutritt für Unbefugte verboten no admission to unauthorized persons
Zu verkaufen for sale
Zu vermieten to let, for rent
Zuwiderhandlung wird strafrechtlich verfolgt we will prosecute
Zwanzigmarkschein twenty mark note/bill
Zweigstelle branch
Zweimal täglich einzunehmen to be taken twice a day
Zweimarkstück two mark piece
Zweiräder bicycles and motorcycles
Zweite Klasse second class
Zwiebeln *[tsveebeln]* onions
Zwiebelringe *[tsveebelring-uh]* onion rings
Zwiebelsuppe *[tsveebelzoop-uh]* onion soup
Zwiebeltorte *[tsveebeltort-uh]* onion tart
Zwischengerichte *[tsvishengericht-uh]* courses served between the main courses
Zwischenlandung stop-over
z.Z. (zur Zeit) at the moment

Reference Grammar

NOUNS

GENDER
All nouns in German are either masculine, feminine or neuter. There are no simple rules for telling which gender a noun is. But to form the feminine of certain nouns the following rule of adding the ending **-in** can be used:

masculine	feminine
der Arzt the doctor	**die Ärztin** the (lady) doctor
der Freund the (boy)friend	**die Freundin** the (girl)friend

PLURALS
Although some general rules can be given, the plurals of German nouns will usually have to be learnt along with the word itself. Some regular plural endings are:

ending of noun	
-e	add **-n**
-heit, -keit, -schaft **-ung**	add **-en**
-chen	no change

For example:

die Stunde	**die Stunden**	the hour(s)
das Auge	**die Augen**	the eye(s)
die Einheit	**die Einheiten**	the unit(s)
die Quittung	**die Quittungen**	the receipt(s)
das Mädchen	**die Mädchen**	the girl(s)

Otherwise German plurals are mostly formed by adding **-e** or **-er**, although sometimes the preceding vowel will have to be changed by adding an umlaut. Here are some examples:

der Preis	**die Preise**	the price(s)
das Flugzeug	**die Flugzeuge**	the aeroplane(s)
der Schuh	**die Schuhe**	the shoe(s)
der Mann	**die Männer**	the man (men)
das Haus	**die Häuser**	the house(s)
die Hand	**die Hände**	the hand(s)
die Nacht	**die Nächte**	the night(s)

Some German words of foreign origin form their plurals just by adding **-s**. For example:

das Hotel	**die Hotels**	the hotel(s)
das Auto	**die Autos**	the car(s)
das Taxi	**die Taxis**	the taxi(s)

ARTICLES

THE DEFINITE ARTICLE (THE)

The form of the definite article depends on whether the noun is masculine, feminine or neuter, singular or plural:

	sing.	pl.
m.	**der**	**die**
f.	**die**	**die**
nt.	**das**	**die**

For example:

der Zug	**die Züge**	the train(s)
die Frau	**die Frauen**	the woman (women)

CASES

The definite article changes according to which case it is in any particular sentence. There are four cases in German — nominative, accusative, genitive and dative. Each has both a singular and a plural form:

	m.	f.	nt.	plural
nom.	**der**	**die**	**das**	**die**
acc.	**den**	**die**	**das**	**die**
gen.	**des**	**der**	**des**	**der**
dat.	**dem**	**der**	**dem**	**den**

For example:

der Wein/das Essen schmeckt gut
the wine/the food tastes good

ich mag den Wein/das Essen
I like the wine/the food

der Geschmack des Weins/des Essens
the taste of the wine/of the food

ich kriege Kopfweh von dem Wein
I get a headache from the wine

Notice that in the genitive case of masculine and neuter nouns an **-s** (or **-es**) is added to the noun:

der Mann the man	**des Mann(e)s** of the man
das Hotel the hotel	**des Hotels** of the hotel

THE INDEFINITE ARTICLE (A, AN)

This also varies according to the case of the noun and to whether the noun is masculine, feminine or neuter:

	m.	f.	nt.
nom.	ein	eine	ein
acc.	einen	eine	ein
gen.	eines	einer	eines
dat.	einem	einer	einem

For example:

ein Mann/eine Frau hat dich gesucht
a man/a woman was looking for you

ich möchte einen Kaffee/eine Banane
I'd like a coffee/a banana

der Name des Berg(e)s/der Straße
the name of the mountain/of the street

ich reise mit einem Freund/mit einer Freundin
I'm travelling with a friend/with a girlfriend

Notice that the genitive endings require an extra **-(e)s** as explained under the definite article.

To express plural ideas such as 'some' or 'any' German very often simply uses the plural of the noun, for example:

haben Sie englische Zeitungen?
do you have any English papers?

ADJECTIVES

If used after the noun to which they relate, German adjectives are quite straightforward:

der Kaffee ist kalt	the coffee is cold
die Bergluft ist kalt	the mountain air is cold
das Wetter ist kalt	the weather is cold

If used before the noun to which they relate then German adjectives must change their endings according to whether that noun is masculine, feminine or neuter and according to whether that noun is used with '**der/die/das**' or with '**ein/eine/ein**'. Endings with '**der/die/das**' are:

	m.	f.	nt.	plural
nom.	-e	-e	-e	-en
acc.	-en	-e	-e	-en
gen.	-en	-en	-en	-en
dat.	-en	-en	-en	-en

For example:

der beste Wein kostet ...
the best wine costs ...

er ist sehr geizig mit dem besten Wein
he's very mean with the best wine

er bestellte den besten Wein
he ordered the best wine

die besten Weine sind sehr teuer
the best wines are very expensive

der Preis des besten Weins
the price of the best wine

Endings with '**ein/eine/ein**' are:

	m.	f.	nt.
nom.	-er	-e	-es
acc.	-en	-e	-es
gen.	-en	-en	-en
dat.	-en	-en	-en

For example:

er ist ein sehr naiver Mensch
he is a very naive person

das Ende eines wunderbaren Tages
the end of a wonderful day

er fährt ein altes Auto
he drives an old car

nach einer langen Reise
after a long journey

Note the plural ending:
  deutsche Autos
  German cars

POSSESSIVE ADJECTIVES (MY, YOUR etc)

As with other adjectives, their form depends on whether the noun they refer to is masculine, feminine or neuter and on whether it is singular or plural. They take the same case endings as the indefinite article 'ein' (see page 108):

	m.	f.	nt.	plural
my	mein	meine	mein	meine
your (sing. familiar)	dein	deine	dein	deine
(sing. polite)	Ihr	Ihre	Ihr	Ihre
his/its	sein	seine	sein	seine
her/its	ihr	ihre	ihr	ihre
our	unser	unsere	unser	unsere
your (pl. familiar)	euer	eure	euer	eure
(pl. polite)	Ihr	Ihre	Ihr	Ihre
their	ihr	ihre	ihr	ihre

For example:

wo sind deine Koffer?	where are your bags?
ich wohne bei ihren Eltern	I'm staying with her parents
in unserem Auto	in our car

COMPARATIVES (BIGGER, BETTER etc)

Comparatives are formed by adding **-er** to the adjective:

    schnell   fast   **schneller**   faster

To say that something is 'more ... than ...' use **-er als ...**:

    billiger als ich meinte   cheaper than I thought

To say that something is 'as ... as ...' use **so ... wie**:

    er ist nicht so groß wie du   he's not as big as you

SUPERLATIVES (BIGGEST, BEST etc)

Superlatives are formed by placing **der/die/das** in front of the adjective and adding **-ste** to the adjective:

ein schwerer Koffer	a heavy bag
der schwerste Koffer	the heaviest bag
die schwersten Koffer	the heaviest bags

A few adjectives have irregular comparatives and superlatives:

gut	good	**besser**	better	**beste(r,s)**	best
hoch	high	**höher**	higher	**höchste(r,s)**	highest
viel	many	**mehr**	more	**meiste(r,s)**	most

PRONOUNS

PERSONAL PRONOUNS

	nom.		acc.		dat.
ich	I	**mich**	me	**mir**	to me
du	you (sing. familiar)	**dich**	you	**dir**	to you
Sie	you (sing. polite)	**Sie**	you	**Ihnen**	to you
er	he/it	**ihn**	him/it	**ihm**	to him/it
sie	she/it	**sie**	her/it	**ihr**	to her/it
es	it	**es**	it	**ihm**	to it
wir	we	**uns**	us	**uns**	to us
ihr	you (pl. familiar)	**euch**	you	**euch**	to you
Sie	you (pl. polite)	**Sie**	you	**Ihnen**	to you
sie	they	**sie**	them	**ihnen**	to them

Note that the German for 'it' depends on the gender of the noun for which 'it' stands:

dein Koffer? ich habe ihn nicht gesehen
your bag? I haven't seen it

kennst du diese Stadt? ja ich kenne sie
do you know this city? yes, I know it

YOU
There are two ways of expressing 'you' in German. They are:

du — used to address close friends, relatives and children and also used between young people (the plural form is **ihr**).

Sie — used to address people the speaker doesn't know well or doesn't know at all (the plural form is also **Sie**).

USE OF 'MAN'
Note the following use of **man** in German:

darf man rauchen? — is smoking allowed?
man sagt, ... — they say ...
daß weiß man nie — you never know

REFLEXIVE PRONOUNS (MYSELF, YOURSELF etc)

Reflexive verbs are those in which the object is the same as the subject, e.g. I wash (myself).
A verb is made reflexive using the following pronouns:

mich	myself
dich	yourself (sing. familiar)
sich	yourself (sing. polite)
sich	himself, herself, itself
uns	ourselves
euch	yourselves (pl. familiar)
sich	yourselves (pl. polite)
sich	themselves

German uses many more verbs reflexively than English. For example:

ich rasiere mich schnell	I'll just get shaved
wir langweilen uns	we're bored
beeilen Sie sich	hurry up
ich freue mich	I'm glad

POSSESSIVE PRONOUNS (MINE, YOURS etc)

Possessive pronouns are formed as follows:

	m.	f.	nt.	plural
mine	**meiner**	**meine**	**meins**	**meine**
yours (sing. familiar)	**deiner**	**deine**	**deins**	**deine**
(sing. polite)	**Ihrer**	**Ihre**	**Ihres**	**Ihre**
his/its	**seiner**	**seine**	**seins**	**seine**
hers/its	**ihrer**	**ihre**	**ihres**	**ihre**
ours	**unserer**	**unsere**	**unseres**	**unsere**
yours (pl. familiar)	**eurer**	**eure**	**eures**	**eure**
(pl. polite)	**Ihrer**	**Ihre**	**Ihres**	**Ihre**
theirs	**ihre**	**ihre**	**ihres**	**ihre**

For example:

ist das Ihr Glas? nein, das ist seins
is that your glass? no, it's his

in seinem Zimmer oder in meinem?
in his room or in mine?

VERBS

German verbs can be divided into two main groups: regular and irregular verbs. Irregular verbs undergo certain variations in different tenses (see the list on pages 115/116).

THE PRESENT TENSE

Present tense endings for regular verbs are as follows:

sagen	
ich sag-e	I say
du sag-st	you say (sing. familiar)
Sie sag-en	you say (sing. polite)
er/sie/es sag-t	he/she/it says
wir sag-en	we say
ihr sag-t	you say (pl. familiar)
Sie sag-en	you say (pl. polite)
sie sag-en	they say

Present tense endings for irregular verbs are the same (although there can be a vowel change in the '**du**' form and the '**er/sie/es**' form — see pages 115/116):

sprechen	
ich sprech-e	I speak
du sprich-st	you speak (sing. familiar)
Sie sprech-en	you speak (sing. polite)
er/sie/es sprich-t	he/she/it speaks
wir sprech-en	we speak
ihr sprech-t	you speak (pl. familiar)
Sie sprech-en	you speak (pl. polite)
sie sprech-en	they speak

There are two very important verbs that do not follow this pattern:

sein (to be)		**haben** (to have)	
ich bin	I am	**ich habe**	I have
du bist	you are	**du hast**	you have
Sie sind	you are	**Sie haben**	you have
er/sie/es ist	he/she/it is	**er/sie/es hat**	he/she/it has
wir sind	we are	**wir haben**	we have
ihr seid	you are	**ihr habt**	you have
Sie sind	you are	**Sie haben**	you have
sie sind	they are	**sie haben**	they have

THE PAST TENSE

Two past tenses are in common use.

The IMPERFECT TENSE is used either to refer to an action that occurred once in the past or that continued over a period of time in the past. For example, **ich sagte** means either 'I said' or 'I was saying'.

The forms of the imperfect are:

sagen	sprechen
ich sag-te	ich sprach
du sag-test	du sprach-st
Sie sag-ten	Sie sprach-en
er/sie/es sag-te	er/sie/es sprach
wir sag-ten	wir sprach-en
ihr sag-tet	ihr sprach-t
Sie sag-ten	Sie sprach-en
sie sag-ten	sie sprach-en

The imperfect of **sein** and **haben** also follow this pattern:

sein	haben
ich war (I was)	ich hatte (I had)
du warst (you were)	du hattest (you had)
Sie waren	Sie hatten
er/sie/es war	er/sie/es hatte
wir waren	wir hatten
ihr wart	ihr hattet
Sie waren	Sie hatten
sie waren	sie hatten

The PERFECT TENSE corresponds to uses such as 'I said' or 'I have said'. It is formed by taking the past participle (see pages 115/116) and using the present tense of **haben**:

sagen	sprechen
ich habe gesagt	ich habe gesprochen
du hast gesagt	du hast gesprochen
etc	etc

Some verbs use the present tense of **sein** instead of the present tense of **haben** to form the perfect tense. Some of the commonest are indicated with an asterisk in the list of verbs on pages 115/116. For example:

ich bin gestern gekommen	I came yesterday
er ist nach Berlin gefahren	he has gone to Berlin
wir sind nicht geblieben	we didn't stay

IRREGULAR VERBS

Here are some of the most important irregular verbs. The parts given are first the 'infinitive' (= to do), second the third person singular present (= he does), third the third person singular imperfect (= he did) and lastly the past participle (= done). An asterisk means that the perfect tense is formed with **sein**.

beginnen *begin*	beginnt	begann	begonnen
biegen *turn*	biegt	bog	gebogen*
bitten *ask*	bittet	bat	gebeten
bleiben *stay*	bleibt	blieb	geblieben*
brechen *break*	bricht	brach	gebrochen
bringen *bring*	bringt	brachte	gebracht
denken *think*	denkt	dachte	gedacht
dürfen *be allowed to*	darf	durfte	gedurft
empfehlen *recommend*	empfiehlt	empfahl	empfohlen
essen *eat*	ißt	aß	gegessen
fahren *drive/go*	fährt	fuhr	gefahren*
fallen *fall*	fällt	fiel	gefallen*
fangen *catch*	fängt	fing	gefangen
finden *find*	findet	fand	gefunden
fliegen *fly*	fliegt	flog	geflogen*
frieren *freeze*	friert	fror	gefroren
geben *give*	gibt	gab	gegeben
gehen *go*	geht	ging	gegangen*
geschehen *happen*	geschieht	geschah	geschehen*
gewinnen *win*	gewinnt	gewann	gewonnen
haben *have*	hat	hatte	gehabt
halten *hold/keep*	hält	hielt	gehalten
helfen *help*	hilft	half	geholfen
kennen *know*	kennt	kannte	gekannt
kommen *come*	kommt	kam	gekommen*
können *be able to*	kann	konnte	gekonnt
lassen *let*	läßt	ließ	gelassen
laufen *run*	läuft	lief	gelaufen*
leihen *lend*	leiht	lieh	geliehen
lesen *read*	liest	las	gelesen
liegen *lie*	liegt	lag	gelegen
müssen *have to*	muß	mußte	gemußt
nehmen *take*	nimmt	nahm	genommen
rennen *run*	rennt	rannte	gerannt*
rufen *call*	ruft	rief	gerufen
schlafen *sleep*	schläft	schlief	geschlafen

schlagen *hit*	schlägt	schlug	geschlagen
schließen *shut*	schließt	schloß	geschlossen
schneiden *cut*	schneidet	schnitt	geschnitten
schreiben *write*	schreibt	schrieb	geschrieben
schwimmen *swim*	schwimmt	schwamm	geschwommen*
sehen *see*	sieht	sah	gesehen
sein *be*	ist	war	gewesen*
sinken *sink*	sinkt	sank	gesunken*
sitzen *sit*	sitzt	saß	gesessen
sprechen *speak*	spricht	sprach	gesprochen
springen *jump*	springt	sprang	gesprungen*
stehen *stand*	steht	stand	gestanden
steigen *climb*	steigt	stieg	gestiegen*
sterben *die*	stirbt	starb	gestorben*
tragen *carry*	trägt	trug	getragen
treffen *meet*	trifft	traf	getroffen
treten *step*	tritt	trat	getreten*
trinken *drink*	trinkt	trank	getrunken
tun *do*	tut	tat	getan
vergessen *forget*	vergißt	vergaß	vergessen
verlieren *lose*	verliert	verlor	verloren
waschen *wash*	wäscht	wusch	gewaschen
werden *become*	wird	wurde	geworden*
werfen *throw*	wirft	warf	geworfen
wissen *know*	weiß	wußte	gewußt
wollen *want to*	will	wollte	gewollt

All verbs ending in **-ieren** form their past participle without **ge-**. For example:

interessieren to interest   **interessiert** interested

Most verbs with a prefix such as **ein-** in **einsteigen** or **ab-** in **abfahren** form their past participle as follows:

einsteigen to get in   **eingestiegen** got in
abfahren to leave   **abgefahren** left

THE FUTURE TENSE
The future is formed by using the verb **werden** together with the infinitive:

zurückkommen (to come back)	
ich werde zurückkommen	I will come back
du wirst zurückkommen	you will come back (sing. familiar)
Sie werden zurückkommen	you will come back (sing. polite)
er/sie/es wird zurückkommen	he/she/it will come back
wir werden zurückkommen	we will come back
ihr werdet zurückkommen	you will come back (pl. familiar)
Sie werden zurückkommen	you will come back (pl. polite)
sie werden zurückkommen	they will come back

NEGATIVES
A verb is made negative by using the word **nicht** after it:

ich bin nicht fertig	I am not ready
er kommt nicht	he isn't coming
sie raucht nicht	she doesn't smoke
ich habe ihn nicht gesehen	I didn't see him

Negatives can also be expressed by using the word **kein**, for example:

ich habe kein Geld	I have no money
keine Sitzplätze	no seats
ich mag kein Bier	I don't like beer

THE IMPERATIVE (GIVING COMMANDS)
The forms used to people addressed as **du** are:

sagen: sag! (say)   **kommen: komm!** (come)

The plural form of this (for people addressed as **ihr**) the forms are:

sagen: sagt! (say)   **kommen: kommt!** (come)

For people addressed as **Sie** the forms are:

sagen: sagen Sie! (say)   **kommen: kommen Sie!** (come)

For example:

warten Sie auf mich!	wait for me
sprich nicht so schnell!	don't talk so fast

TELLING THE TIME

what time is it?	wie spät ist es? *[vee shpayt ist ess]*
it is ...	es ist ... *[ess ist]*
one o'clock	ein Uhr *[ine ōōr]*
seven o'clock	sieben Uhr *[zeeben ōōr]*
one a.m.	ein Uhr nachts *[ine ōōr nachts]*
seven a.m.	sieben Uhr morgens
one p.m.	ein Uhr nachmittags *[nachmittahks]*
seven p.m.	sieben Uhr abends *[ahbents]*
midday	zwölf Uhr mittags *[tsvurlf ōōr mittahks]*
midnight	Mitternacht *[mitternacht]*
five past eight	fünf nach acht *[foonf nach acht]*
five to eight	fünf vor acht *[for]*
half past ten	halb elf *[halp elf]*
twenty-five to ten	fünf nach halb zehn *[nach halp]*
twenty-five past ten	fünf vor halb elf *[for halp]*
quarter past eleven	Viertel nach elf *[feertel nach]*
quarter to eleven	Viertel vor elf *[feertel for]*

CONVERSION TABLES

1. LENGTH

centimetres, centimeters
1 cm = 0.39 inches

metres, meters
1 m = 100 cm = 1000 mm
1 m = 39.37 inches = 1.09 yards

kilometres, kilometers
1 km = 1000 m
1 km = 0.62 miles = 5/8 mile

km	1	2	3	4	5	10	20	30	40	50	100
miles	0.6	1.2	1.9	2.5	3.1	6.2	12.4	18.6	24.9	31.1	62.1

inches
1 inch = 2.54 cm

feet
1 foot = 30.48 cm

yards
1 yard = 0.91 m

miles
1 mile = 1.61 km = 8/5 km

miles	1	2	3	4	5	10	20	30	40	50	100
km	1.6	3.2	4.8	6.4	8.0	16.1	32.2	48.3	64.4	80.5	161

2. WEIGHT

gram(me)s
1 g = 0.035 oz

g	100	250	500
oz	3.5	8.75	17.5 = 1.1 lb

kilos

1 kg = 1000 g
1 kg = 2.20 lb = 11/5 lb

kg	0.5	1	1.5	2	3	4	5	6	7	8	9	10
lb	1.1	2.2	3.3	4.4	6.6	8.8	11.0	13.2	15.4	17.6	19.8	22

kg	20	30	40	50	60	70	80	90	100
lb	44	66	88	110	132	154	176	198	220

tons

1 UK ton = 1018 kg
1 US ton = 909 kg

tonnes

1 tonne = 1000 kg
1 tonne = 0.98 UK tons = 1.10 US tons

ounces

1 oz = 28.35 g

pounds

1 pound = 0.45 kg = 5/11 kg

lb	1	1.5	2	3	4	5	6	7	8	9	10	20
kg	0.5	0.7	0.9	1.4	1.8	2.3	2.7	3.2	3.6	4.1	4.5	9.1

stones

1 stone = 6.35 kg

stones	1	2	3	7	8	9	10	11	12	13	14	15
kg	6.3	12.7	19	44	51	57	63	70	76	83	89	95

hundredweights

1 UK hundredweight = 50.8 kg
1 US hundredweight = 45.36 kg

3. CAPACITY

litres, liters

1 l = 7.6 UK pints = 2.13 US pints
$\frac{1}{2}$ l = 500 cl
$\frac{1}{4}$ l = 250 cl

pints
1 UK pint = 0.57 l
1 US pint = 0.47 l

quarts
1 UK quart = 1.14 l
1 US quart = 0.95 l

gallons
1 UK gallon = 4.55 l
1 US gallon = 3.79 l

4. TEMPERATURE

centigrade/Celsius
$C = (F - 32) \times 5/9$

C	−5	0	5	10	15	18	20	25	30	37	38
F	23	32	41	50	59	64	68	77	86	98.4	100.4

Fahrenheit
$F = (C \times 9/5) + 32$

F	23	32	40	50	60	65	70	80	85	98.4	101
C	−5	0	4	10	16	20	21	27	30	37	38.3

NUMBERS

0 null *[nool]*
1 eins *[ine-ss]*
2 zwei *[tsvy]*
3 drei *[dry]*
4 vier *[feer]*
5 fünf *[fœnf]*
6 sechs *[zecks]*
7 sieben *[zeeben]*
8 acht *[acHt]*
9 neun *[noyn]*
10 zehn *[tsayn]*
11 elf *[elf]*
12 zwölf *[tsvurlf]*
13 dreizehn *[drytsayn]*
14 vierzehn *[feertsayn]*
15 fünfzehn *[fœnftsayn]*
16 sechzehn *[zecHtsayn]*
17 siebzehn *[zeeptsayn]*
18 achtzehn *[acHtsayn]*
19 neunzehn *[noyntsayn]*
20 zwanzig *[tsvantsicH]*
21 einundzwanzig *[ine-oont-tsvantsicH]*
22 zweiundzwanzig *[tsvy-oont-tsvantsicH]*

30 dreißig *[drysicH]*
31 einunddreißig *[ine-oont-drysicH]*
32 zweiunddreißig *[tsvy-oont-drysicH]*
40 vierzig *[feertsicH]*
50 fünfzig *[fœnftsicH]*
60 sechzig *[zecHtsicH]*
70 siebzig *[zeeptsicH]*
80 achtzig *[acHtsicH]*
90 neunzig *[noyntsicH]*
100 hundert *[hoondert]*
101 hunderteins *[hoondert ine-ss]*
110 hundertzehn *[hoondert tsayn]*
200 zweihundert *[tsvy-hoondert]*
201 zweihunderteins *[tsvy-hoondert ine-ss]*

1000 tausend *[towzent]*
1987 neunzehnhundertsiebenundachtzig
     [noyntsayn-hoondert-zeeben-oont-acHtsicH]
1,000,000 eine Million *[ine-uh millee-ohn]*

1st erste *[airst-uh]*
2nd zweite *[tsvyte-uh]*
3rd dritte *[drit-uh]*
4th vierte *[feert-uh]*
5th fünfte *[fœnft-uh]*
6th sechste *[zeckst-uh]*
7th siebte *[zeept-uh]*
8th achte *[acHt-uh]*
9th neunte *[noynt-uh]*
10th zehnte *[tsaynt-uh]*